THE KEEPER

THE KEEPER

★

A LIFE OF SAVING GOALS
AND ACHIEVING THEM

★

TIM HOWARD

WITH ALI BENJAMIN

HARPER

An Imprint of HarperCollins*Publishers*

B
HOWARD

HarperCollins books may be purchased for educational, business, or sales promotional use. For information, please e-mail the Special Markets Department at SPsales@harpercollins.com.

FIRST EDITION

Designed by William Ruoto

Frontispiece by Kevin C. Cox/Getty Images

Library of Congress Cataloging-in-Publication Data has been applied for.

ISBN: 978-0-06-238739-4
ISBN: 978-0-06-239426-2 (International Edition)
ISBN: 978-0-06-239628-0 (Signed Edition)

14 15 16 17 18   OV/RRD   10 9 8 7 6 5 4 3 2 1

For my mom, who gave me everything
And for Alivia and Jacob, who are my everything

CONTENTS

AUTHOR'S NOTE

The game I play has a different name in the U.S. than it does in the rest of the world, and I'm one of the few people who uses both. When I'm playing for my club team, Everton, in Liverpool, England, I refer to the sport as football, but when I'm playing for the U.S. National Team, I call the sport soccer. In this book, I have decided to go with the latter.

PART ONE

USA VS. BELGIUM: PREGAME
ARENA FONTE NOVA
SALVADOR, BRAZIL
JULY 1, 2014

Even from the locker room, I can hear the rumbling of the crowd. The drumbeats. The chants: USA! USA!

I believe that we will win.

I spent the past 24 hours doing what I always do: I stuck to my routine and stayed focused. Just as I've done today, warming up.

I started, as usual, by getting dressed in the same order—right leg before left for shin guards, socks, and shoes. Then I taped my fingers in precisely the same pattern I always follow. On the field, I checked the orange cones, right to left, with my feet, moving the one that my goalkeeping coach leaves off center deliberately so I can realign it.

This whole process might seem crazy to everyone else, but to me, nothing makes more sense. It's the only way I know to feel calm and in control.

It's the routine I've had since my first game at Everton, when

I finally had the experience and conviction to take control of my own preparation. Eight years and 500 games later, it still works—it puts my head in the right place, a place that tells me I can handle whatever comes my way.

I can't know what's coming. I only know how to make myself feel ready for it.

A few feet from where I'm standing now in the locker room, Michael Bradley looks intently at our center-back Matt Besler. *When they put Lukaku in,* Michael says, his voice measured, assured, *you've got to close him down alright?* Michael moves on to DaMarcus Beasley, our left fullback. *When Mirallas comes on, you can't let him get behind you.*

Jürgen Klinsmann moves through the locker room clapping players on the back. He's upbeat as he makes the rounds. He speaks to Julian Green, quietly, in German. Whatever he says, Julian smiles.

Nearby, Clint Dempsey pulls his yellow captain's armband over his bicep. His hardened jawline, his steely eyes tell me all I need to know: it's on.

There's a poster on the wall of the locker room, a close-up image of a bald eagle, staring straight ahead. The words next to it:

WE CAN AND WE WILL.
ONE NATION, ONE TEAM.

Something is in the air. I can feel it. Actually, I've been feeling it since we arrived in this country, every time I spotted an American flag next to a Brazilian one on a clothesline, every time I heard strangers shouting to us, "I believe!"

I believe that we will win.

I believe that we have everything we need this time.

We are strong. We have speed and power and grit. The fight is in us.

We've been beating powerhouse countries for over a decade.

We've earned a spot as the top team in our region; we've even beaten Mexico on their home turf for the first time in history.

We've beaten Spain in the Confederations Cup, making us the first team in 36 games to conquer the defending European champions. We've surprised the soccer world again and again and again.

Last night, Michael Bradley looked me straight in the eye and said the thing that everyone seems to be feeling, but which they haven't yet dared to say out loud: "I really think we can beat Belgium. I think we can get to the quarterfinals."

I believe that we will win.

Dempsey calls us over. *Let's get this done for our country, okay?* We're pumped now. *Anyone else have something to say? Tim?*

No. I've said it all. Marked up the white tactics board and tapped it again and again, reminding our defenders of our strategy.

Dempsey locks eyes with me, then says to the group, *Let's bring it in on three.*

We place our hands in a circle. Dempsey counts, and we respond in unison. *USA!*

We walk out of the locker room. In the hallway, I see the two Belgian players who also happen to be my Everton mates: Kevin Mirallas and Romelu Lukaku. We hug, but we all feel the tension; we're not teammates today. We're opponents.

Belgium's starters line up; we fall into place beside them, our eyes fixed straight ahead. Nearby, children wait, ready to take our hands.

The referee stands between us, holding the ball.

That ball: I ask the ref if I can hold it. Another ritual. I turn it over in my hands, feeling its curve against my keeper's gloves.

Then I make the sign of the cross.

Michael bellows, "Come on, boys."

Almost there.

That's when I say the same prayer I always do before a game, the one for my children: I pray that they'll know how much I love them, that they'll be protected from harm. This is the prayer that grounds me, that puts everything in perspective.

We walk out of the tunnel, and the stadium erupts.

It's all color and light and sound. The green of the field, the ref's neon jersey, the blue stands that surround us. Flags and scarves and banners everywhere, in red, white, and blue. The thunderous roar of that crowd.

When I reach the field, it's time to bend down and touch the grass; then the sign of the cross, again. Two more rituals.

I believe that we will win.

Somewhere in that roaring crowd sits my mom. Simply knowing she's there gives me the old feeling I had as a kid playing rec league soccer, when she'd move closer to me during a tough moment, lending me strength—telegraphing the message, simply by her presence: *You'll be okay, Tim.*

I know others are watching back in the States. My old coach. My dad. My kids. My brother. Laura.

And so many more. Nearly 25 million people in the U.S. watched our last game against Portugal—50 percent more than had tuned in to either the World Series or the NBA Finals. At this very moment, people are crowded into public spaces all over the U.S., watching together. Twenty-eight thousand in Chicago's

Soldier Field. Twenty thousand in Dallas. Ten thousand in the small city of Bethlehem, Pennsylvania.

They're out there right now, wearing Uncle Sam hats, stars-and-stripes T-shirts, their faces painted red, white, and blue. They're out there for us. They believe in us.

I believe that we will win.

When the whistle blows, I cross myself for the third time. The final ritual.

We can do this. I am certain of it. We can win today. And if we do, if we advance to the quarterfinals, it will be the greatest thing I've ever done for my country.

This is going to be the game of my life.

IN NEW JERSEY, ANYTHING IS POSSIBLE

All my saves are rooted in New Jersey—every leap, every block, every kick and dive and fingertip touch. All of them were born in Jersey.

I spent my childhood following my older brother, Chris, around Northwood Estates, our apartment complex in North Brunswick. While "Northwood Estates" might conjure images of rolling hills and English gardens, the reality was far more modest: a group of functional brick buildings, with 250 units in all, wedged between Routes 1 and 130. We were the far outer edge of the suburbs, a stone's throw from a pizza shop and not much else.

A few miles away were the manicured streets of the Fox Hill Run development, where some friends of mine lived. I was always taken aback by the upper-middle-class luxury of their homes: high ceilings and white carpets and light streaming in through skylights. They had pool tables in finished basements, huge backyards with pools and hexagonal gazebos where their parents sat sipping glasses of wine. *If you could make it to Fox Hill Run*, I thought, *you really had it made.* But if Jersey gave me anything, it gave me perspective. A few miles in the other direction lay a rough apartment complex with a reputation for gang violence and corner crack deals.

In our New Jersey, we heard a medley of languages—Spanish, Polish, Punjabi, Italian, Hebrew. Leaving our apartment each day, we were often hit with a pungent and mysterious odor; it took years before my brother and I figured out that it was the smell of curry bubbling, the nightly fare for a Sikh family who lived in an adjoining building. One of the kids in that family, Jagjit, rode his bike with us, occasionally stopping to adjust his turban.

In that eclectic, multinational mix, I fit right in.

My own father, who moved out before I formed my first memory, is black, a Woodstock hippie turned long-haul trucker. My mother is white, born in Hungary to a teacher and a former POW. Although deeply shy with others, Mom was always affectionate and loving with me and Chris.

The world around me was so diverse, so filled with different ethnicities and experiences that I never bothered to wonder about my own skin until I was ten years old.

"Why does your skin have that dark color?" a white classmate asked one afternoon.

I looked at my arm and considered his question. My skin *was* pretty dark, now that he mentioned it. I shrugged.

"My family went to Florida," I said. It was true. We had been to Florida . . . about 20 weeks earlier. "I guess I still have a tan."

We didn't have much. My mother raised me and Chris in a small, one-bedroom apartment—my "bedroom" was supposed to be the dining room, and my brother's room was in the basement. Mom paid for food and rent from her meager earnings working for a distributor of packing containers—an hour commute in each direction. By the time I got older and we needed money for travel soccer teams and uniforms, Mom had to supplement her day job with shifts at a roadside home furnishing store.

Mom's worry about money was constant. "Turn off the lights!" she always pleaded as Chris and I tumbled from room to room, wrestling and smacking each other in the head. "You're wasting energy!"

She clipped coupons before our weekly trips to Pathmark, and then filled the cart with generic-brand boxes of food. For housewares, we'd head to U.S. 1 Flea Market, where we found garage sale prices. For clothes, it was always Sears; the knees on their pants were reinforced with double the fabric, so they lasted longer.

On winter mornings, we'd wake up shivering and walk into the tiny kitchen. There, Mom turned on all four stovetop burners for us to huddle around and get warm.

Mom's long hours at work meant that Chris and I were latch-key kids, left to our own devices after stepping off the school bus. After seven hours struggling to sit still in the classroom, these wild, unstructured afternoons were blissful freedom.

In Northwood Estates, we could always find a game being played somewhere—street hockey or touch football or Manhunt in the woods. Chris and I dashed over to the basketball hoop to play some pickup, or headed to the scrubby field to hit a baseball. Sometimes we tossed footballs while dodging cars in the parking lot.

I wanted to play everything.

I wanted to *win* everything.

It didn't matter to me that most of the kids organizing the

games were years older than I was, bigger and tougher and more skilled in every way. I still wanted to be as good as they were—*better* than they were—so I jumped in and played hard, no matter how much I got knocked around.

And I did get knocked around.

Once, on the basketball court, a kid named Jimmy fouled me so hard I dropped to the ground. Jimmy was three years my senior, and a terrific basketball player, tough as nails. I'd seen him get into a fistfight with another player, a brawl so rough that Jimmy had started bleeding from the eye and lip—only to return immediately to the game as if nothing had happened.

From the ground, I looked up at Jimmy, and he stared back at me, unblinking. It was as if he was saying, *I don't care how old you are. I'm not going to let you win this game.*

I met Jimmy's stare. *Well, I'm not going to let you win by knocking me down.*

I got up. He tossed me the ball, and we started playing again.

If things got out of hand, though, Chris was right there for me. My brother might have punched me regularly around the house—often delivering a blow to the gut so hard it knocked the wind out of me—but he was also always the first to stand up on my behalf. He was fearless that way. During another basketball game, I got into a scuffle with a wild kid named Darren. Chris was on crutches at the time, but when Darren hit me, Chris was off his crutches in an eyeblink, punching the daylights out of him.

"Quit messing with Tim!" Chris cried as he pummeled Darren. He punched that kid so hard we would later learn he'd broken Darren's nose. "Just play the game."

Later that night, though, Chris punched *me* in the gut. "I saved your butt, jerk."

I hit him back, so fast I barely tapped him, then turned on my heels. If he caught me, he'd start pounding me the way he did Darren. So I ran like hell, knocking over lamps and books as I barreled through the apartment with Mom begging us to please, for goodness sake, calm down.

It was business as usual for the Howard boys.

Each night when Mom got home from work, she set her purse down and headed straight for the pantry to scrape together some sort of dinner for us. By now Chris and I were hungry as bears. We devoured anything and everything she put in front of us: hot dogs, mac and cheese, cans of beans, bowls of Pathmark cereal for dessert.

After dinner, we were at it again, wrestling and rolling around on the carpet.

"Please, no Clash of the Titans tonight," Mom might say. She called us that—Clash of the Titans. We were both big kids, all limbs and elbows and energy, and we did a lot of damage when we got brawling.

Mom longed to put a record on, hear a few bars of Joan Baez or close her eyes and sing along with James Taylor's "Fire and Rain" before doing the dishes—enjoy a few minutes of peace in her own home. She begged us to settle down, please, *please* be a little quieter. When we didn't, she finally broke. She started shouting in Hungarian, her native language—throaty curses that neither Chris nor I understood. To us, her words sounded like gibberish. And although she was steaming by now, ready to toss us out the apartment window, we couldn't help ourselves: we'd start laughing at all of Mom's crazy sounds.

"Enough," she snapped. "Downstairs." She chased us out of

the kitchen and out of the living room, down to the basement, where we fell to the floor holding our stomachs. We were laughing that hard.

Thursdays were spent with Poppa and Momma—my mom's parents—in their split-level home in the nearby town of East Brunswick.

Poppa had this crazy trick; he could fall asleep in an instant. It was something he picked up while he was prisoner of war, a forced laborer, in 1944–45, given no rest.

Once he was released, he tried for almost a decade to go to a university. But under Soviet communist rule, only peasants and laborers could earn a higher degree; he labored on factory floors instead. During the 1956 Hungarian student uprising, the first major threat to Soviet control of the country since the end of World War II, Poppa had helped organize factory workers. The uprising had inspired a revolution, then the revolution invoked a backlash. Poppa was informed he would be tried for treason—a certain death sentence. So Momma and Poppa escaped Hungary under the cover of night with my mother, then six, and her infant brother, Akos, in tow.

Poppa told us these stories as my Momma and my great-grandmother—my Poppa's mom—bustled around the kitchen preparing stuffed cabbage and dumplings and meat dishes heavy with paprika. My great-grandmother was a tiny little thing, always in an apron, the wrinkles on her face deep and hardened. As the food bubbled on the stove, my brother and I listened, completely rapt, to Poppa's thickly accented tales. Later, I'd drift off to sleep, wondering about the kind of strength it took to survive a prison camp, to march with your hands on the shoulders of the prisoner in front of you so that you could sleep standing up.

When Poppa had arrived in New Jersey with his family, they had nothing whatsoever. He found a job as a factory janitor at Johnson & Johnson, and over the next three decades he slowly worked his way up through the ranks of the company. By the time he retired, he'd become a senior research scientist, a number of patents in his name.

This house we sat in every Thursday, with its tidy lawn and middle-class comforts, was testament to Poppa's success in America—proof that freedom and hard work made everything possible.

My Nana, my father's mom, lived in a neighborhood where the air was rife with danger and the threat of crime; it was nothing like Poppa's East Brunswick.

I never knew my paternal grandfather, who had left Nana and their five young kids to fend for themselves. Somehow Nana managed to support those kids working on cafeteria wages; she served meals in the dining hall at Rutgers University. Nana's children stayed near to her, and then had their own kids. We cousins met up at Nana's—sometimes fifteen of us all at once. We ran around screaming and shouting at each other, slamming doors as we tore around her apartment. When the chaos got to be too much, Nana called out, "Where's my switch? I'm getting my switch." Then she opened the back door, snapped off a branch from a scrubby bush growing outside her door, pulled off the leaves, and started waving the thing around. If we didn't move fast, we'd feel that switch hitting the back of our legs. So we burst out of the house, running for our lives, this huge caravan of kids all scared to death of the strongest, toughest grandmother imaginable.

Still, for all her switch-waving, Nana seemed to have more

internal peace than anyone I've ever known. Nana's life had been a hard one, yet she had a quiet calm, as if none of the troublesome things around her—the gang graffiti or worries about her kids or long hours scooping stew into bowls—could bring her down. That peace came from faith. Nana took us often to her church, Mount Zion African Methodist Episcopal in New Brunswick. It was one of those congregations where people seemed to take in the Holy Spirit with every breath, where the choir belted out gospel tunes for hours at a time, stretching their arms toward the sky. I was mesmerized by the sheer joyfulness of it all, by the voices uplifted in song, by the wildly dancing feet. It was so infectious I couldn't stop myself from clapping along.

I was no stranger to churches. Mom's family was Catholic, and my favorite night of the year was Christmas Eve. When I was little, I climbed up into my mother's lap during midnight mass, drifting in and out of the service dreamily. Even as I grew older, I'd sit close to my mom, lean against her as I heard her voice singing that all was calm and all was bright. There was a such beauty to these Catholic services, a quiet reverence shrouded in mystery that to this day I can't separate from the feeling of being protected and loved by my mother.

But Nana's church was something altogether different—what with the dancing and shaking of tambourines, and people singing and calling out *Amens* and *Mmm-hmms* and *That's rights* at the top of their lungs as Reverend Hooper stood at the front of the church, praying with outstretched hands.

I remember the first time I saw someone overtaken by the spirit there. It was an old woman who'd been dancing and singing like everyone else, until something strange began to come over her: her hands shook, then her arms, and soon her entire body.

Her mouth opened, and she began to wail in a kind of ecstasy, stretching her arms toward heaven. That's when her wails turned into words—rapid-fire words like none I'd ever heard. It wasn't my mom's Hungarian, or any of the languages people spoke in Northwood Estates. It didn't sound like an earthly language at all. She shouted up at the sky in what seemed to be a secret tongue known only to her and God.

I glanced nervously at Nana, but she wore a knowing smile on her lips.

"She's caught the Holy Spirit," Nana said.

Whatever this woman had caught, it was electric. It was pure. It was unlike anything I'd ever seen.

That was my New Jersey: Sikh immigrants and the sprawling lawns of Fox Hill Run. Hungarian paprikash, and scrappy games of pickup basketball. The force of Jimmy's fist, and the sting of Nana's switch. Pathmark coupons and flea markets and old ladies suddenly speaking in tongues. The idea that you could start a new life as a janitor, and bit by bit work your way up and into your own split-level in the heart of East Brunswick's middle class.

New Jersey was promise. New Jersey was the American Dream. New Jersey was the world, and the world could be yours for the taking—all you had to do was show up, day after day, give it everything you had, and keep the faith.

It was in New Jersey that I first understood this: anything is possible.

GOALS THAT MATTERED

If only you'd apply yourself, Tim . . .
You're a good kid, but you lack ambition.
If only you worked as hard in the classroom as
you do at sports . . .

wasn't much of a student. Actually, that's an understatement: I despised school. I couldn't sit still, couldn't focus, desperately wanted to be anywhere but at my desk.

Mom always said that as a baby, I'd been oddly alert to the environment around me, sounds and sensations somehow amplified. I screamed every time I was changed, because I hated the feel of cool air on my skin. I hollered when I was bathed; the water was either too warm or too cool. I didn't sleep through the night until I was seven. Mom might spend hours getting me to sleep—playing Chuck Mangione records, stroking my face, trying in vain to help me calm down enough to close my eyes. When I finally did, she'd tiptoe out of the room, praying that I'd stay asleep. Twenty minutes later, though, if a floorboard creaked or a faraway police siren sounded, my eyes popped open again.

I was terrified of heights. I startled easily. I was acutely sensitive to even slight changes in light. It was as if, Mom has always said, all my nerve endings were outside my body instead of tucked safely under my skin.

Nowhere did the environment around me feel more horrible than the classroom. I hated school, hated everything about it—the *tick tick* of the clock on the wall. The hum of the fluorescent lights overhead. The screech of chairs scraping across floors, the hardness of the seat beneath me.

And worse: all those long, long hours of sitting still.

I couldn't understand how other kids tolerated it all like it didn't even bother them. For me, the school day was unbearable.

I escaped the only way I knew how: I became the kid who raised his hand five, six, seven times a day, asking to go to the bathroom. When it wasn't the bathroom, I'd say I needed to go see the nurse—not because there was anything physically wrong with me, but because anywhere, even the nurse's office, was better than being stuck in the classroom. I'm pretty sure that the first record I ever set was Boy Most Likely to Leave the Classroom—and I wasn't even in second grade yet.

"Oh, Tim," my teachers would sigh when I squirmed in my seat or failed to answer a question. "If you'd only pay attention . . ."

I wasn't a troublemaker. I wasn't impertinent. The teachers liked me. But year after year, the comments on my report cards and summer-school forms basically came down to a single point, and it was 100 percent accurate: I seemed to get nothing whatsoever out of all those long hours I spent in the classroom. To me, the days at Arthur M. Judd Elementary School were just something to be endured. They were what I had to do until I could burst into the open air and get to the things that really mattered: sports.

When I was six, my mom signed me up for sports leagues. First, she signed me up for T-ball. Because I was a big kid, standing head and shoulders above all the other boys my age, the coach put me in the outfield.

But nothing happened in the outfield. I stood there and waited as a bunch of short kids swung and missed. At best, they might send a ground ball rolling toward first base. So as I stood around in the field, I'd make up an imaginary game in my head. *"And he hits the ball into the outfield . . , it's over the center fielder's head . . . he's rounding third base and the crowd goes crazy . . ."*

By the time the other team had gotten three outs, I was running wild all over that outfield, waving my arms and shouting, completely caught up in this imaginary game.

Then we tried recreational soccer. My first team was called the Rangers, and we wore green T-shirts.

I had no skill whatsoever. None. I couldn't dribble or trap a ball or even complete a pass. But I was fast. I ran past the other kids, got to the ball first, and blasted it up the field.

During one early game, I remember an opposing player's dad—one of those type-A parents on the sidelines, the kind coaches can't stand—kept shouting to his son, "Don't let the jolly green giant get the ball!"

Then, a minute later, "Go get that jolly green giant!"

He was talking about me, of course, the tall kid in the green shirt. I looked over at the sideline and met my mom's eyes. *It's okay, Tim,* she seemed to be saying. *You keep playing.*

It was only when I heard the dad yell, "Don't let that Puerto Rican giant get the ball," that I stopped. I turned to the man.

"I'm not Puerto Rican!" I shouted. If he was going to keep screaming about me, he might as well be accurate. "I'm Hungarian!"

Pelé famously called soccer "the beautiful game." That's exactly right: it's an amazing, beautiful game—filled with explosive power and almost ballet-like grace.

I couldn't have explained back then exactly why I fell so hard for soccer. If asked, I might have said something simple, like "I like running and sliding," or "It's fun to score." But through the lens of time, I can see, even in those early, clumsy moments on the rec field, all I'd later come to cherish about the game.

I could sense, for example, the game's fluidity, its continual ebb and flow. It's something I still appreciate—soccer, even in youth leagues, is played without stop, except for a single halftime break. By the time they're pros, players move back and forth between two goals, up to 120 yards apart, covering as many as seven miles in a single match—more than twice that of basketball players, five times that of U.S. football players, and 14 times as much as major-league baseball players.

I could sense the potential for artistry, although I wouldn't have used that word at the time. It was so much more difficult to control a ball with one's feet versus one's hands. To do this, you had to be nimble and skilled.

I could also sense, even then, how a single moment of brilliance or indecision can change everything. That, of course, is what gives soccer its knife's edge excitement. Entire games, entire seasons, might turn on a single play—a 60-yard solo run, a deflection in the box, an acrobatic bicycle kick, a goalkeeper's fumble in the final minutes of a championship match.

Because I was tall, and relatively fearless, the coach of the Rangers wanted me in goal.

But I didn't want me in goal. Standing in goal was as bad as standing in the outfield in T-ball. It wasn't where the action was. If I was standing in goal, I couldn't score.

Playing up front, I was always one goal away from being a hero. As a goalie, I was one goal away from being a villain.

"If you play goalie for half the game," Coach pleaded with me, "I'll let you be the striker for the other half."

I sighed, and did as I was told, restlessly watching the action I wasn't involved in.

Then suddenly, the other team would race down the field and the ball would sail right at me. At that moment, I felt the weight of the whole team—which, to a kid, meant the whole world—on me.

I wanted so badly to stop the ball. At the same time, I was terrified I wouldn't.

Often I did stop it. But when I didn't—and when the other team's parents started cheering and the kids who weren't in green began leaping all over the field—I knew what it felt like to be fully exposed, all alone at a moment of spectacular failure.

It was too much. I often started crying right there on the field.

When I did, my mom got up. She stepped closer to where I stood. Then she caught my eye.

It's okay, Tim, her look said. *You'll be okay.*

Mom's presence was enough to make everything better.

I took one deep breath and got back in the game.

I was ten when the symptoms began to appear.

First came the touching: I walked through the house tapping certain objects in a particular order. *Touch the railing. Touch the door frame. Touch the light switch. Touch the wall. Touch the picture.*

The pattern might vary, but there was always a specific rhythm, and it had to be followed. Exactly. If it wasn't—if I tried to resist, or if Chris knocked into me at the wrong time—I had to start all over again, until I got it right.

It didn't matter if I was starving and dinner was on the table. It didn't matter how badly I needed to go to the bathroom. I had to obey the pattern inside my head. I *had* to touch these things, and in exactly this order. It was urgent.

One part of my brain, the logical part, understood that these rituals were irrational, that nothing bad would happen if I didn't practice them. But knowing that only made things worse. If it wasn't rational, then why couldn't I stop?

What was wrong with me?

Then similar things started happening outside of the house, on my way to school. Each day, I walked to school carrying a bag full of books. I remember that bag so clearly: it was an Auburn University duffel bag that my mom had picked up at TJ Maxx. I can still feel it in my hand.

I spotted things along the way—a rock, for example. There was nothing special about the rock's shape or texture or color; it looked like every other rock. But suddenly, that rock was special, the most important object in the world.

Pick up that rock, my mind commanded. *You'd better pick up that rock.*

I tried my damnedest not to. I gritted my teeth and stared ahead, trying to convince myself that everything was okay, that I could leave the rock. I might manage to walk a few steps before my heart started pounding.

Go back, my body urged me. *Pick up that rock.*

If I resisted, I became physically uncomfortable. My stomach churned. I might break out into a sweat. I started to breathe harder, feeling like the oxygen had been sucked out of the air around me. Sometimes I wanted to throw up then and there.

For some inexplicable reason, the fate of the universe rested on this one act: picking up that rock.

Finally, I gave in, I turned around, got the rock, and dropped it in my bag. I felt a flood of relief.

Everything was okay now. The universe was back in control again.

Over the following weeks, my Auburn bag became filled with rocks and acorns and dirt and flowers and grass stems—all the crap I was driven to pick up on the way to school. As I arrived, I waved to the crossing guard, as if having to haul this enormous bag around was perfectly normal—*Oh nothing, just my books and things, have a nice day!* As if I hadn't just lost a fierce battle with my own brain. As if I didn't feel these compulsions to do things I could never in a million years understand, much less explain.

Next came the tics.

Each started the same way: with an uncomfortable sensation in some part of my body—a heightened awareness, an *urge*. The feeling could be relieved only by some specific motor action. I started blinking, for example—forceful, deliberate blinks that I couldn't stop. I began to clear my throat over and over.

Then there were facial jerks. Shoulder shrugs. Eye-rolling.

With each of them, it was the same pattern: that awful sensation welling up, the one that could only be relieved, inexplicably, by some action. As soon as I did it, I felt normal again. Seconds later, the cycle would repeat itself. Terrible sensation. Buildup of stress. Action. Relief. In school, teachers snapped at me in class—*Sit still. Stop clearing your throat.*

Other kids laughed. *What's going on with your face?*

At home, Mom stayed quiet, but I could feel her watching me. I saw how her eyes zeroed in on whatever part of my body I'd moved, the flicker of concern that passed over her face. It was the same look that she had when she realized Chris and I had outgrown our winter coats and needed new ones. It was the same look she had when she pulled out her checkbook and a calculator, opening one bill after another and sighing.

I could tell it worried the hell out of her.

I hated that I was adding to her anxiety. I hated that I couldn't knock it off, be a little easier on a woman who deserved some peace of mind.

But, of course, that was impossible.

On the soccer field, though, my whole world changed. While the ball was far away, my mind might still order me around (*touch the ground, twitch, snap the Velcro on the goalie glove, cough, touch the goalpost, blink*). But the closer that ball came, the more my symptoms receded. The tics, the crazy thoughts, the conflicting mental messages—poof! They were gone in an instant.

So were the details around me. Players, colors, people on the sidelines, they all blurred and fell away. Only one thing remained in sharp focus, its every detail vivid: the ball, moving toward me.

I would kick it or catch it or parry it. Or it would elude me and I'd have to pick it out of the net while the other team celebrated.

Either way, whether I had succeeded or failed, that's when everything became crystal clear again—players, colors, spectators, scoreboard.

And then, too, the intrusive thoughts. *Touch the ground. Touch the post. Twitch, jerk, cough.*

When I was 11, I developed a new symptom, the worst one yet: I had to touch people before I talked to them. When I say "had to," that's exactly what I mean: if I didn't touch them first, I literally couldn't form the words.

It was like touching the person opened the door to my thoughts, allowed vague ideas to flow into concrete words. But if I didn't touch the person, everything in my brain just kept thumping against the door, unable to escape.

At school, I tried to hide this tic through casual touches—I might punch a kid lightly in the arm, or tap him on the opposite shoulder from behind, as if trying to make him look the wrong way. Sometimes I faked bumping into them.

At home, I touched my mom on the shoulder. One tap. Then I could talk.

She glanced down at the place I just touched. She didn't say a word.

After a while, when I stepped toward her, she began stepping backward, slightly out of reach.

"Go ahead," she encouraged. "What were you saying?"

But I couldn't tell her. I stood there mute. *Just tell her,* my brain screamed. *Tell her something.*

No words came. I was helpless—yet again—to control my own brain, my own body.

Mom took me to a pediatric neurologist. He peppered us with questions about my behavior. If I'd had any doubts about whether I'd been hiding my symptoms, that visit made it clear: I hadn't been. Mom described it all: the compulsive touching, the twitching, the blinking. She'd noticed everything.

The doctor put words to my symptoms. I had obsessive-compulsive disorder, or OCD, and Tourette Syndrome, TS—a double whammy of brain difference, a worrisome one-two punch.

OCD is an anxiety disorder, one that brings conscious intrusive thoughts and compulsions—*Touch the bannister. Pick up that rock. You'd better do it or something terrible will happen.*

TS, on the other hand, creates almost unconscious physical urges.

The two are closely related—at least a third of TS patients have OCD. Sometimes it's even hard to tell the difference between a tic and a compulsion. But while tics stem from an urge in a specific part of the body—either completely unconsciously or through a premonitory sensation that's satisfied only by the tic—OCD bubbles up as conscious thoughts in the mind.

"His certainly isn't the worst case I've ever seen," the doctor said to Mom. I wondered then what the worst case might look like.

What Mom already knew, and I learned over time, is that most people don't understand TS. They think of it as a "cursing disease," a disorder that makes people swear uncontrollably. That's how it's usually depicted on television. It's a trope, because it makes a great punch line. And sure, that form exists, but it's rare—fewer than 10 percent of all diagnosed TS cases. But there are myriad possible tics. In fact, TS looks different in everyone who has it—I've heard it called a "fingerprint condition," and that's exactly right. No two people have the same case. Some people echo other people's words. Some hoot, some cough, some hiss or bark or grunt. There are motor tics, too—in fact, it's not TS unless a person has both vocal and motor tics—like nose wrinkling, grimacing, kicking, or even jumping. Complicating matters, even in a single person tics often change over time, too.

So now we had a name for my urges, but not much else. There was no reliable treatment or cure. Some children did extremely well on medications; others moved from cocktail to cocktail, each one causing different side effects to little avail.

But the doctor explained some other things, too—curious things. He said that he'd seen some examples of people with these disorders having some special gifts—an ability to hyperfocus, to stick with a task until it's 100 percent mastered. He'd also seen a kind of hypersensitivity—an ability to see and feel and smell things that others couldn't.

Mom described my challenges as a baby—how sensitive I was to sights and sounds and touch, as if my whole body were one exposed nerve.

The doctor nodded. "Sure. That fits with what I've seen in some patients."

As we walked out of the office, he said, almost as an afterthought, "Mrs. Howard?"

She turned around.

"I've been doing this a long time," he said. "And there's one thing I'm absolutely sure of: with every challenge a kid faces, there's some flip side. I have no way to prove it, but I believe this: there's always a flip side."

Soon after, my mother met with teachers and administrators at my middle school. She'd gone in armed with all the information she could find: photocopies of books she'd gotten from libraries, pamphlets she'd ordered from organizations, copies of every article she'd been able to find. These were the days before the Internet, of course; Mom had to work hard for the information she had.

She sat in the classroom, a nurse, teachers, administrators, and the district psychologist arrayed in a semicircle around her. Not one of them picked up any of her handouts.

One teacher even asked, "Are you sure Tim has Tourette Syndrome? Because you know, Mrs. Howard, there are so many labels these days that people use to excuse bad behavior."

Well shit, my mom thought. *Now I'm going to have to fight these people, too.*

Before she'd gone in, she felt alone. Now she felt worse than alone; she felt outnumbered.

She cried the whole way home.

But it was true what the doctor said about an ability to hyperfocus—at least when it came to sports.

I watched a documentary about Pelé, then spent hour upon hour in the backyard trying to master his techniques—step-overs, cut-backs, stop-and-gos. I practiced day after day, sometimes not even hearing my mom when she called me in for dinner.

I discovered that an Italian cable television station broadcast games of AC Milan, the European Cup soccer champions.

Saturdays became devoted to studying Roberto Donadoni's artful footwork, the way the ball seemed almost Velcroed to his foot as he dribbled down the field.

When the USA qualified for the World Cup in 1990—the first time in 40 years my country reached that big stage—I watched it on television, thrilled for our ragtag group of college players and semipros. There were even some New Jersey guys on the team: Tab Ramos and keeper Tony Meola. I jabbered on and on about these guys to my mother as she rattled pots and boiled water for our evening's mac and cheese. Then I headed back outside with my ball to practice some more.

The thing is, all those teachers were right: if I had given school that same focus and attention I gave to my athletic pursuits, I'd have had endless potential. But I knew I would never care about homework the way I cared about making myself faster, stronger, quicker, more agile.

From recreational soccer leagues came traveling teams. The more I played, the more I began to understand what the doctor had said about enhanced perception. I *could* see things somehow, things that other people didn't seem able to.

I could see, for example when a game was about to shift, could sense the attacking patterns before they happened. I knew exactly when the winger was about to cross the ball and whose head it would land on.

I could see the flicker of a striker's eyes before he pivoted. Sometimes I even saw it in time to warn my defender.

I noticed things off the field, too.

I was beginning to see how different my mom was from the other soccer parents, the ones who rolled up in Lexuses and SUVs. The demographics of my New Jersey had started to shift. North Brunswick had once been the outer edge of the suburbs. Now new communities popped up all around us, massive homes occupying space that had previously been farmland and woods. These were every bit as grand as Fox Hill Run, often more so. The families moving into these houses formed the fabric of the New Jersey soccer world.

I also saw the way my mom avoided others parents' eyes, stood apart from them as they talked about kitchen renovations and gym memberships. I observed her shoulders round as she got closer to them, as if she were sinking into herself. It was almost like she wanted to disappear.

It was as if simply being around these other parents—their crisp sweaters embroidered with tiny polo players, their absolute sense of belonging—diminished her, sucked some of the life right out of her.

I could see she felt less than them somehow.

If she was going to keep bringing me back to the field, week after week, no matter how out of place she felt, the least I could do was to make her proud. So, with my mom in my peripheral vision, I ran even faster and kicked even harder, imagining that I was Donadoni himself, one of the greatest in the world. When I scored a goal, I turned to Mom, eager to make sure she'd seen it.

She always had.

On Mother's Day in my sixth-grade year, I played striker in a game during a cold, driving rain. Mom stood on the sidelines, apart from the other parents. She held a tiny umbrella for a while, but it was no use; the rain flew in from the side, pelting her face. Mom finally closed the umbrella, dropped it to the ground, and held her hands up to shield her eyes from the torrent.

I hadn't gotten her a Mother's Day gift. I didn't have an allowance, and I didn't have a dime to my name. I couldn't imagine a time when I would have enough money to buy flowers or perfume or even a decent umbrella.

But this game: this was something I could do for her. I could race down the field, splashing through puddles as I ran. I could slam that ball past the other keeper, score one for our team.

When I did, I turned to her and shouted over the heads of the other players, "Happy Mother's Day, Mom!"

Even today, all these years and games later, I can still remember the expression that came over her face as she stood there, dripping wet on the sidelines. That smile on her face, pure and radiant against the battleship-gray sky, showed me everything I would ever need to know about love.

MY OWN PRIVATE SOCCER ACADEMY

You ready to work harder than you've ever worked in your life?"

The man in front of me—a short, redheaded Irish guy—had an intense, restless energy. He looked like an oversized kid, the scrappy kind that was always ready for a fight. His eyes fixed on me with such hardness, such expectation, that I couldn't quite tell if the guy was going to train me, or eat me.

Mom had brought me here, to the GK1 Club, so I could spend a few hours with Tim Mulqueen, the goalkeeping coach of Rutgers University's men's team.

Rutgers was a powerhouse. The previous year, they made it to the NCAA championship final, losing to UCLA in a penalty kick shootout. This year, 1991, they'd been ranked number one. One of their defenders, Alexi Lalas, had earned the Hermann Trophy for the best collegiate soccer player in the nation.

When Tim Mulqueen offered goalkeeping training for youth players, parents all over New Jersey clamored to give their college-bound hopefuls that extra edge.

Mom had scraped up $25 for a single session with Mulqueen.

He looked me up and down. "Okay, Tim. Go get in goal." I started to jog toward the edge of the field.

"Sprint!" Mulqueen called after me.

I sprinted.

That afternoon, Mulqueen—Coach Mulch, as he was known to his Rutgers players—pushed me harder than anyone ever had. Before then, other coaches might fire four or five volleys at me at a time.

Not Mulch. He hammered ten in a row, so fast it was hard to get back on my feet between them. The moment I saved one, another was already whizzing past me.

"Recover faster," he barked. "You can do better than that."

Then he launched five more rockets.

"Some games are like this," he said, sending another one flying at me.

"They keep coming at you." And another.

"You've got to be ready." Yet one more.

He watched me carefully, in a way he hadn't been watching the others.

"Move your feet closer together," he said. I did. He kicked a hard low ball at me, and I stopped it.

"Good," he said. "Let's do some more of those."

When my mom came to get me, he ran over to her. "Mrs. Howard," he said, "you've got to bring Tim back."

Mom looked down. I knew she wanted so many things for me—warmer mittens, math tutors, sessions with a psychologist who could help me with my OCD. If we couldn't afford those things, $25 a week for goalkeeping training was out of the question.

"This is, um . . ." She paused. ". . . a one-time thing."

"Your son's got something, Mrs. Howard. He's got something I haven't seen."

I let those words sink in. *I had something.*

Mom shook her head. It was impossible, of course.

"I don't care about the money." Mulch looked intently at her now. "You bring him back. No charge. Ever."

To this day, I believe the offer Mulch made that day—to work with me, for free, indefinitely—was as important, as life altering, as any I've ever had.

As we walked toward the car, Mulch called after me, "See you next week, Tim Howard!" Then he added, sharply, "Don't be late!"

I trained with Mulch week after week. Eventually, we'd work together every day, year after year. The man was true to his word: he never asked for so much as one penny.

Within a year, a prominent New Jersey family put together a club team, hand-selecting the county's—and then later the state's—best young players to surround their own son on the field. Mulch was the guy they hired to coach us.

Mulch prided himself on his notoriously tough practices—he was like the Bobby Knight of youth soccer. His practices were so brutal, in fact, that kids often vomited on the field. Over time, it became a kind of joke: *practice hasn't started until someone has thrown up.*

Sometimes parents complained, but Mulch shrugged. "Sounds like you need another coach, then."

He wasn't going to change his approach for anyone.

Of all those kids, Mulch pushed me hardest.

When other kids played badly, Mulch jogged over to me. "This is on you, Tim. Fix it."

Me? I was standing all the way back here. I couldn't help what was happening in midfield.

"Come on," he'd push. "How do you make it better?"

I watched them for a minute.

"Well," I said. "They're pushing up too fast and leaving big gaps in the middle."

"Right," Mulch said. "So talk to your midfielders. Tell them what they need to do differently." And then he stood there while I directed our midfielders to close up the center and force the opposing forwards wide.

If a kid came to practice even 40 seconds late, Mulch would yell at me. "Go have a word with him."

"Why me?"

"'Cause I'm making you the leader. Go."

And if I hesitated even a moment, if I sat there blinking, wondering *why is that my job*, Mulch snapped. "What the hell's the matter with you? Go!"

Once, when our club team—the Central Jersey Cosmos—played a game in South Jersey, a few of the families got stuck in traffic on the way down. Mulch stormed over to me as I put my cleats on. "Four of your teammates are late, Tim." He was fuming.

"Yeah," I said. "I know."

He stood there with his arms folded.

"And?" I said. Nearby, players were already on the field, and I was ready to go warm up with them.

"And so you don't get to play," Mulch said.

"What?"

I thought he must be kidding, but his face was dead serious.

"Nope. Not when your teammates are late like this."

"That's not fair!" I hadn't been late. It's not like I had any control over those parents. Besides, there was no one on that team—no one—who was half as good a keeper as I was. He was putting the whole damn team in jeopardy.

"So I want you to make sure no one is ever late for a game again," he said.

Our club team practiced in front of the Middlesex County correctional facility. As we played, the inmates watched through their bars. They called out to us, hooting and hollering and whistling. We did our best to pretend not to hear the catcalls and F-bombs.

I was pretty good at tuning them out, but when the ball flew past the post or rolled over the end line and I had to fetch it, their calls came back into sharp focus.

"Come on back here, boy," the prisoners called to me.

"Hey, kid!" they called. "You come on over here, and I'll teach you how to play games."

I picked up that ball and sprinted back toward the goal, toward my teammates. Back toward my mom. Mulch. Back toward everything that made me feel safe.

As I moved up the ranks of youth soccer, Mom drove me all over the state—and eventually all over the East Coast—for my different teams.

Although I continued to play midfield on my school team, I was by now a full-time goalkeeper everywhere else. I'd come to appreciate the subtleties of the position, especially the mental part. I liked anticipating three moves ahead, then setting up our defense so it would be ready for any possible danger. And when the opposing team was able to get behind our back four, I loved flying between the ball and the net, doing everything in my power to stop it.

The night before we left for each tournament or game, I packed and repacked my bag. Obsessively. Hours would pass, and I was unfolding and refolding and reorganizing. *It's good now*, I told myself. *Leave it alone. Just go to sleep.*

But in the same way my OCD drove me to touch household items in a particular pattern, there was a right way to pack my bag, and a wrong way. Somehow I knew—with that familiar mounting sense of dread—that I'd packed it the wrong way. So I got out of bed again, unzipped my bag, and started all over.

Not right yet. Do it again.

Still wrong. Try again.

There was always a team hotel somewhere, but it was invariably too expensive for Mom. She and I stayed separately in motels a notch down in quality, always on strips lined with fast-food restaurants and car dealers and pawnshops. Instead of eating out, we looked for a grocery store. There we bought store-brand peanut butter and jelly. In the motel room, we made a pile of sandwiches and ate them while we watched television.

I think about those trips now, though—all those nights in roadside motels. Since those days, soccer in America has become more organized, more structured, more about tournament schedules. It's about team hotels and long rides in minivans capped off with dinner at a burger joint.

I worry for the kids who can't afford that. It's become even harder for working families today than it was for my Mom. They have less recreational time, less wiggle room in their budgets.

And what does that mean for those kids who aspire to play at the highest—most expensive—level?

In much of the rest of the world, kids begin playing soccer in pickup games—a loose, often barefoot scramble in scrubby patches of dirt or smack dab in the middle of the street. These future Messis and Ronaldos don't have uniforms or coolers full of juice boxes. Sometimes they don't even have a ball; they make do with whatever they've got handy.

We could use a little more of that in America—a little more scrap, a little more pickup, a little less structure. U.S. Soccer and the U.S. Soccer Development Academy are trying to change the travel team culture today, and I'm glad about that. The truth is, until we get that right, I'm not sure we'll ever become the nation of soccer champions that we all want to be.

When I was 13, I was selected for the Olympic Development Training Program, ODP, which at that time helped identify high-caliber young players for international competition. That became my pathway to the Youth National team—first the Under-15s, then the Under-17s, then the U-20s.

I was proud to put on the USA jersey, but the pride I felt at the time was more personal—more ego—than it was patriotic.

All of us had been the best in our towns . . . then our counties . . . then our states . . . then our regions. Being here, at a national youth team training camp, was confirmation: we were now the best in the country.

That felt pretty damned sweet. Especially for a kid with TS who sometimes got laughed at by his peers.

I didn't know it then, but on the other side of the globe, kids half my age were entering soccer youth academies—hypercompetitive talent factories. Life in these academies was—and is still—intense and regimented, devoid of the joy one generally associates with childhood. Academy scouts scour every nook and cranny of the soccer landscape, hoping to find a prodigy who might have the potential to someday make the senior team.

When they identify a prospect, they scoop him up, then move him into the high-stakes academy, where he eats, drinks, and breathes soccer. He often lives away from home, training night and day. He goes to school on a modified schedule.

He works with professional coaches and trainers and nutritionists and physiotherapists. He is drilled and evaluated; his progress tracked in thick dossiers.

If he can last, he watches most of his friends get cut and disappear. He watches new prospects arrive and compete for his spot, so he works harder. If he can survive this Darwinian process, if he can withstand the pressures and the demand for excellence, he'll be ready for a professional career by the time he leaves.

Someday, I'd be competing with these guys.

I didn't have some fancy European incubator of talent. But what I did have turned out to be every bit as valuable:

First, I had Mulch driving me. Second, I had a rough-and-tumble world that was filled with every kind of sport, often with kids who were older, bigger, and faster—completely out of my league. Last, I had this weird brain that hyperfocused on sports, pushing me to do things again and again.

It was like I had my own little private soccer academy.

"IT WILL TAKE A NATION
OF MILLIONS TO
HOLD ME BACK"

The world was astounded when FIFA announced that the 1994 World Cup would be held in the United States. Sure, the U.S. had the resources, but America was *not* a soccer country.

Truth is, it was pretty much the only non-soccer country on the planet.

The folks at FIFA wanted to change that by giving us a taste of the world's greatest sporting event. But they required something in return: in exchange for our hosting the World Cup, we had to launch a major professional soccer league.

Both the 1994 World Cup and the league that grew out of it would have a profound influence on my life.

I'd always followed all the local pro teams, particularly the New York Giants and New York Knicks. But soccer was a different world—played professionally only on faraway soils, seen on television rarely and even then, mostly in highlights.

When my friends and I played pickup sports, we never imagined ourselves as soccer players. We fantasized about being Patrick Ewing or John Starks, or Phil Simms or Lawrence Taylor—players in the NBA or NFL.

But the World Cup changed all that. My club and high school teammates and I buzzed about the marquee matchups. We watched them together on TV. We cheered our hearts out for the USA.

Tony Meola, the goalkeeper I'd followed in '90, was back, as was midfielder Tab Ramos. Now these Jersey guys were taking on the world on their home turf.

I went to a World Cup game in California with the Youth National team. It was that infamous match against Colombia in which Andrés Escobar, one of their defenders, scored an own goal for which he was later murdered back in his country. I knew the rest of the world took soccer seriously, but I didn't realize how much until I heard the news of Escobar's death.

Mulch was scouting that game, and he sat next to me in the Rose Bowl. During the match, he kept pointing at Meola. "That should be you," he said. "Someday, I want it to be you out there."

And to make sure that I understood, he looked me in the eye.

"One of these days, that's going to be you."

The next year, I made the World Youth Championship team—the Under-17 equivalent of the World Cup. The tournament, held in Ecuador, fell at exactly the same time that my club team, the Central Jersey Cosmos, would be going to Regionals.

Some parents of the other team members were outraged that their star keeper might not go to the Regionals. They confronted Mulch. "You're not going to let Tim go to the world championships, are you?"

It wasn't even a choice, Mulch told them: of course I'd go to the world championships.

They were furious and approached my mom. They used words like *selfish. Shirking one's responsibility. Abandoning one's team.*

Mom watched them wag their fingers and fold their arms over their chests.

You don't understand, she felt like shouting. *You don't understand, because your kids have options. They can go to college, because you can pay for it. If they struggle academically, you get them tutors. But that's not our reality. Tim gets C's and D's, even with summer school. He can't sit in a classroom for more than a few minutes, and I'm not sure he'll ever hack it in college. My greatest hope for him—maybe my only hope for him right now—is that somehow, someday, he'll be able to use his athletic skills to pay his rent, and maybe make a car payment.*

Can't you understand that? Can't you understand how important the world championships are to his being able to do that?

They couldn't. We were from different worlds.

I went to that world championship.

U.S. Soccer gave us ten dollars a day for spending money, and they hammered home the idea that we were representing our nation, that this was an honor that they could take away in the blink of an eye.

We lost all three games in the group stage, to Japan, Ecuador, and Ghana, but it was a valuable experience for three reasons.

First, I had a taste for soccer on the international stage.

Second, I had a new appreciation for all that my mom had given me. We'd seen tremendous poverty there, shantytowns perched on hillsides. I had thought that my family was poor. Suddenly I understood how lucky we were.

Third, I had more than $200 in my pocket. I hadn't spent any of the money U.S. soccer had provided.

I gave it to my mom so she could use it for groceries and clothes.

Meanwhile, my TS symptoms continued.

Sometimes in class, I heard kids whisper. *Watch Tim. He's going to jerk his head.*

Watch Tim, he's going to twitch.

To spite them, I'd focus all my attention on not having a tic. At the front of the classroom, the teacher was rambling on about quadratic equations, but I wasn't listening. I was too busy pretending that the urge wasn't welling up inside of me until I was about to burst. Eventually, when I couldn't hold back any longer, I jumped up and went to the bathroom. There, I let loose, relieved to be left in peace to twitch and cough, move around and make noise freely.

But when I trained with the Youth National Team, I got to do more than step out of class for a few minutes. I missed school for weeks at a stretch, several times a year as I traveled the globe.

These weren't glamorous trips. They were as grueling mentally as they were physically.

It's not merely that we traveled in bare-bones style—during one trip to Chile, for example, it was so cold we slept in our USA Soccer parkas and still couldn't stay warm.

It's also that we were under the microscope. The coaches and administrators scrutinized our every move—what we wore, what we ate and drank, how we spoke to each other. You could tell they were sizing up our potential to represent the nation as senior players one day.

I especially clicked with the guys from California. I'd grown up surrounded by Type-A East Coasters, so I marveled at the Cali boys' laid-back, casual vibe. Although they were in constant motion on the field, they otherwise never seemed to be in a hurry.

By the time I got to the U-20s, I'd made some real friends among them. I liked Nick Rimando, a fellow keeper who was a jolly prankster in the locker room, but reliable and solid on the field. I also liked a kid named Carlos Bocanegra. Carlos was a pretty boy—a Tom Cruise look-alike with hoop earrings and big baggy jeans. He was so mellow, I sometimes wanted to check to see if he had a pulse.

Carlos would have been easy to dismiss if he hadn't been such a powerful defender on the field.

In the hotel, Nick and Carlos and I pulled our fair share of stupid pranks—we filled garbage cans with water, leaned them up against other players' doors, then knocked and ran. By the time they opened their door—water tumbling into their room—we'd be cracking up down the hall.

On one trip, Nick and I almost got ourselves kicked off the youth team. We were in Düsseldorf, Germany, staying in a little cottage. We snuck out after curfew to wander around town, looking for the party scene. We didn't find it, but it was exhilarating to be roaming a foreign country in the middle of the night. When we finally returned, at 4 a.m., we couldn't find our way back into the cottage. We tried to pry open every window, even climbed up on the roof and attempted to drop down through a skylight. Mercifully, we eventually got back in and managed to pretend we'd been sleeping all along.

If we'd been caught back then, who knows if they'd have ever let us play for the U.S. senior team.

I had great school friends, too. I forged lifelong friendships with my buddies from the basketball and soccer teams.

Every weekend, I slept over at the home of my best friend, Steve Senior. One night, when I was 16, I told Steve that my brother had come home with a tattoo on his leg—a big panther.

"It's the most badass thing," I said. "I want one of my own."

"You should do it," Steve urged. "That would be so cool."

A few weeks later, I walked into a craphole tattoo parlor in a sketchy neighborhood.

Since you have to be 18 to get a tattoo in New Jersey, I did the only logical thing: I borrowed Chris's ID, waved that thing around as if it were my own, and asked for a tattoo of a Superman sign, with the name HOWARD, below my bicep.

Walking into the studio, I'd felt like the coolest guy in the world. Then the needle hit my skin, and it hurt like crazy.

I couldn't sit still through the pain. I squirmed and jumped and grimaced and squeezed my eyes tight so tears wouldn't roll out.

The artist was a big, mean hairy guy in a black tank top.

"Sit still, kid," he commanded. "I'm not going to finish if you keep jumping around like that. You'll have a half-tat. Is that what you want? A half-tat?"

In school the next day, I didn't tell anyone that I'd wanted to cry like a baby in that chair. I simply flexed my arms, showing it off—my Superman tat—to Steve and all my other basketball buddies, as if I were the bravest guy on the planet.

I knew of exactly one other person on this earth with TS: Mahmoud Abdul-Rauf, the point guard for the Denver Nuggets. I'd watched him whoop it up on the basketball court, sometimes earning himself technicals for his outbursts. I'd watched him startle his teammates or opponents with his grunting.

But I'd also seen him dazzle people on the court, nailing one three-pointer after another. In interviews, Abdul-Rauf described touching things in ritual patterns. His obsessive drive to make everything feel exactly right. Sometimes, that meant tapping or jerking his head. Sometimes it meant putting on his clothes in a precise order. Sometimes it meant practicing his skills over and over, until he led the league in free-throw percentage.

It confused people. A major sports figure with Tourette? How could anyone be sure he wouldn't have an episode at the wrong moment and cost his team the game?

I understood. I understood the way the symptoms faded in those critical moments.

If anything, Abdul-Rauf said, his TS helped him. It drove him.

To a high school kid with TS, an aspiring athlete myself, Abdul-Rauf was an inspiration. *If this guy can do it*, I thought, *maybe I can, too.*

Mulch continued to push me on the field. He never left me alone. I'd stand in goal and he'd make me tell him what I was seeing.

He was my guide to the tactical. *When the ball comes in from the left, you look to the right; that's where you're going to find your open players.*

He was my guide to the physical. *Feet closer together. Drop down faster. Now get up, that ball is coming right back.*

He was my guide to the mental. *Let that ball come to you, Tim. Don't rush toward it.*

He was my guide to the practical. *Ball goes over the post? Don't go get it right away. First, take a minute, talk to your defenders, use the moment as a mini-time-out.*

While some keepers are tempted to punt the ball down the field, particularly in the final minutes of the game—do anything to send it as far away as possible—Mulch taught me to think. *Throw the ball if you can. When you throw it, you have control over where it goes. Send it right to your teammate's feet.*

If I didn't get it exactly right—if, say, I threw it to a player and he gained control with his chest, or his thigh—Mulch made me do it all over again.

"That was a crap throw, Tim. Get it to his feet this time."

Major League Soccer began its play in 1996, the year I turned seventeen.

In those frenzied, heady start-up days, the MLS was part professional league, part three-ring circus. Plenty of aspects were made up on the fly, like some of the goofy-sounding team names—the Dallas Burn and the San Jose Clash, or the clunky New York/New Jersey MetroStars. There were some bizarre rules meant to appeal to American audiences. Official time was kept on a clock that counted backward, not forward. No game could end in a tie; there was a shootout to determine the winner. Salaries for most players were hardly what you would think of as major league. The minimum salary, $24,000, didn't go a long way in a city like New York.

But to a soccer-loving kid with big dreams, MLS gave me a tangible goal.

ESPN and ABC agreed to televise games and a few of the earliest matches drew large audiences at the Rose Bowl and Giants

Stadium. All the big names from the U.S. team at the 1994 World Cup signed on, and a few international stars from the World Cup, like Carlos Valderrama, Jorge Campos, and Marco Etcheverry did too. My old hero, Roberto Donadoni, joined the New York/New Jersey MetroStars, as did Tab Ramos and Tony Meola.

Then Mulch was hired as their goalkeeping coach—as well as for the New Jersey Imperials, which was like a minor-league team associated with the MLS club.

I felt my own world colliding with the one I'd only dared imagine.

We were getting to the end of high school, and I had some decisions to make. I'd had some interest from colleges, local powerhouses like Rutgers and St. John's. Some dangled promises of basketball or soccer scholarships. College was the obvious way to go, the path that everyone around me hoped to follow. My friends from the soccer and basketball teams were taking their SATs and applying to schools all over the country. My youth World Cup buddies Nick Rimando and Carlos Bocanegra were both heading to UCLA to play soccer.

Shouldn't I be considering that route, too?

But I could barely sit through my high school classes. How could I possibly keep up with college studies while devoting myself to the soccer team? Why would I even want to try?

Why subject myself to four years of being distracted from the one thing I truly cared about?

One night, Mulch sat down with me and my mom.

"Listen," he said. "Tim can get started professionally by playing for the New Jersey Imperials."

He made sure my mom understood: the Imperials weren't the MLS—they were more like the soccer equivalent of the Durham Bulls.

"He'll get to play a lot, and if all goes well, he can move up to the MetroStars next season. But it means skipping college . . . Mrs. Howard, you've got to be okay with that."

I already knew what Mom would say.

"Tim," she said, "I want you to have a complete life. That means you've got to make your own decisions."

I didn't even hesitate. I wanted to give soccer everything I had. I turned to Mulch. "Let's go pro."

So that was the plan. But even if I could make it to the MLS after a year, there was no established career path for an American soccer player. It wasn't like the NBA or the NFL.

I'd probably never earn more than my grandfather did at Johnson & Johnson. It was possible I'd never even come close.

This was a total leap of faith.

I played so many games during those years, I couldn't count them if I tried.

But there's one that goes down in local folklore, and it wasn't even a soccer game.

North Brunswick's biggest basketball rival is St. Joseph's High School. My senior year, St. Joe's had this big-time player, a sophomore that everyone kept talking about: Jay Williams. Later, Jay would play for Duke and be selected the number two pick in the NBA draft by the Chicago Bulls. My North Brunswick basketball team had a good run that year—good enough that we were heading to the county championships. Our opponents? St. Joe's.

I would guard Jay.

Today there's some mythology about what happened that night. If you ask my old coaches or any of the guys who were rooting for me, they'll tell you all about how I shut down the great

Jay Williams. They'll swear by it, saying things like *Tim owned Jay . . . that game is proof that Tim could have played in the NBA.*

But I was there. I know what the reality was.

I had some strong defensive plays, including one critical block during the final minutes. And it's true we won the championship that year.

I'm telling you, though: Jay was breathtaking. I was accustomed to being the strongest athlete around. But Jay was a perfect blend of agility, grace, and power. He had explosive ability on both ends of the court. He was simply the best I'd ever seen.

That feeling I had playing against him was one I wouldn't have again for six years. That next time, I'd be standing on a field in Lisbon, watching a teenager named Cristiano Ronaldo.

I signed with the New Jersey Imperials, and I started playing games three months before I graduated from high school.

I was 18 years old. I had a Superman tattoo, and someone was paying me to play a sport I loved.

My senior quote, in the yearbook that would come out after I'd already started playing professionally, was based on a lyric from Public Enemy: *It will take a nation of millions to hold me back.*

You remember everything I taught you about taking your leadership seriously?" Mulch asked.

"Yeah."

"It won't be fun and games anymore. Now that you're a pro, you'll be responsible for other people's livelihood," he said.

He narrowed his eyes. "You'd damn well better not forget what I've taught you."

LIKE NOWHERE ELSE

I made $250 a week playing for the Imperials—the equivalent of a $13,000-a-year salary—and I felt flush. We trained at the Fairleigh Dickinson University campus, in Teaneck, nearly an hour's drive along the New Jersey Turnpike. I got an $800 1984 Nissan Sentra—a stick shift, spots of rust above the exhaust. To this day, that little Sentra is still my favorite of all the cars I've ever had. That funny little box on wheels gave me freedom.

The Imperials had some local legends, college stars like Rutgers University's Dave Masur. But we also had players with day jobs, who worked long hours as plumbers and pipefitters in the Bronx and Long Island City, then commuted to New Jersey to train with us. Many were in their thirties with family obligations and bills to pay. These guys seemed almost prehistoric to me, a carefree 18-year-old.

The Fairleigh Dickinson campus flanks the Hackensack River. Each day, we arrived for practice to find the field covered with Canadian geese. We had to start doing ball drills to shoo the birds away. However, they never failed to leave reminders of their presence on the grass.

Our locker room was comparable to the one at my high school, and our "uniforms" were basic, 1950s-style cotton gray T-shirts. There was no money for airfare, so we rode a bus up and down the East Coast, from Vermont to Myrtle Beach. After each game, we'd load the two front seats with refreshments—pizza boxes stacked in one, beer in the other—and dig in. The Irish players led us in drinking tunes and the rest of us sang along.

Occasionally, the league pulled some publicity stunt to draw larger crowds. At my first away game, against the Myrtle Beach SeaDawgs, they fielded a guest player, Laura Davies, the English professional golfer. It was after the second round of an LPGA event in Myrtle Beach. To be eligible to play in the game, she'd signed a four-year contract with the SeaDawgs, worth $1. The SeaDawgs offered $500 to any player who assisted on a Laura Davies goal. The stunt worked; the game attracted over 2,220 fans—far more than our usual audience of family members and friends. And I've got to hand it to Laura Davies: she had some nice touches on the ball.

We were a ragtag team in an unglamorous league. But playing for the Imperials afforded me the comfort of knowing that I could make mistakes—even some of the same stupid ones I made in rec league—and there would never be more than a couple hundred people to witness them.

One time, we scored a great goal. I ran to midfield to congratulate my teammates, and while I stood there, the other team executed a quick kickoff and launched the ball into my empty net.

Thank goodness that game wasn't on television . . . and that it happened in the days before YouTube.

I made enough of an impression as the Imperials' goalie to be called up to the big leagues; I joined the MetroStars for their 1998 season as a backup to Tony Meola.

When the MLS was formed, everyone expected the MetroStars to dominate. After all, they had Tab Ramos, the creative linchpin of the U.S. team in the 1994 World Cup. Tab had just returned to the States from playing in Spain. There he'd earned the kind of money the rest of us could only dream about. The Metros had signed other big names, too, including the great (albeit aging for a soccer player—he was 34 years old now) Roberto Donadoni.

That year, they also acquired Alexi Lalas. Famous for his mountain-man look, featuring a wild mop of fiery red hair and a matching beard worthy of ZZ Top, Lalas had been the first American ever to play in the venerated Italian Serie A and he had emerged as one of the more colorful personalities at the 1994 World Cup.

But somehow, bringing together all those marquee players didn't stop the MetroStars from losing in every way imaginable. The tone was set in the team's home opener before a boisterous crowd of 46,000 that watched, slack-jawed, as an Italian defender named Nicola Caricola scored the only goal of the game in the 89th minute. Unfortunately his shot went into his own net.

Now, almost two decades later, people still talk about the "Caricola Curse"—as of this writing, the team (now the New York Red Bulls) has still never won an MLS Cup.

Whatever their struggles, I was thrilled to be playing soccer for a living. My salary had jumped when I moved to the Metro-Stars—I earned the minimum salary, $24,000 a year. It might not be enough to move out of my mom's apartment, but it felt like real wages: the income of a grown-up.

The team was a hodgepodge of alpha males. First of all, there was Tab, a guy who could instantly cool whatever room he might enter. Guys might be horsing around, loosening up with a game of "soccer tennis"—they'd tape a line down the center of the locker room, knocking the soccer ball back and forth with their heads. But when Tab walked in, or decided things were too relaxed, he'd cut that game short with one word: *enough.*

All of us obeyed.

Then there was Alexi Lalas. Alexi was like the anti-Tab, an extrovert who liked cranking heavy metal in the shower. Alexi would turn on Ratt or Guns N' Roses, blasting it loudly, singing along from behind the shower curtain. Tab would walk over and snap off the radio without speaking. Then Alexi would step out of the shower dripping wet. He'd turn it up louder, and Tab's face would burn red.

And then there was Tony Meola. Man, I was terrified of Tony. He was a hulking presence, with shirt-stretching biceps and a chest as broad as a Hyundai. After the 1994 World Cup, he'd tried out for the New York Jets, nearly nabbing a spot as a place-kicker. And his personality was equally big and brash—he was unafraid to let everyone know that he was the best. Tony could do anything; briefly, he'd even played the lead role in the Off-Broadway hit show *Tony n' Tina's Wedding.*

And when Tony was ticked off—which was often—he could make guys cower.

Keepers train together, one guy standing in goal while the others fire shots at him. When Tony sent balls toward me, they either flew past my head or skidded past me on the ground. I dove all over the box in a futile attempt to stop them. Tony rolled his eyes.

And when I kicked balls at him, Tony would grow exasper-ated.

"What the hell is that?" he shouted, flinging up his massive arms as another of my shots ballooned over the net. "That ball sucked."

Or worse, he might remind me that I shouldn't be there, sneering, "This isn't high school, you know."

Once, he turned to Mulch in frustration, throwing a hand in my direction. "I've gotta train with this guy? No wonder my performance is dropping off."

Later that practice, Mulch said quietly to me, "Just do what you do, Timmy. You keep your head. Be a good teammate. Be yourself. He'll come around."

Maybe, I thought. *But I'm not so sure.*

I tried to be friendly.

"Good luck, Tony," I might say before a game.

"Have a good game," I'd offer.

If he responded at all, it was always a quick *thanks* muttered in a low voice. More often than not, though, I got no response at all. Not a word, not a glance, not a nod. Just Tony, slapping on his gloves and walking away as if I hadn't said a thing.

A good attacking player will gladly hit a hundred shots in a row at you if you let them. So Tab Ramos and I stayed on the field as everyone else headed to the locker room. At first, many of his balls whizzed past my head.

After a while, I got better at stopping his shots.

Then we did it some more, and I began to save the majority of them.

I hyperfocused, like I did when I was a kid. I measured myself against Tony, and I saw the gap between us closing.

I marked off my progress. I dove. I reached, I stretched.

Whether I saved it or watched it billow the net, I got up and walked back to my line, ready to do the whole thing again.

Keepers can shine when their team is losing . . . and the Metro-Stars gave Tony plenty of opportunities to excel.

In August, though, Tony argued a little too vehemently with a referee late in a match against the Miami Fusion. He was fined $1,500 for "major misconduct" and slapped with a one-game suspension. Until then, he had played every minute of the season's previous 24 games. Now he'd be missing the home match in Giants Stadium against the Colorado Rapids. The MetroStars would have to rely on the number two goalkeeper to save the day.

I was that guy.

When I get nervous or excited, my tics go wild. In the moments leading up to the game, I probably cleared my throat about five hundred times.

Then, in the locker room, on my stool, was a handwritten note:

YOU'RE GOING TO DO GREAT TODAY. TONY

There's pretty much a single moment I remember from that game. It was the 63rd minute, and the MetroStars were ahead when Jamaican striker Wolde Harris, one of the top MLS scorers back then, came racing toward me. He was yards from the goal when he fired a hard shot a few feet to my right. It's almost impossible for a striker to miss from that close in, but Tony had been launching rockets at me for five months. My reflexes were sharp. I reached out my right hand and stopped that thing, dead.

All these years later, that was the one. That was the singular moment: my hand touching the ball, and knowing that I'd blocked a point-blank shot in my MLS debut.

A half hour later, we walked off the field, victorious. Tony stood in the tunnel, dressed in street clothes. He ran toward me and wrapped his arms around me. It was like getting hugged by a grizzly bear.

"You did good, Tim," he said. His voice was so animated, so happy—so unlike the Tony who'd been giving me one-word answers. "You did really, really good."

From then on, Tony became like a big brother—always tough, always direct, but also always looking out for me. When we were on the road, we'd go out to dinner and dissect every one of Tony's saves, every angle of play, from whatever game the MetroStars had just played. At the end of the meal, he always reached for the check.

"Keep your money," he'd say, waving away my cash with a bulging arm. "I've got this one."

The MetroStars slumped badly as the season progressed. We led the league in ejections, with nine, and we ranked third in yellow cards.

Then our head coach, Alfonso Mondelo, was abruptly fired and replaced by Bora Milutinovic, who may have led four countries into the second round of the World Cup—Mexico in '86, Costa Rica in '90, the U.S. in '94, and Nigeria in '98—but had no idea what awaited him in Jersey.

Bora had his work cut out for him.

Before the next season started, Bora gave the MetroStars a makeover. He traded Tony and Alexi to Kansas City. Tony was replaced with Mike Ammann, an irreverent guy, beloved in the locker room for his off-the-cuff imitations and attempts to wind up Tab.

But Bora's efforts were no more successful than any other coach's had been. By June 1999, our record was 4–9, and we were dead last in the Eastern Conference.

On June 20, we played the Kansas City Wizards; with a record of 3–10, they were the bottom team in the Western Conference. This was the polar opposite of a championship match; we were battling it out to see which of us was the worst of the worst.

They embarrassed us, 6–0.

Ordinarily, after a thrashing like that, we'd tuck our tails between our legs and try to move on. But there was something about this particular humiliation. Something that said we were a club that couldn't get it right.

We had hours to kill before our flight home from Kansas City. "Get food," advised Bora. "Go shopping."

The bus dropped us off in downtown Kansas City. Bora and Mulch went off to Barnes & Noble. Tab went shopping alone.

The rest of us piled into an Irish pub called O'Dowd's. There, we drank.

And drank.

It turns out people can drink a lot—a whole lot—in a few hours in Kansas City, especially after taking a thumping on the field. By the time we headed to the team bus, some of the players were stumbling drunk.

As we stepped onto the bus, the song "Jack and Diane" by John Mellencamp was playing. As soon as Mike Ammann heard it, he started singing along. He tripped as he made his way to the back of the bus, but he didn't stop singing.

The rest of the O'Dowd's crowd, following him, all joined in. By the time we were seated, we were all belting out the lyrics as if we were a bunch of middle school kids on a field trip.

> *. . . let it rock, let it ro-oll . . .*
> *Let the Bible Belt come and save my soul . . .*

Bora turned around and looked at us. A bunch of the guys were rocking out the drum solo, waving invisible drumsticks in the air.

You could see the exact moment Bora realized his players were plastered; his face went white, then turned red. He was livid.

Behind him, Tab stared out the window, his jawline hard.

When the next song came on, the drinking crew sang that one together, too—sloppy and loud.

Tab whipped around and snapped, "Would you shut up?! We lost six–nothing."

But of course we knew that. We hadn't simply lost. We'd proved that we weren't just the worst team in the Eastern Conference. We were the worst team in the whole damned MLS.

There was nothing to do but burst out laughing at Tab's fury.

It was like the bus was divided right down the middle. The boys in the back were obliterated, crooning and laughing. The front of the bus sat there stone-faced, pretending not to hear any of it.

It was a moment that could have only happened in the MLS. It sure wouldn't have been tolerated on any of the national teams where Bora had once coached. First of all, those teams would have traveled by private plane; they wouldn't have had hours to kill in a bar in the first place. But beyond that, getting this hammered in public would have resulted in fines; we'd have lost a month's salary easily.

Fortunately, the MLS in those early days was like nowhere else in the world.

GROWING UP

Mike Ammann came and went, and by 2001, not long after I turned 22, I became the starting keeper for the MetroStars.

That was the year I grew up—the year I became a man.

By this point, it had been years since I'd sat in a classroom trying to hide my tics. I was tired of running from TS, tired of hiding my symptoms.

I'd been thinking a lot recently about Mahmoud Abdul-Rauf. It had genuinely helped knowing there was someone else out there with TS—a pro athlete at that, succeeding at the highest level in his field. But Abdul-Rauf had left the NBA in 1998, and I knew of no other athletes—no other public figure at all—with TS now. Who was out there to prove to today's kids that TS didn't have to hold a person back?

I approached the MetroStars publicity director and said I wanted to come out publicly with TS. He did a double take, as if he didn't understand what I was saying. My guess is that he— like most people—thought of TS primarily as a "cursing disease." Then I saw the lightbulb go off for him. *Oh,* that's *what's going on.* That's *why he's always clearing his throat.* That's *why he's so damned twitchy.*

I told him something else, too: I told him I wanted to start working with kids in the community who had TS. I asked if he could help me find an organization that would be open to my involvement.

He put me in touch with Faith Rice, a New Jersey native who was launching a new nonprofit aimed at assisting Jersey families affected by TS. Faith and I spoke first by phone. She told me that her own son, Kim, had TS, and that she'd spent two decades running herself ragged trying to help him.

Kim was 27 years old now, finally settled in a job where he felt comfortable. But it had taken too long, Faith said, and there hadn't been nearly enough support. She had big plans, a crummy basement office strewn with discarded office furniture, and not a whole lot else.

But she was determined. "As you know, Tim, kids with TS are going to have to stand up for themselves every day for the rest of their lives."

We met for lunch—me, Faith, my mom, and Faith's son Kim.

Faith was an itty-bitty thing, but she charged into that restaurant like a miniature pit bull. I could tell from my first glimpse of her that she had plans for me as well as for herself—plans for the whole wide world, even.

Kim's symptoms were pronounced. He jerked his neck and shoulders dramatically. He grunted, and once in a while let out a loud yelp, as if he'd been kicked. The restaurant wasn't crowded enough to be noisy; the few customers present couldn't help but hear him. Strangers made eye contact with each other, as if to say, *What's up with* that *guy?*

Kim noticed and shrugged. "I'm used to it. Mom and I were at Costco recently; she could hear me from one end of the store to the other."

Although Kim's symptoms started at age seven, he wasn't diagnosed until 17. "I never knew it was an actual condition," he said. "I just knew I was different. I asked friends sometimes if they ever had these urges. When they said no, I felt really, really alone."

"And I felt so alone trying to help him," Faith added. "Doctors couldn't tell us what he had. Once we finally figured it out, we couldn't find information, we couldn't find guidance, we bounced from doctor to doctor trying to find someone who could help."

I glanced at my mom; I felt sure she was thinking about how hard she'd worked to find information, how little there had been.

As Faith spoke, my eyes kept drifting toward Kim. This was the first time I'd ever spent time with anyone else who had TS. Although Kim's vocalizations were louder, his motor tics more pronounced than mine, I saw myself in him. There were so many similarities between our stories: the inexplicable urges . . . wondering what in the world was happening . . . feeling alone.

My mom, I could tell, glimpsed her own mirror image in Faith.

Driving home that day, Mom said, "Kim's symptoms were pretty severe, huh? I didn't realize how lucky we were that your symptoms are mild."

Then I was silent. I knew Mom hadn't meant any harm, but there was something wrong with that word. *Mild*. Nothing about TS had ever felt mild to me. It was a condition I'd spent half my life trying to hide, trying to conquer.

But no matter how hard I tried, TS had won, every time.

"Mom," I finally said. "I know it may seem like that to you. But I don't imagine TS ever feels mild for anyone."

She thought about that for a while. Then, without speaking, she reached over and took my hand.

When the MetroStars released the news—a starting keeper with Tourette Syndrome!—it got picked up by the New York *Daily News*, the Newark *Star-Ledger*, *USA Today*. I got a feature in the *New York Times*, a profile in *Sports Illustrated*.

Faith put me right to work, too. I began hosting events for kids with TS after MetroStars games. I'll never forget my first one. By now, I'd signed hundreds of posters. I'd given dozens of interviews. I'd already received and responded to countless letters from children, always telling them the same thing: *You can do anything anyone else can do.*

But this was the first time I was in a room full of people with the same condition I had.

It's a funny thing, looking out at a crowd of kids with TS. You see movement—head jerks and quick arm motions, leg kicks and eye blinks. You hear coughs, hums, hoots, yelps.

TS is equal opportunity. Which means every sort of kid was there in that room: every color, every background, every age. They wore hoodies and jeans and baseball caps, like all kids do. They had crew cuts and ponytails.

If they were remarkable at all, it was for how wonderfully ordinary they were.

"I'm Tim Howard," I said to that fluttering room. "I have Tourette Syndrome. I live with TS. I try to excel with TS. What I don't do is suffer from TS. And you don't have to, either."

Some other things were happening that season, too. I was playing well, but I became aware of a new sort of pressure. I was beginning to understand what an emotional roller-coaster ride I had signed on for—the way your whole world, your whole sense of self, could rest on the outcome of a single game. Win, and you feel euphoric. Lose, and it's like a punch to the gut—it knocks the air right out of you.

Mind you, as athletes go, I was small-time—earning my keep with a losing team in a league where few Americans could name more than a handful of players. But still, I heard a faint voice inside my head warning: *Don't rely on winning for your peace and comfort. Find something else. When you find it, cling to it with all your might.*

I thought about my Nana, the inner peace she'd always projected. It was exactly what I craved for myself.

I called her.

"Hey, Nana," I said. "I'd like to go to church with you this weekend, if that's okay."

"Well, Tim," she replied, "you know that's more than okay with me."

I loved going to Mount Zion. I loved that it brought me and Nana closer together. It felt like there was no hierarchy in place, no egos raging. Pauper or millionaire, the place welcomed everyone with open arms—all those hugs from congregants, each of whom sought and often found their own spiritual refuge there. Not one of them cared if I'd won or lost my last game.

A teammate and I started a Bible study. Once a week, a group of us met at a Barnes & Noble to read and discuss passages that moved or puzzled us.

In addition to the Bible study group, we started a pregame prayer session that still exists today. We found a chaplain to lead it, and quietly mentioned it to a few other players who might appreciate it.

Each time we met, the chaplain chose a scripture that seemed especially connected to that week's game. He might talk about courage, or fear, or playing for the glory of God. When he was done, players might ask him to lead a prayer for the team's health and safety. If one of us had a family member traveling to the game, we prayed for their safe arrival.

They were quiet moments, just a few minutes of prayer. By the time I walked out of that room, I felt ready to play in a way I hadn't before. I felt renewed.

I remain a religious man to this day. But over time, my faith would change and mature. It would become more complex, more private, much harder to define.

I look back now on those afternoons in the Barnes & Noble, amid the whir of espresso machines and the dings of cash registers, as well as on all those tiny pregame chapels. I see now that I was reaching to grab hold of something that would ground me. I had come to my faith seeking stability. I yearned for purpose in the years to come.

And big things were coming—that was for sure.

I *want to go to Europe.*

Just as graduating to a travel team was the obvious next step from the Brunswick recreation league, a move from MLS to Europe became the way forward.

European clubs are institutions, often more meaningful than local governments or cultural landmarks. The best players on earth wind up in Europe.

If I was going to become the best, that's where I needed to go.

But to get there, I needed an agent. I had already encountered a number of them—the strong-handshake, fast-talking, name-dropping types. These slicksters often hung around in locker rooms, team and league events, and road hotels. The more success I had, the more they gravitated to me. And when they approached me, they acted as if *they* were the sole person who could bring me vast fortune and fame.

Their bluster held me back, kept me from committing.

Then I met Dan. A lawyer with a master's degree in history from Oxford University, Dan never planned to be an agent. But he loved soccer and had attended the University of Virginia Law School at a time when UVA was the top college team in the country. When MLS launched in 1996, a number of those UVA players had called him to ask for help with their contracts. Now he had a solid list of MLS clients, including guys like Eddie Pope, Ben Olsen, and Josh Wolff, all of whom I knew and respected.

We met in a midtown Manhattan restaurant for lunch. Dan asked me about my goals, and I said one word: "Europe."

The waiter poured water. Dan sat quietly, waiting until our glasses were full. Then he replied, "That's a great goal. But Europe isn't one thing. It's many different clubs, within different leagues, within a whole lot of different countries."

It was a thoughtful, low-key response—so different from the other agents I'd talked to who heard "Europe" and immediately said, "Done."

"You're a good goalkeeper," Dan continued, "but even so, a move to Europe isn't going to be easy."

He explained some of the obstacles. First, European clubs rarely recruit internationally for goalkeepers the way they recruit for strikers, attackers, and center-backs. Most countries believe they can produce their own keepers.

There was also the language barrier. A midfielder or striker might be able to get away with speaking a different language than the rest of the team. But not the guy whose job involves organizing the defense.

"England's your best option," Dan explained. "But even if there's interest there, it will be difficult to get a work permit." A player can be sure of obtaining a work permit only if they've played 75 percent of their country's national team games over a two-year period. I hadn't.

To get a permit, then, I would have to go through an appeals process. Those appeals, particularly for Americans, were often declined.

"In the meantime," Dan said, "I'd recommend you focus on other European countries without such tight restrictions. Maybe you can even get an invitation to train at one of these clubs in the MLS off-season—it's often a great way to fuel interest."

By the time lunch was over, my European dreams in some ways felt farther away than ever. But in another, important way, they felt more real, more concrete, than they ever had: now I understood the obstacles. I had a sense of what it would take to overcome them. And thanks to Dan—who I already decided would be my agent—I had a plan.

It was a good year. I played every minute of every game that season. Although I let in plenty of goals—I can still remember, for example, a San Jose rookie phenom named Landon Donovan netting his first-ever MLS goal against me that season—I finished strong. I had a 1.33 goals-against average (the average number of goals per game conceded over the course of a year), a pretty impressive record, considering how much time the MetroStars spent defending. By the end of the season, I was named to the MLS All-Stars, and I was voted MLS Goalkeeper of the Year, the youngest-ever player to earn that honor. I was also selected as part of the league's "Best Eleven." Perhaps most rewarding of all, I was named MLS Humanitarian of the Year for my work with Tourette Syndrome awareness.

I put those trophies in a box and sealed them up. I was afraid if I looked at them too much, if I had them on display, it would make me complacent. I wanted to stay hungry.

Dan and I thought carefully about which country, which league, which club, might be the best fit for me. Holland is one of the stronger soccer countries in Europe. Its top league, the Eredivisie, isn't rich like England's Premier League or Germany's Bundesliga, but it's good.

In the winter of 2001–2002, an elite Dutch club, Feyenoord, was looking for a goalkeeper. They invited me to train with them for two weeks—essentially giving me a tryout. I felt confident, physically and mentally ready. I'd had a great MLS season and I'd been getting looks from the U.S. National Team. I was so pumped, in fact, that when I stepped off the overnight flight to Holland, I didn't even bother to stop at my hotel before heading straight into my first training session.

It was a good two weeks. I trained my ass off. I liked the team, and felt like I fit in. By the end, I fully expected that Feyenoord would make an offer.

But they didn't. Instead, they told Dan that they thought I

had great potential, but that they didn't feel sure enough to make a move.

Okay, so now what? I decided that I would aspire to be the best goalkeeper in MLS for a few more years, try to push my way into the U.S. National Team. Europe would come when I was a slightly more established commodity. And I had some luxury there; goalkeepers tend to have longer careers than field players.

But it wouldn't be long before my whole life would turn upside down.

"WE'VE GOT OUR EYES ON YOU"

People's lives can change when—and where—they least expect it. Mine took a sudden turn in August 2002, at a place called "Club Poogo," which wasn't actually a club. It was Clint Mathis's basement.

Clint had joined the team a few seasons ago, transferring from the LA Galaxy. It didn't take him long to charm everyone; as soon as he scored his first goal for the MetroStars he'd lifted his jersey to reveal an "I ♥ NY" T-shirt. The fans ate it up.

Before he left for the 2002 World Cup, Clint shaved his head into a Mohawk. While there, he scored a sensational goal against South Korea in their home stadium, earning the U.S. a 1–1 draw. In that one instant, Mathis looked like the best striker on earth. He helped the team to advance to the knockout stage, where we beat archrival Mexico in what was then the biggest-ever matchup of the regional powers. By the time the U.S. team arrived home after reaching the quarterfinals for the first time in our history, Clint had become the face of American soccer. He appeared on the covers of *Sports Illustrated* and *ESPN The Magazine*, and even bantered with Jon Stewart on *The Daily Show* about how to grow out a Mohawk.

Clint was the kind of guy who liked nothing better than a good party, so when he purchased a town house in East Paterson, New Jersey, he refinished the basement to look like a nightclub. Midnight-black walls. Velvet ropes. Funky red velvet furniture and a huge red pool table to match. There was also an enormous glass bar, complete with working taps and tiny bulbs casting a red glow over fake ice. He even had a sign custom-made with the words CLUB POOGO spelled out in red neon.

It was there, beneath Mathis's twirling disco ball, that I met my future wife, Laura.

She was there visiting Ross Paule, who had recently been acquired by the MetroStars. Ross was a quiet, hardworking family man who'd become a regular at our pregame chapels. The dude had 24 cousins, and Laura was one.

I noticed Laura immediately. It was hard not to: with her flirty girl-next-door vibe, she was dazzling enough, I swear, to light up this whole dark basement.

We spoke only briefly that night—I remember I learned that she was a loan officer at a bank, that she loved animals, that she'd been an All-City basketball player.

I'm sure I blinked and cleared my throat eight million times during our chat. My tics come out especially fiercely when I get nervous or excited. This time I was both.

Before she left, Laura asked, "You guys are playing the Dallas Burn next month, right?"

I nodded. Near me, I could hear Clint's unmistakable Southern drawl, *Who needs another beer? Anyone? Anyone?*

"Well," Laura said. "Maybe I'll drive up to Dallas to see you play."

As I watched her walk up the stairs, Clint came over to me.

"Timmy, my friend. Can I get you another drink?"

Laura disappeared from view.

"Nah," I said. "I'm good."

The truth was, all I wanted was another chance to talk with Laura—in Dallas, or here. I'd have followed that girl to Timbuktu.

A few weeks later, Laura and Ross's brother Ryan drove 450 miles—7 hours, round-trip—to see us play in Dallas. Afterward, I ran into her in the lobby of the Embassy Suites hotel. She was waiting for the elevator with Ryan and Ross.

"You want to come hang out with us?" Ross asked me.

Of course I did.

Upstairs, Laura and Ryan sat together on the sofa, while Ross and I took the armchairs on either side. We talked about the game we'd played that day. It was our fourth match against the Burn that season, and the first time we'd won—Clint had scored on a header in the second minute.

There was a long, awkward silence. Finally, Ross glanced at me, then at Laura. He stood up. "Guys, I'm going to bed," he said.

Almost immediately, Ryan followed him.

Laura and I were alone.

It didn't matter that I was a pro athlete who'd been named the best goalkeeper in the MLS. It didn't matter that I'd been invited to play for the U.S. National Team in exhibition games. I was learning that a guy can accomplish all these things and still get jittery when he's left alone in a room with a girl he likes.

When I looked back up at Laura, she patted the sofa next to her, smiling. "Well, don't be so shy all the way over there. Come on and sit with me. We'll watch some TV together."

Feeling like I was back in seventh grade, an insecure kid who became tongue-tied around pretty girls, I got up and moved to the couch.

Laura clicked through the channels until she saw Denzel Washington on the screen and stopped. Denzel was saying, "You think football is fun?"

"*Remember the Titans!*" Laura exclaimed. "One of my favorite movies."

It was a favorite of mine, too.

So we watched it together, quoting memorable lines out loud, and when it was over I didn't get up to go. Instead we talked some more, about Memphis and basketball and her days at Christian Brothers University. I told her about my Hungarian family, about my Nana's church, about twitching and blinking and coughing my way through middle school.

We moved on to my high school basketball rivalry with Jay Williams. I told her about Mulch and my burning desire to play in Europe.

I told her about playing for the U.S. Men's National Team— I'd played several games now, along with my friend Carlos Bocanegra, from the youth team. Carlos and I were the new kids on the block—not quite experienced enough to sit at what we called the "grown-up table," so we hung around together during training camp, watching the older players and trying to pretend we weren't completely intimidated.

Laura and I talked about everything that mattered, or so it seemed, and we didn't stop until after the sun came up. When the clock said 6:15, I realized that the MetroStars bus would be leaving for the airport in 45 minutes.

"I guess I've got to go," I said.

"I have a funny feeling we'll talk again soon," she said, grinning widely.

I grinned right back. "Yeah," I said. "Me, too."

We did talk again soon—later that day, in fact, then every day and night thereafter. Our conversations often lasted for four or five hours straight. It wasn't long before I visited her in Memphis. She introduced me to maybe a hundred relatives—uncles and aunts, cousins and nieces and nephews, her parents, her brother Jerry— and though I struggled to keep the faces and names straight, I loved being around this enormous family. I loved the way they welcomed me as if I'd always been one of them.

Within a few months, Laura and I were already imagining the dog we'd get together.

"Let's name him Clayton," she said, and I agreed.

Pretty soon we moved on to the child we'd have, too.

"We'll name our son Jacob," she said.

Once again, I agreed.

It was wonderful in all the ways that falling in love is wonderful—we felt carefree and giddy. Laura was easy to talk to, easy to laugh with. And so, so easy to fall in love with.

The end of that MetroStars season, on the other hand, was anything but easy. We still weren't clicking as a team, and I was starting to worry that we never would. Not only had we lost our final three games of the year, we were one of only two MLS teams that failed to reach the playoffs.

Then I heard rumblings.

Bob Bradley's in.

Bradley's going to be our coach.

We hired Bob Bradley.

Bob had coached at Princeton, so he'd been active in the New Jersey soccer world. He was tactically smart, he drove his team hard, and he was a straight shooter who told you exactly what he thought.

When your team is struggling, when you've endured loss after loss and you're trying to find the light, and then you hear that a guy like Bob Bradley is coming to your rescue, you think, *Hey, maybe this is the end of all that other nonsense. Maybe Bob Bradley's going to change things. Finally.*

As the 2003 season kicked off, things were going well for me on all fronts—I was head over heels for Laura. Bob Bradley was, in fact, coaching the MetroStars. I was selected to train with the national team in Los Angeles; because the starting keepers Kasey Keller and Brad Friedel were busy in their English Premier League seasons, I saw some quality playing time. Dan had negotiated a better contract for me, so I was making decent money—not the European mega-salary that I'd dreamed of, but good money nonetheless.

Then one day, still early in the season, my phone rang, displaying a number I didn't recognize. When I answered, the voice on the other end spoke quickly, in a crisp British accent.

Tim Howard? Tony Coton here. I'm the goalkeeping coach at Manchester United. We've seen some tapes of you play, and we're a bit interested. No need to do anything. Just wanted to let you know we've got our eyes on you. Maybe we'll even come see you play some-time down the road. Take care.

When you get a call like that, things register in different stages. *British voice . . . not a name I know . . . Manchester United.*

And then: *Holy cow. Manchester United!*

After Coton hung up, I stared at the phone. It had happened so fast, part of me wondered if it had happened at all.

Manchester United was the most famous club team in the world. It held the record for the most English Premier League titles: fifteen in total, seven of them in the previous decade alone. A few years ago, they'd become the first team in history to win a "continental treble"—the Premier League, the FA Cup, and the UEFA Champions League, all in a single season.

United not only attracted stars, they *made* stars. Irish legend George Best, the so-called "fifth Beatle" who inspired the line "Maradona Good, Pelé Great, George Best," had played for Man U. Peter Schmeichel, one of the greatest goalkeepers of all time, was also a Man U guy. Bobby Charlton, Eric "the King" Cantona, David Beckham—all played for United.

The manager, Sir Alex Ferguson, had won his knighthood for services to English soccer.

Had that call really happened?

Manchester United could have any goalkeeper in the world. I was a 23-year-old kid from New Jersey. Sure, I had some talent, but I was young and relatively inexperienced. Feyenoord hadn't felt compelled to sign me. And let's face it: in the last World Cup, I'd been ranked the number four keeper for the U.S. National Team, behind Kasey and Brad and Tony. I had yet to play in any international match of consequence.

I dialed Dan. "I just got this crazy phone call . . ." I said.

Next, I phoned Laura to tell her about Coton's call. I could scarcely believe the words coming out of my mouth: *Manchester United. Tony Coton. Said they're watching me.*

"Oh my goodness, Tim!" she exclaimed. "That's so great!"

Later, she confessed that she immediately called her brother after we spoke. "Hey, Jerry?" she asked. "What's Manchester United?"

During the MetroStars preseason in March 2003, I was selected as an alternate keeper for a U.S. game against Venezuela.

Kasey would be there, too. We'd train together for a week.

I explained to Laura how big this was. Kasey had been playing in the Premier League for over a decade now; he was a veteran of three World Cups.

"He's an outstanding keeper. The best in America at the moment," I told her. "During a 1998 game against Brazil, he made ten saves. Some from point-blank range. It's incredible. Ten saves!" It was true. Not only had the U.S. upset one of the best teams in the world; Kasey had earned a shutout. One particularly spectacular save had so impressed the famed Brazilian striker Romário that he'd interrupted play to shake Kasey's hand. Romário later said that it was "the best performance by a goalkeeper I have ever seen."

Kasey turned out to be full of contradictions. He was affable as well as competitive, a family man who watched *Barney* with his kids yet blasted heavy metal whenever he got the chance. His reputation was so intimidating that the rest of us were in awe, yet he didn't bring a shred of ego to the field.

"Really great," he might tell me if I'd made a save he liked, and what Kasey said, he meant. I could hear it—the same animated tone I'd heard from Tony Meola after he'd gotten to know me.

I watched Kasey get ready for the Venezuela match. The guy was totally relaxed. No clenched jaw, no apparent jitters.

I realized something about him then: *Everything that could happen in this sport had already happened to him.* Over the course of his career, Kasey had faced thousands of shots coming at him from every angle, every speed. He'd stared down some of the best strikers in the world. There was nothing left that could surprise the guy; he'd already seen it all.

Kasey recorded his 29th career shutout for the U.S., against Venezuela that day. Just as I once chased the standard set by Tony Meola in training with the MetroStars, I now stalked Kasey. There was still a big gap between us, I knew. But if it was experience that could close it, then experience was the thing I needed most of all.

I tumbled that phone call from Tony Coton around in my head over and over again. *Maybe we'll come see you play sometime. We've got our eyes on you.*

In March, Coton called again. He'd be coming to Houston to see me play in a U.S.-Mexico exhibition game, one of my first starts with the national team. It would be the first match between the two teams since the U.S. had knocked Mexico out of the World Cup the previous year.

The U.S.-Mexico rivalry is among the most combative in all of soccer. No opponent stirs both our pride—and our ire—more intensely than Mexico.

For decades, the rivalry was one-sided. Mexico dominated CONCACAF—the Confederation of North, Central American and Caribbean Association Football—and it was simply assumed that our neighbors to the south would always kick our ass. El Tri had a rich soccer history, and for a long time Mexico was the only nation outside South America and Europe considered worthy of hosting a World Cup.

But in recent decades, the U.S. had steadily improved, play-ing with increasing skill and fostering a relentless fighting spirit. Since 1999, we'd had five clean sheets against Mexico on home soil. The U.S. shutout of Mexico in the 2002 World Cup had been more than a historic victory; it confirmed a shift in the re-gional balance of power.

The game that Tony Coton would see on May 8 had been billed as *La Revancha en la Cancha*. Revenge on the Field. Mexico was planning to take back their honor.

Most of the seats had been snapped up within the first five days of sale. Between the high stakes and Tony Coton's presence in the stands, there would be a whole lot riding on those 90 minutes.

"TO WHOM MUCH IS GIVEN"

Laura and I celebrated her 26th birthday at the swank W hotel in Times Square. We'd been dating for seven months—long enough for me to be sure.

This was the girl.

When Laura arrived, there was a bubble bath waiting for her surrounded by candles in Laura's favorite scent, warm vanilla sugar.

"What is this?" she gasped upon entering the bathroom. I smiled. The surprises wouldn't end here.

Behind the closed door, I could hear her sinking into the tub.

That was my cue to scatter rose petals on the floor. Then I pulled out the dozen roses I'd hidden in the closet.

Tonight, I'd ask her to marry me.

A while later, I heard the sound of water draining out of the tub, followed by a blasting hair dryer. I fired up a Freddie Jackson CD and waited. The bathroom door opened and Laura emerged, stunning in a black dress and heels. I pressed play, and the first few piano chords of "You Are My Lady" filled the suite.

For a moment, Laura froze. She stared at the rose petals and then at me, slowly raising her hands to her mouth and holding them there briefly. "Tim," she said, "what *is* this?"

I took her hand and led her to the window, the lights of Times Square twinkling behind us. As I went down on my knee, her eyes darted all over my face. Then I pulled the ring from my pocket.

"I want to spend the rest of my life with you, Laura," I said. I had no idea what that life would look like yet, no certainty about where it would take place—the U.S.? Europe?—or how far I'd get as a soccer player.

All I knew was that I wanted her by my side.

Laura threw her arms around me. "I can't believe it," she murmured, then said it again. And again. "I really can't believe it." She looked at the ring. "Tim," she said, "yes."

Within minutes, she'd picked up her phone and dialed.

"Mom!" she said. "Guess what!?"

May 8. Houston. Show time.

The crowd at *La Revancha en la Cancha*—all 70,000 fans, overwhelmingly pro-Mexico—was deafening. The stadium was a sea of green El Tri jerseys. My body vibrated from the noise.

But out there in front of me was a team I knew could handle the next 90 minutes: Carlos was at the heart of our defense, Clint Mathis was in midfield, and Landon Donovan, the boy wonder, was up top.

I glanced toward the stands.

Somewhere in that stadium is Tony Coton, I thought.

Mexico put us under pressure right from the start, and their fans made such a racket that my defenders couldn't hear me shouting at them.

Twenty-four minutes in, El Tri thought they had drawn first blood when Jesús Arellano's shot from the edge of the box arrowed toward the top corner. I have a pretty decent vertical leap—something that was always helpful in both basketball and goalkeeping—and I needed every inch of it. Launching myself as high as I could, I was able to get my fingertips to the ball, barely deflecting it to safety.

I was hoping that Tony hadn't taken that exact moment to go to the bathroom because I was proud of that save. The game ended in a scoreless draw—a shutout. Dan called me after.

"How did Tony like the match?"

Dan thought for a moment. "He didn't give us a final answer. He said he saw what he needed to."

"Anything else?"

"Well," Dan said with a laugh, "he wanted to check out the Galleria Mall. I dropped him there on my way to the airport. Tony was excited about the pounds-to-dollars exchange rate. He brought an extra suitcase to fill up for the trip home."

It was the biggest game of my life. Tony saw what he needed to see and then went to the mall to fill an empty suitcase. What the . . .

"For now," Dan said, "we're just going to have to wait."

The wedding plans were in full swing. We'd be married in November, after the MetroStars' season ended, at the Racquet Club in downtown Memphis.

The guest list was already at 250 people, with new names being added by the hour. Laura pored over every detail: Floral bouquets. Bridesmaid dresses. Photographer portfolios. One day, she phoned me, absolutely giddy. "I found my dress, Tim! I love it, and I can't wait to marry you in it!"

Then Dan got *the* call. Manchester United wanted me. They

wanted me to join the team at the start of the Premier League season, which was only a few weeks away.

In England, every game matters. There are no playoffs. The championship is given to the team with the best record over the season. The difference can be one game over the course of a 38-game season. Even in the Premier League weeks off, teams play other competitions, like the FA Cup or League Cup.

All this means that players don't miss a game. Ever. Not even to get married to the warmest, most adorable Southern girl in America.

But will you actually play at Manchester United?" That's what everyone—teammates, family members, my mom—wanted to know. It was a polite way of saying that I wouldn't.

Which made sense. After all, I was young and unproven. And Man U had Fabien Barthez, goalkeeper for the 1998 World Cup champions, France. I figured I'd sit on the bench, as I had under Tony Meola.

But I was hungry. And this was Manchester United. I'd have gone there to wash cars if they'd asked me.

Some serious obstacles still stood in my way. First, Manchester United had to buy me out of my contract with MLS. In Europe and other soccer leagues around the world, players are routinely bought and sold. There's a tacit understanding among clubs that a good player shouldn't miss out on the big break of his career, or a chance at exponentially improved earnings.

But MLS didn't buy that logic. It had only a few American stars, and it didn't want to lose them. Bayern Munich tried to acquire Clint Mathis immediately after the 2002 World Cup.

MLS asked for more money than Bayern would pay; Clint was only able to move to a lesser club in Europe years after when his MLS contract expired. That was the MLS strategy: don't say no outright; instead, quote a price that's out of reach. Or, if the club doesn't balk, keep moving the finish line until it gets frustrated and ends the negotiation.

As soon as Manchester United decided they wanted me, Dan got to work. Every few days, sometimes more often, he would give me an update.

Man U made an offer.

A few days later, *MLS has agreed to make a counterproposal.*

We're getting closer, he'd say, his voice calm as always. After each call, I would phone Laura, then Mom, trying to sound nonchalant. Then I would get back to practice, determined to stay 100 percent focused on my MetroStars career.

Just keep blocking shots, I'd think. *Keep getting between the ball and the net.*

Negotiations got bogged down. Both sides had dug in and were holding firm. Dan made a suggestion. "What if you offer to make up the difference from the first year of your salary? Even doing that, you'd still earn seven figures next year. And you'll be at Man U."

"Done," I replied.

Now I needed that elusive work permit. Manchester United would be presenting my case to an appeals panel. If four out of the six panelists agreed to grant the appeal, I'd get my permit.

Still, there was no guarantee. Players are denied work permits all the time. Cobi Jones, one of the most accomplished American players, had been turned down. So had Brad Friedel, even after submitting multiple applications. If the same thing happened to me, I could forget Manchester United, forget the million-dollar contract they'd dangled in front of me.

All this work—the hopes, negotiations, the phone calls, the scrambling to pull together myriad documents for Manchester United—would be for nothing. I'd be going nowhere.

I needed character references from other players. Manchester United asked former U.S. captain John Harkes, the first American to play in the Premier League, and they asked Kasey Keller and Brad Friedel, among others. Most signed without question.

However, Man U told us that Friedel had refused to submit a statement on my behalf.

"You're kidding me," I said. Friedel was among what was then a handful of American players in the Premier League; his influence was huge. Having himself been denied several times, he understood better than anyone exactly what was at stake. Why wouldn't he vouch for me?

I mean, who would sabotage his own countryman like that?

In the end, very little gets in the way of what Manchester United wants to do. I got my work permit. Apparently Alex Ferguson himself appeared at my hearing and said that I would be his goalkeeper.

Almost immediately, the headlines began appearing:

UNITED WANT AMERICAN WITH BRAIN DISORDER—
   The Guardian

MANCHESTER UNITED TRYING TO SIGN DISABLED
   GOALKEEPER—*The Independent*

WE SWEAR IT'S TRUE: TOURETTE'S SUFFERER TARGET FOR
   UNITED—*The Mirror*

I never read the articles below the headlines. I didn't need that kind of garbage cluttering up my brain.

I played my final game for the MetroStars—against the New England Revolution, in Foxboro, Massachusetts—on Saturday, July 12, 2003.

In the locker room, Bob Bradley announced to the team that I'd be captain for the day—a classy gesture that I've never forgotten.

After, I walked from our hotel—the team was staying at a Sheraton that looked like a fake brick castle—to the South Shore Plaza mall, and headed to Macy's. There I bought the clothes I would wear when I signed my name to the Manchester United contract. I thought I'd picked out a pretty sharp outfit—pinstriped suit, dress shirt, and tie, all in coordinating shades of light blue and navy.

I shook Bob's hand. Thanked him for everything.

"I hope we can work together again," I said.

"Good luck to you, Timmy."

Then Dan, Laura, and I took an overnight flight to England.

It was a whirlwind trip of 36 hours. After landing, we drove to the Manchester United training ground in Carrington. The first team was on the field, going through some punishing drills. Right in the middle of them was none other than Sir Alex Ferguson himself. He came over to greet me. Then he stopped the session and called over the team.

"This is Tim Howard," he said to them. "New keeper."

Now I was shaking hands with some of the biggest names in English soccer.

The Neville brothers, Paul Scholes, Ryan Giggs, Nicky Butt—nearly all of the renowned class of 1992—all except David Beckham, who'd recently left for Real Madrid. In 1992, Ferguson had replaced the older, experienced players on the team with these guys. *You'll never win with kids*, he'd been warned by pundits. But these kids went on to win the league, and in the process, they became United legends. And Ferguson had sealed his reputation as one of the brilliant managers of all time.

There were other faces I recognized: Rio Ferdinand, one of the world's most famous defenders . . . Roy Keane, the captain with the legendary temper . . . Ruud van Nistelrooy . . . Fabien Barthez.

These guys were international stars, every one of them. Now they were all right in front of me. In a few hours, they'd be my *teammates.*

I spent the next four hours in various doctors' offices. Manchester United wanted to rule out any existing or potential medical problems before they sealed the deal. So I shuttled between technicians and physicians, who measured my lung capacity and joint functioning, took my blood pressure, calculated muscle mass and dental needs. I had CT scans, stress and blood tests, an electrocardiogram, and an echocardiogram. They found no surprises, so the signing was on.

When all that was over, we went to look at several houses, owned by Manchester United, where we'd live for at least the first year. I'd never lived in a house before—when I left my mom's apartment, I moved into a one-bedroom with my brother. These Man U homes weren't just any homes, either: they were beautiful, spacious, and overflowing with English charm.

I tried to picture actually living in one of these homes with Laura, but the whole prospect still seemed dreamlike, as if I were imagining someone else's life.

We finally picked a beauty on Hawthorn Lane in Wilmslow, a brick Tudor with six bedrooms and expansive country gardens. It had huge bay windows, touches of leaded glass, skylights, built-ins, and double French doors—far fancier than even the Fox Hill Run homes I used to marvel at back in Jersey.

And it was mine. *Ours.*

On our way to Old Trafford stadium for the signing, Dan gave me some great advice. Listening to it would be one of the wiser things I've ever done.

"Tim," he said. "This is a lot of money. But your career is front-loaded; you have only a short window when you'll be able to earn this much. So conserve it until the basic concerns are off the table."

"What are the basics?"

"However you define them. Decide what you think you'll need to live on over the long term, and sock that money away. You'll be tempted to spend a lot of it, but keep your eye on that long term."

We headed to Old Trafford to sign the contract that would change my life and to announce to the world that I had joined Manchester United.

I would now be earning $1.4 million per year, and double that if I actually played regularly. I was jumping from the bottom team in MLS to one of the best teams in the world's top league. I didn't feel exactly like Cinderella, but the whole thing was enough of a fairy tale to make me wonder when the clock would strike midnight.

After, we went outside to have a photo taken in front of Old

Trafford—they'd given me a red Manchester United scarf to wear around my neck, maybe to underline how official it was. Hundreds of fans had already gathered. To see me. They knew exactly what I looked like from all the pictures in the English papers when my transfer was announced.

"Welcome, Tim!" they shouted.

"Look, it's Tim Howard!"

"Gonna be the next Peter Schmeichel, are ya?"

I held up a Man U jersey as the fans cheered. I was still dressed in the navy suit with pale blue pinstripes from Macy's. It would be months before I realized that the suit I'd so carefully chosen featured the team colors of United's bitter crosstown rival, Manchester City. This was a massive faux pas in English soccer, and one of many things I'd learn only in retrospect.

Laura and I huddled together on the flight home, talking about the wedding. It would have to be postponed until the Premier League season ended.

"Or we could . . ." I said, my voice trailing off.

"What?" she asked.

"Why don't we get married before I go."

"*Before* you go?" she asked.

"Yeah," I answered. "Why not?"

"Tim," Laura said, looking at me with both caution and surprise. "Your first game is in a couple of days."

"So let's go to City Hall as soon as we land," I said.

It seemed so obvious now.

"Oh my goodness, Tim," she said. "We could. We could just do it."

Laura had already bought a wedding dress, ordered stacks of

engraved invitations, put down deposits with photographers and florists. But I could see by the way her eyes sparkled that she liked the idea.

"Doesn't it feel right?" I asked.

"Tim," she said, "it feels perfect."

We'd be landing in Newark, but New Jersey makes you wait 48 hours to marry after applying for the license. We didn't have 48 hours.

In New York, the waiting period is just 24 hours. That we could manage.

Mom picked us up at the airport.

"Mom," I said once we'd settled in the car, "can you take us into New York? City Hall. We need to get a marriage license."

It rained on July 18, 2003, but no one seemed to notice or care. Laura and I didn't, anyway; if the sun wasn't shining, it sure felt like it was around 3 p.m. when we were married in Central Park. It was an impromptu ceremony that marked the line between what had been and what would be. Only ten people could attend the ceremony on such short notice.

Afterward, we celebrated at the Chart House in Weehawken, directly across the Hudson River from Manhattan. We were taking photographs outside when word got around the restaurant that a professional athlete was on the deck. The next thing I knew, people started coming out to snap their own shots.

Everything in my life is about to change, I kept thinking. *The world I know, the people I love, I'm leaving it all behind.*

I wrapped my arm around Laura's waist.

But I'll have Laura. My wife will be with me.

Laura spent her first day as a married woman flying back to Memphis to begin the process of saying goodbye to her friends, family, and hometown—the only place she'd ever lived. I hopped on a plane to join my new team and get ready for our first match. I'd travel with them to a couple of friendly matches in the U.S., then we would head together to Portugal to play Sporting Lisbon.

Before I left, I scribbled out some words that had been rattling around in my head. They were from Luke 12:48, the parable of the faithful servant: *To whom much is given, much is required.*

Without knowing why, I tucked the piece of paper into my day planner. I had no idea how often I would unfold it and read that line, again and again. I'd even pull it out more than a decade later, fresh off the field in Salvador, Brazil, after the U.S. lost in overtime to Belgium in the 2014 World Cup—the most eventful game of my life.

I remember telling myself that I was taking all the excitement in stride. And I suspect that anyone who knew me then would agree; they'd say I played it cool, never got rattled.

Looking back, however, I can see that I was the same kid who'd tried to act tough while getting his first tattoo, then squirmed in his seat.

I was a wreck.

My first match for United, against the Italian giant Juventus, would be held, ironically enough, in New Jersey—at Giants Stadium, where the MetroStars played their home games. When I walked out onto the field, I remember being in utter shock. Yes, it was still Giants Stadium, but it was transformed. There was a capacity crowd. The atmosphere was electric.

There's a photo of me, taken moments before kickoff. I'm

smiling, but it's not the assured-looking grin I usually see in photos of myself. This smile is shy, even sheepish. I look like a little kid. A little kid asking himself, *Do I even belong here?*

The whistle was about to blow.

What I felt, most of all, was fear.

PART TWO

USA VS. BELGIUM: WARNING SHOTS
ARENA FONTE NOVA
SALVADOR, BRAZIL
JULY 1, 2014

Belgium's a formidable team. Twelve of their players are in the Premier League. Their keeper, Thibaut Courtois, hasn't lost a game for Belgium in 20 international matches. They have Chelsea's Eden Hazard, one of the most gifted midfielders in the world. Eden won the Professional Footballers' Association award for best young player this season; he was runner-up for PFA best player, too. They have Marouane Fellaini, whom I'd played with at Everton before he transferred to Manchester United; I've seen firsthand his rugged tackles and aerial challenges. And they have Rom, a game-changer.

Belgium has power and pace and skill.

Thirty seconds in, Jermaine brings the ball just over the line into Belgium territory. His pass is intercepted by Kevin De Bruyne, who gallops down the right wing toward me. He's youthful and fresh-faced with red hair and freckles, but he's got unbelievable velocity with the ball at his feet.

On my right, I can sense Divock Origi also making a run. Origi is another young Belgian. I know he's good because he's starting in place of Romelu.

Origi races past our defender, Omar Gonzalez. De Bruyne passes him the ball.

He's got a clear shot.

Origi pulls back his right foot and snaps it forward.

Then it's just me and that ball.

Time stretches. The world around me retreats—the stadium, my teammates, Origi himself.

It all happens in a fraction of a second. My brain flickers back and forth between the ball and my own body. I measure the ball's angle, its speed. I adjust my body.

And then *Whap!* The ball hits my leg.

The world returns in a flash. I saved it.

I shake my fist and bellow at my defenders. *Get fucking tighter!*

I need it to be absolutely, 100 percent clear: this cannot happen again.

Forty-five seconds on the clock. I'm focused now. My blood is pumping.

I've made my declaration—to myself, to the world. That ball's not getting through.

"YOU'RE NOT IN AMERICA ANYMORE, SON"

It was like I'd gone to Jupiter. As if I'd rocketed not merely into a different league, different country, different culture, but onto a different planet altogether.

Before I left the States, Mulch had shaken my hand and said, "Tim, go represent the 732." I laughed; 732 was our Jersey area code.

"Always," I'd said. Then I'd pulled him in for a hug.

It wasn't long before the 732 would vanish in a haze with the rest of Jersey's hardscrabble charm. In this new world, flashbulbs popped, people swarmed team buses and screamed as if we were the Beatles. Security guards in neon jackets pushed back crowds that were ten people deep, all of them craning their necks, hoping for a glimpse.

A glimpse of us.

Manchester United is often talked about in purely financial terms—the most valuable soccer brand in the world, worth nearly $3 billion today. But for me this was even more of a cultural shift than a financial one.

A full-time staff of 600 supported the team. On game day, those ranks swelled to 1,200—nearly a hundred employees for every player on the field. During our preseason tour of the U.S., we traveled by private jet, chartered by the club from its owner, the Dallas Mavericks. It was a stunning 767 fitted with custom leather seats designed for the comfort of even the tallest NBA star—a far cry from the economy-class flights with the Metro-Stars, let alone the long-distance bus trips I'd taken with the Imperials.

By the time I arrived in Carrington for my first day of training with Manchester United, I would find a brand-new Mercedes waiting for me in the parking lot.

"You mean they're just giving it to you?" Laura asked when I called to tell her. She was still weeks from joining me in England.

"Yeah," I said. I could hear the disbelief in my voice. I was only a few years removed from my $800 Sentra; I still remembered the feel of that plastic steering wheel. "They're just handing me the keys."

I probably felt the full power of the Man U brand when we played Sporting Lisbon, the last of our preseason friendlies. We had won all of our previous U.S. games, but that streak ended abruptly in the Portuguese capital.

Sporting had this kid playing for them—a skinny, baby-faced 18-year-old with blond highlights in his hair. He had everything: speed and athleticism, touch and vision. He danced over the ball, tormenting our defenders before leaving them in his dust and bearing down on Barthez.

The kid was sensational. And every time he touched the ball, the stadium turned into a giant party. The fans knew something special was about to happen, and they were right: the kid performed astonishing tricks with the ball, then shrugged, as if to say, "Oh, that's nothing." It was a kind of look-at-me showmanship that bordered on arrogance, but it was impossible to take your eyes off him.

Later, in the locker room, I heard my teammates rave. *Ronaldo,* they exclaimed. *Cristiano Ronaldo.*

I stayed quiet, taking it in, heartened by the fact that even the best players in the world were still capable of being awestruck.

When Ferguson came into the locker room, Rio Ferdinand and Nicky Butt rushed up to him.

"That kid, gaffer," they exclaimed, using the British term for boss, "we've got to sign that kid."

Barely a week later, Ferguson announced that Cristiano Ronaldo had become a Manchester United player. He would wear the number 7 shirt made famous by David Beckham.

It all seemed so simple. We saw him. We wanted him. We got him. One game, one glimpse of this kid, and suddenly we had the most promising young player any of us had ever seen. All it took was roughly $20 million and the aura of Manchester United.

Training was grueling—the pace, the intensity, the physicality. My teammates were, to a man, better than anyone I'd ever played with. They were stronger. They were more technical. They were faster in every way. It's probably not an exaggeration to say that some of the balls they sent my way reached speeds greater than my old Sentra ever had.

I had to react more quickly, be more decisive. Most of all, I had to *win.*

At Man U, my potential didn't matter. Effort didn't matter.

Winning was the sole currency. Winning had made my teammates rock stars. If I was going to hold my own, I'd have to *win*.

I called Kasey Keller in London.

"So . . . uh . . . what do I need to know?" I asked. It was a stupid question, too broad to be meaningful. But how could I summarize how it felt to have gone from the soccer boondocks of MLS to the bright lights of the Premier League? It was impossible to explain the relentless pressure, the feeling that gnawed at me: *I'm not quite ready for this yet.*

Kasey thought for a while, then answered simply, "Well, Tim, I guess my advice to you would be this: make as many saves as you can."

In Europe, soccer seasons tend to open with a "Super Cup"—one champion playing another for best-of-the-best status. In England, that super-championship is the Community Shield, where the winner of the Premier League meets the winner of the FA Cup. The game doesn't count in the standings; it's a glorified exhibition.

Manchester United was the Premier League champion. Which meant that we would face Arsenal, the FA Cup champion. It was two heavyweights slugging it out before the season officially kicked off a week later.

Arsenal, like Man U, is one of the great Premier League powers. The London club had a pantheon of international stars, a slick passing game, and plenty of attacking flair. In their hundred-year history, they'd already won 9 FA cups and 12 First Division and Premier League titles.

Hours before the game, Tony Coton told me I'd be starting.

Not Fabien Barthez, who'd been the regular keeper. Me. Apparently it was on the strength of those friendlies I'd played in America. I'd made some tough saves against Juventus and Barcelona, and Ferguson decided to shake up the starting keeper position.

In the locker room, I saw a gray-and-white Manchester United goalkeeper's jersey on a hanger with my name on it. I looked at it, marveling, *I'll be wearing that today. I'll be wearing that when I play for Manchester United.*

Roy Keane, the captain, called the team in. Already, I was impressed with his take-no-prisoners attitude and blunt talk. He was known for being a hard man—a guy who didn't give a crap about conventionality or politeness or anything he personally deemed as bullshit. He wanted to win, and he was going to tell us how. What wisdom would he impart in this all-important moment?

He reminded us of some tactical strategies, but then he said—in what I'd learn was his gruff, no-nonsense manner, "Just pass it to a red shirt, guys. It's as simple as that: take the ball and pass it to another player in red."

The game was a war from the first whistle. Seconds in, Phil Neville got a yellow card for a hard tackle on Arsenal's Patrick Vieira. Then Arsenal's Ashley Cole was booked for a clumsy challenge on Ole Gunnar Solskjær. We took the lead when Mikaël Silvestre scored on a header off a corner kick, but Arsenal responded moments later when Thierry Henry—Arsenal's all time goal-scorer—won a free kick about 35 yards out.

With free kicks in scoring range, the goalkeeper sets up a defensive "wall"—a line of players, shoulder to shoulder, 10 yards from where the ball is spotted. The idea is to close off parts of the goal to the shooter, reducing the total area to be covered by the keeper.

The number of men you might put in your wall depends on many variables. Generally, you're trying to cover as much of the goal as you can, without blocking a clear view of the ball or leaving their attackers unmarked. Against Henry, I called for a three-man wall and positioned myself in the unprotected area of the goal.

But Henry struck his shot with such power and precision that it rendered the wall useless. The ball flew over it and tucked inches inside the right post.

I dove, stretching my body flat out, but I couldn't reach it.

At halftime, Ferguson just about took my head off.

Ferguson was famous for what the media referred to as his "hair dryer treatments," so-called because he'd blow such blistering air at you, it felt like your hair was being straightened.

"A three-man wall!" he shouted, the muscles around his jaw so tight I could see them flex. "Against Henry! You needed four men on that wall. You've got to *think*"—he jabbed both index fingers at his forehead—"when you play this game."

My teammates were quiet. I had heard enough about Ferguson to know that they'd all been through this themselves. But frankly, it scared the wits out of me.

"If you *cannae* handle the fucking stage"—his Scottish accent was coming through loud and clear—"I'll send you right back to the MLS."

The disdain in his voice when he said "MLS" was palpable.

I've made plenty of mistakes as a keeper, that's for sure. I'll make plenty more before I'm through. Granted, the three-man wall turned out to be the wrong strategy, given the free kick that Henry ultimately took. But the thing is, he might have opted for an entirely different shot. What if he had kicked it high and to my left? Then a four-man wall could have made it harder for me to see the ball.

There had been no way to know what a world-class player like Henry would do; in the moment, all you can do is make a judgment call.

But I wasn't going to say that to this legend of English soccer—and certainly not while his eyes were bugging wildly out of his head. I looked down at the ground and let him berate me— longer, I might add, than seemed necessary, all things considered.

His final words to me were soaked in derision. "You're not in America anymore, son."

Neither team scored in the second half. The match was still deadlocked at 1–1 at the final whistle. Since there's no overtime in the Community Shield, the game would be settled by a penalty kick shootout.

Sometimes people ask me how I feel about penalty kicks, the ultimate high-stakes moment of a game. My answer is simple: I love them. I have loved penalty kicks since I was 12 years old. I have no proof, but I believe that my heightened senses—the flip side of my TS—makes me better able to read the shooter, to anticipate balls better than most keepers.

And while it's true that the likelihood of actually making a save is fairly low, a keeper doesn't need to stop them all. If you can save one or two, you generally end up a hero.

Plus there's something about that moment standing in goal, just you and the shooter. There's not a time when you're more alert, more alive, more attuned to absolutely everything around you.

Most of the time, a penalty kick is a guessing game. Which

way will the shooter send the ball? Which way should you dive? You can try to make it an educated guess—keepers spend a tremendous amount of time studying videos of different shooters' PK histories. You can also try to read the player's body language, a tiny motion he might make in his run-up to the ball that hints at the direction of the shot. In that case, you might have a fraction of a second to decide.

More often than not, though, it's a crapshoot.

Paul Scholes was up first. The stadium was silent. As Scholes prepared to take the kick, Arsenal's keeper Jens Lehmann danced all over the box, jumping back and forth trying to distract him. Didn't work. Scholes put it away.

Then I faced down the Brazilian Edu. I couldn't read him, and I didn't know enough about his tendencies, so I guessed. I dove left.

Although it was the correct choice, his shot was just beyond my reach.

1–1.

Rio Ferdinand scored; I stopped van Bronckhorst.

2–1.

Then van Nistelrooy missed and Arsenal's Sylvain Wiltord stepped up. I guessed wrong again. I flew one way, the ball sailed past me the other way. I was so mad at myself I kicked the ball into the upper corner of the net. 2–2.

United's Solskjær: score.

Arsenal's Lauren: score.

United's Forlán: score. Now we were up 4–3.

Arsenal had only one bullet left in the chamber.

The kicker was Robert Pirès, a French international who the previous year had scored the winning goal in the FA Cup final.

Pirès was generally regarded as one of the best players in the league.

If I could stop him, we'd win.

That summer I had watched the French national team on television and happened to see Pirès take a penalty kick. For some reason, that image stuck in my head. Standing now in the goal, with Pirès directly in front of me, I saw the entire shot play out in my mind almost like I was watching a video replay—could picture the ball's precise trajectory, how it veered sharply toward the low right corner of the goal.

So that's where I dove. I had to extend my body fully, reach toward it with everything I had. Even before I made contact with the ball, I knew: I had this one. I forced it wide.

Half of the stadium—the roughly 30,000 fans in red shirts—sprang to their feet and went berserk.

I got up, barely registering the red jerseys that were already tearing toward me. Instead, I turned toward the fans and raised my arms in victory.

By the time I wheeled around, Mikaël Silvestre was wrapping his arms around me. We were still embracing when John O'Shea flew toward us in a leaping hug. Then Ruud was there, encircling his arms around the three of us. The rest of the team piled on top: Giggs and Keane and Ferdinand, all those legends playfully punching my stomach and rubbing my bald head.

We'd won. Even better, we'd won on penalty kicks.

The Man U fans jumped up and down all over that stadium. They waved flags and twirled scarves in the air like lassos. In front of them stood Sir Alex Ferguson. He looked as if he had forgotten, by now, all about that three-man wall.

In the wake of the Arsenal victory, I was named the starting goalkeeper. Manchester United soon began negotiating Barthez's transfer to the French club Marseille. It happened in an instant. That, I knew, was one of the risks of playing soccer at this level. If I didn't perform, there would be somebody right behind me who'd be thrilled to jump into my place. The gap that separated me from my competition would never be more than a game. Or a coaching change. Or an injury.

Privately, Fabien was always friendly. Publicly, he made statements like *I blame only myself if I lose my spot.* This from a guy who had won the Premier League the previous season and won the World Cup and European Championship with France and was now watching as his job was handed to a 24-year-old straight from Major League Soccer.

Here, in the most competitive position on the world's most competitive team, he was nothing but classy.

If that should happen to me someday, I thought, *I hope I'll handle it the same way.*

Laura arrived a few weeks later, on a drizzly morning. Manchester is a gloomy town—almost always gray and rainy. But Laura is all bright colors, all sparkle. When she emerged from customs, it was like she'd brought all the sunshine of Memphis, all the warmth of home with her.

"I'm here!" she exclaimed. "I can't believe I'm finally here!"

We collected her bags, dragged them out to the new Mercedes—"Verrrry nice," she said approvingly.

Before I turned on the engine, I looked at Laura.

My wife.

It was a strange moment for me. I'd been so caught up in the excitement of the last couple of months—it had all been heady and frenetic. Falling in love, and traveling between Memphis and New Jersey, meeting each other's families, getting engaged, planning the huge wedding that never happened. Our whirlwind trip here to sign with Manchester United. Back to the States for the tiny impromptu wedding that happened instead. The series of exhibitions I had played for my new team as Laura took apart her old life in Memphis, to be reassembled now with me.

She'd said so many times, *I can't wait. I can't wait to get there. I can't wait to start living with you.*

Now she was here. Our life together—whatever it looked like—was about to begin. We were about to drive to our new house, the near-mansion that she and I had selected just a few weeks ago. (Was it just a few weeks ago? Already it felt like forever)

Sitting there with her in that car, my hand on the ignition, I realized I had no idea how to do this thing I was about to do—perform my job to the best of my abilities and live with a wife in this dark, damp country.

I took a deep breath, and started the engine. The wipers made steady sloshing noises as we drove through the rain. I felt my face twitch a little as I stared straight ahead.

I'm going to have to figure this out, I thought.

We lived about a block from Wilmslow's Grove Street, a pedestrian shopping plaza. It was a neighborhood of "footballers." As we strolled over to Grove Street, we passed Bentleys and Aston Martins, a sure sign that soccer players were about. At the end of the shopping plaza sat a Starbucks. There, I might spot some of my teammates or guys from the other big clubs in the area.

Walking home, Laura would offer her views on whomever we'd seen. Her opinions rarely had anything to do with their game: it was all about how much they'd been caught up in the weird egocentric world around us.

She liked Cristiano Ronaldo, for example—liked how boyish and friendly he was. Cristiano had come to England with his mother, a sturdy, thickly accented Portuguese woman who looked like she'd just left the island of Madeira. Within a year, his mom would be decked out in Prada sunglasses and $2,000 handbags. But Cristiano would never stop doting on his mom, something that always impressed Laura.

She adored Paul Scholes, because he'd quit the national team to spend more time with his kids. Laura appreciated family guys who hadn't let the money go to their heads.

But others, like Roy Keane, she couldn't bear. "Ugh," she said. "I can't stand that guy. He walks around like he thinks he's bigger than God."

I laughed. Laura was American, through and through—and she had no patience for the huge egos that dominated English soccer.

I happened to like Roy. Sure, he was quick to rage, loose with profanity, and often itching for a fight, sometimes even with his own teammates.

And granted, he could be arrogant. But he had every right to be. He was the captain of Manchester United and he had led them to countless trophies; he actually was every bit as good as he believed he was. Besides, he had that quality I'd always appreciated in people: you knew where you stood with the man. He gave it to you straight, even if "straight" meant his words were shouted, and came strung together with F-bombs.

Once, when Laura and I were walking home from Starbucks, we ran into Brad Friedel. I was prepared for it to be a pass-and-nod—no greeting, only a perfunctory acknowledgment that we'd seen each other. Brad had different plans.

"I'd like to come by and talk to you about what I did," he said. He paused before adding, "You know, with regard to your work permit."

I knew exactly what he meant, of course. He was talking about his refusal to help me out with my work permit papers. I had also learned something else. The legal team at Manchester United—the ones who had originally applied for my papers—had already told me that Brad hadn't merely refused to sign a statement on my behalf, he had actively tried to block my transfer. He'd written to the appeals committee suggesting that I shouldn't be given a work permit at all.

I hadn't asked for an explanation, and I certainly didn't need one. But I wasn't going to stop him from dropping by.

"Sure, Brad," I said. "Anytime."

A few days later, he showed up at my door with a folder full of documents.

Laura arched her eyebrows at me. *This will be interesting,* she seemed to be saying. Then she disappeared; she cared for Brad about as much as I did.

Brad began to explain his own struggle getting a work permit.

Would have signed for Nottingham . . .

Had to wait until '97 . . .

Problems at Newcastle, too . . .

Permit for Liverpool denied . . .

He showed me one document after another as he spoke without a pause. I glanced at the papers and passed them back. The crux of his presentation was this: if *he'd* had this much trouble getting a work permit, why should he make it easy for me?

"It's a matter of principle, you see," he said.

A matter of principle? Whatever his principles might have been, I knew they were different from my own.

Besides, the simple fact was that Brad Friedel had tried to undermine the best opportunity of my career. If he'd have succeeded, it could have dealt a tremendous blow to my lifelong earnings and career . . . and for what clear benefits?

I'd always be the kid from Northwood Estates watching my own mother scrimp and save. I can tell you right now: that's not something I'd do to anyone. Ever.

After an hour of show-and-tell, Brad stood up.

"Oh, and one other thing," he said. He spoke casually, as if presenting it as an afterthought, "just so you know: Manchester United was interested in me at the same time. So, obviously, there was a real conflict of interest."

I thought about the way Manchester United had signed Cristiano Ronaldo within days of that preseason friendly. I had a feeling that if Manchester United wanted the pope to play in goal for them, they'd have been able to arrange that.

"Okay," I said. I wasn't going to argue with him. I shook Brad's hand, and we parted ways.

It was amicable enough. But as far as I was concerned—and to borrow a favorite phrase from the Brits—the guy could sod off.

I naively thought that I could maintain some sense of a private life in England. Once I arrived in Manchester, I'd given an interview to the *New York Times*. When the reporter asked me about Laura, I'd said, "That's private."

Boy, was I in for a rude awakening.

It's hard to express the degree of fanaticism within the Premier League. There's nothing quite like it in the United States. In the U.S., we've got our share of superfans, men and women who live and die by their team's fortunes.

But in the States, loyalties are divided across sports. We've got the NBA. The NFL. National Hockey League. Major League Baseball. We've got NASCAR and, yes, Major League Soccer, too. We've got college sports—March Madness and the BCS.

Now imagine if the most rabid fans from each of these different sports coalesced around a single team within a single sport. Imagine that their dedication runs deep, through multiple generations over a century. Imagine that reports about their sport are broadcast around the clock—in every pub, every restaurant, every hotel lobby in the country.

Now imagine being a player in their midst.

Most of the time, it's incredible. I love the passion, the commitment. It's a joy to see perfectly ordinary people leap out of their seat in a state of pure ecstasy. I don't even mind hearing the expletives pour out of their mouths toward the players on the field.

But once in a while, I come across someone who takes it too far. One night, for example, Laura and I were at a pub with a friend when a man stumbled up to our table. "Tim Howard," the guy bellowed, "you don't know shit about goalkeeping."

Suddenly, the din of the voices around us grew quiet. The man's face was flushed and his words slurred, probably from a few too many pints. Other than that, he looked like a normal guy in his forties—probably somebody's husband, somebody's dad, a midlevel employee of some company.

I felt my heart beating faster, felt that rush of adrenaline through my body. The same thing happened to me before each game; it was what allowed me to stay alert, to sense danger on that field, to stop the ball reflexively, without thinking. But there was no ball to be stopped here, only some red-nosed jerk with a paunch telling me how to do my job.

Laura looked right at me, as if silently saying, *Keep your cool, keep your cool.*

"You know I pay your wages, right?" He continued: "I've got a season ticket, so I'm the one who's paying you."

As his friends dragged him from our table, I could still hear his voice: "You're a wanker, Tim Howard. And don't you forget who pays your salary."

Our guest's jaw hung open. He gave a little shake of his head, as if to trying to dislodge the unpleasant encounter he had witnessed.

"So," he said. "This happen a lot?"

I shrugged. I could feel my heart pounding. "Sometimes," I said. What I wanted to do was get up, find this guy, grab him by his shirt collar. I wanted to remind him that his season ticket entitled him to one thing only: to attend the game, to scream and cheer virtually anything that wasn't racist or homophobic. And then to go home.

It sure as hell didn't give him the right to interrupt dinner with my wife and friend.

Laura and I did our best to try to acclimate to life in Manchester. Our first order of business was to get a dog.

Clayton was a goofy puppy who flopped all over the house, always getting in trouble. He needed to be in constant motion or he'd start chewing the furniture or scratching at the doors. He reminded me of myself and my brother, running roughshod all over Mom's apartment back in New Jersey.

"He's going to destroy this house!" I'd exclaim. Then I'd try to scold him, and Laura would swoop him up. She'd pet behind his ears and say, "Aw, but he's just learning. And he's such a good boy.

"Aren't you a good boy, Clayton?" Then that dog would go bounding around the house all over again.

Clayton took forever to housebreak; we'd come in from the grocery store, only to find piles and puddles staining the hardwood floors of our beautiful Manchester United home.

We'd stand in the doorway, temporarily paralyzed by the constant havoc of this furry little creature.

Then Laura would go into action mode. "You get the paper towels," she would say. "I'll get the plastic bag."

I was playing well. In my first nine games, I posted six clean sheets, and had allowed only three goals. By January, I'd started in 29 matches, posting a 22–5–2 record, with 14 shutouts.

The tabloids turned around their screaming headlines pretty quickly.

The bestselling *Sun* noted, THIS YANK'S NO PLANK.

The *Express* agreed: YANKEE DOING DANDY.

And the more sober-minded broadsheets chimed in as well. "If the American goalkeeper has a weakness," the *Telegraph* observed, "there has not been a team who have located it."

Before long, the home crowd had even made up a chant for me. Sometimes when I stopped a shot, I'd hear the Man U supporters singing to the tune of "Chim Chim Cher-ee" from *Mary Poppins*:

Tim Timminy,
Tim Timminy,
Tim Tim-eroo
We've got Tim Howard and he says "Fuck you!"

It was a play on my TS, of course. And while it wasn't remotely accurate, I could live with it. It beat being called "retarded" and "disabled," anyway.

Again and again, I was compared to Peter Schmeichel, the "Great Dane," former United keeper widely considered to be among the top ten in history. In a Reuters poll more than 200,000 fans had ranked him the best goalie of all time.

During one interview, Tony Coton said he believed that I could even surpass Schmeichel. Halfway through my first season, Schmeichel himself said that I could be "a United legend."

It was flattering, but every time I heard someone spout this kind of hyperbole, I wanted to say, *Wait. Please wait.*

I'd spent my entire life comparing myself to others. I knew exactly how I stacked up against Schmeichel. I had talent, I had drive, and I had a heck of a lot of potential. But I wasn't in Schmeichel's class. Not by a long shot.

I knew something else, too. As hard as I was working, and as lucky as I'd gotten, it was just a matter of time before I made a mistake. A big one.

THE LONGEST SEASON

Six weeks after the Community Shield, we met Arsenal again in a match that would go down in soccer folklore . . . and not for its outstanding play. Still scoreless in the 80th minute, the game turned ugly when Ruud van Nistelrooy and Arsenal's Patrick Vieira both went after a high ball, and Ruud jumped on top of Vieira, knocking them both to the ground. Vieira kicked out at Ruud—a deliberate, nasty cheap shot. Already on a yellow card, Vieira was given a second one for the foul on van Nistelrooy, which resulted in automatic ejection.

When the game ended, the Arsenal players surrounded Ruud. Martin Keown, who had a history of bad blood with the striker, got right up in Ruud's face, bringing his arm down hard on the back of his neck—he clocked the guy. Ray Parlour, Ashley Cole, and a few other Arsenal players joined in, jostling and taunting Ruud for missing a penalty kick in stoppage time. Roy Keane tried to pull Ruud out of there. As he did, three more United players, Cristiano Ronaldo, Quinton Fortune, and Mikaël Silvestre, entered the fracas, ready to defend their besieged teammate.

From the end of the field, I watched it escalate, swelling to a bench-clearing 25-man melee. Here were some of the world's top pros pushing and shoving as if they were in the schoolyard.

What is happening?

It was adrenaline, of course—the same chemical that kick-started my rage when the middle-aged drunk approached me in the restaurant—and I'd soon come to learn how much it could dominate players' lives, both on and off the field.

Arsenal's win that day was just the beginning of an incredible run that would see them go through the season unbeaten and earn them the moniker "the Invincibles." But by the time we played them again, I would no longer be on the field.

The winters come quickly in Manchester and last for a long, long time. By early September, the average daytime temperature is in the 50s, often dipping to near-freezing at night. Manchester sits on the 53rd North parallel—as far north as many parts of Alaska. It's dark by 3 p.m., and shops are shuttered by 5 p.m. The color of the sky ranges from slate gray to ink black.

And then there's the rain, thin and persistent. The dampness seeps into your bones. Not long ago, a Manchester resident tracked the weather for an entire year, taking meticulous notes, and found that rainy days outnumbered dry ones by 198 to 167.

That winter, taking Clayton out for walks with Laura became the best part of my day. Each afternoon, we strolled over to Carrs Park, a mix of woods and meadow along the Bollin River where Clayton would romp with his canine playmates, splash along the riverbanks, and pee on every available tree. At night, exhausted, we'd all curl up, close our eyes, and sleep.

I loved that dog. I loved that he didn't know anything about goals or games, about hot-headed managers or boastful teammates. I loved that he wasn't impressed when he heard passersby whisper *Tim Howard . . . Manchester United . . . yeah, that's him.*

Most of all, I loved the way Laura looked at Clayton, how her eyes went soft just because he thumped his tail on the floor. And when I checked out—because of anxiety before a game or disappointment after one, or when I was too spent from a tough training session to utter a word—Clayton would step in wagging his tail and make Laura laugh. Even when I couldn't.

I often lingered after practice. Just as I had enlisted Tab to fire balls at me back in our MetroStars days, now I asked Ruud van Nistelrooy to open up a can of thunder. Ruud was happy to oblige, sending balls in with swerve and dip at speeds up to 90 mph. But no matter how long we stayed out there, we were never the last to leave the field. That's because no one could outwork Cristiano Ronaldo.

Cristiano has always had plenty of flash—the underwear commercials, the diamonds in each ear, the fleet of fast cars, the supermodels. And sure, he might strut into the locker room wearing shades and an air of superiority. But what I remember most vividly about him isn't his cockiness. It's how hard he trained.

As Ruud and I headed toward the locker room after practice, eager to put on warm, dry clothes and get home to rest and recover, Cristiano was still out there dribbling the ball around the perimeter of our training ground.

I remember watching him one afternoon as the rain pelted down. He kept on working on his ball tricks while the rest of us took shelter inside.

That guy's going to be the best in the world one day, I thought.

Laura took control of the domestic details, from masterminding travel schedules and grocery lists to investigating local restaurants; she soon knew whom to turn to, and for what. With my fat new paycheck, we suddenly had money rolling in and nowhere to put it, so she researched investment options and hired advisors when necessary. Understanding that Manchester United players should dress the part—in the fashion equivalent of the luxury cars they drove—she even bought my clothes.

But that financial windfall caused some problems for us. Almost as soon as I'd signed with Manchester United, friends and loved ones began asking us for money. Within a few months' time, I easily could have handed over hundreds of thousands of dollars.

Meanwhile, I kept thinking about Dan's advice. *My career is front-loaded. I have no idea what will happen from here. Take the basics off the table.*

So I said no to any handouts, and I was amazed to see how quickly past relationships could fall apart.

We didn't socialize a whole lot, but Laura carved out space for a few friends. Once a week we'd have dinner with Claudio Reyna, a U.S. star who played for Manchester City in the Premier League, and his wife, Danielle, usually at their place. Sometimes another U.S. player, Eddie Lewis, and his wife, Mari, joined us. With their kids running around, the guys and I would talk soccer while Danielle and Laura and Mari chatted about everything but. Danielle cooked, and we'd all relax over some wine.

Because Laura didn't like to stay alone in our big house, she often slept at Claudio and Danielle's whenever I had away games. She stayed in a room with their young son Jack, who was then four years old.

"Oh, Tim," she'd say. "He's the sweetest little thing." There was a wistfulness in her voice as she described watching Jack's little chest rise and fall as he slept.

Her smile reminded me of the one my mom had given me when I made that Mother's Day goal. Laura was going to make an amazing mom one day.

In late September, Rio Ferdinand, our best defender, missed a routine drug test. It was a stupid mistake, not a sinister dodge; he'd simply forgotten to show up after practice as planned. As soon as he remembered, he'd turned around and returned to the training grounds . . . only to be told it was too late.

He was tested 24 hours later, with negative results. But that didn't matter to the Football Association. Nor did it matter that he offered to have a hair follicle test, which would have registered results for the prior six months. Even when Alex Ferguson went absolutely apoplectic, demanding appeals, the FA was unmoved.

They fined Rio 50,000 pounds—about $82,000. Worse, they banned him from playing for eight months. He'd miss the entire second half of the current season, and some of the next.

It was a sucker punch to our defense and it meant more pressure on me to raise my game.

By March, I'd been playing soccer for 14 consecutive months. I'd gone from the MLS preseason in January 2003 to the regular season, and from there straight into the Premier League campaign. Even the holidays offered no respite. I trained on Christmas morning, and played a game the very next day.

Manchester United's season wouldn't finish until the very end of May. I was still staring down three more months of nonstop competition, game upon game upon game, without pause.

Never before had I faced stakes this high, for this long, at this level of intensity.

On the way to matches, I sat near the front of the bus and stayed quiet, while Ferguson played cards in back with Roy Keane and Ryan Giggs and Gary Neville, laughing and bantering from the hotel to the stadium. I closed my eyes and cleared my throat and tried to focus on my breathing.

I needed to concentrate.

When you win, you don't question it. You don't wonder how you pulled off that save or why you happened to play well in that particular game but not some other one.

It's only when you lose that the self-examination begins.

I can pinpoint the day it started for me: March 9, 2004.

The top teams throughout Europe compete in the UEFA Champions League tournament—by far the most important, prestigious club competition. Earlier in the season, we'd played six Champions League games. We'd won five, and advanced to the round of 16.

We'd meet FC Porto, a club in the top league of Portuguese soccer. After playing them home and away, the team with the highest aggregate score would move on. In the event of a tie, whichever of us had the most away goals (weighted more heavily than home goals) prevailed.

We were the clear favorite, and we expected to win. But the first game, played at Porto, didn't go as planned. Although we took an early lead, Porto's striker Benni McCarthy sent two brilliant goals right past me. We lost 2–1.

Ferguson was so enraged he refused to shake hands with José Mourinho, Porto's new manager, still a relative unknown.

Mourinho responded by mocking Ferguson to the media, saying, "I understand why he is a bit emotional . . . you would be sad too if your team gets as clearly dominated by opponents who have been built on ten percent of the budget."

In the second game, a header from Paul Scholes gave us the lead in the 32nd minute. If the score remained 1–0, we'd be tied on aggregate at 2–2—enough to win, with the help of our away-goal advantage.

We held the line for nearly an hour. But with two minutes left in injury time, Phil Neville was called for a foul outside the penalty area. Benni McCarthy—the guy who scored on me twice in the last game—would take the free kick.

I organized the wall. McCarthy struck his shot. The ball flew past the line of defenders, curling toward the net.

I've replayed that moment a thousand times since. I know exactly what I did wrong. I had two options: catch the ball, or parry it into a safe area, beyond the box. A truly top keeper, an experienced keeper, would have had the confidence to do one or the other.

Today I'd have that confidence. A decade ago, though, I was still raw, not assured enough to act decisively. I knocked the ball right back into the danger zone: Smack dab in front of the six-yard box. Porto's Francisco Costinha pounced on the rebound. His shot came sailing toward my right. I dove. I stretched. I extended my hands as far as I could. It's possible the tips of my gloves even grazed the ball. Then it slid into the far corner of the net.

Before I even hit the ground I understood: we were out of the Champions League.

I lay facedown on the field for a moment. I looked up in time to see Costinha's triumphant leap, fist pumping in the air. Then his teammates throwing themselves on top of him. Then Jose Mourinho's now-famous manic dash down the touchline—arms toward the sky, dark trench coat flapping behind him in the wind. This celebration, which would be replayed again and again, essentially announced his arrival on the European stage.

Porto would go on to win that year's Champions League title. In time, Mourinho would be considered one of the greatest managers in all of soccer.

But all I knew, lying there on the turf, was that it was over for us.

And that was on me.

BENCHED

Criticism hurts. But nothing hurts more than knowing you could have done better.

I took the blame for that Champions League loss—in the papers, among the fans, with Ferguson, and with my teammates.

"That's not fair," said Laura. "Phil Neville made the foul. The ball went past ten other guys before it got to you. And where were your defenders on the rebound? They didn't follow the shot."

She'd look at me earnestly. "Tim, honey. It's not your fault."

But I knew better. Stopping that ball, keeping it from hitting the net, was my job. It was the job I signed up for when I came to Man U. If I couldn't take the heat, I shouldn't have been standing in that box.

Mulch called me to see how I was doing. He was working for the Kansas City Wizards now, and he'd caught the last five minutes on the bus ride home from his game. I knew him well enough by now to know that his heart must have sunk down to his toes when he heard what I'd done.

"Listen, Tim," Mulch said. "This is just another step in the journey. You'll have other games. You'll have other saves."

I thanked him, but it didn't matter.

That voice inside me was saying as it had all along, *You kept calling me the next Peter Schmeichel, but I knew I wasn't there yet.*

I could be someday. I swore I could be, but I was 24 years old, still young for a keeper. I was fresh from the MLS. I needed time. But time was a luxury I wasn't about to get at Manchester United.

Five days after Porto, we played our crosstown rivals, Manchester City, and lost 4–1. After that, Alex Ferguson announced that our backup keeper, Roy Carroll, would be playing in the next three games. It meant I'd be on the bench for our second Premier League match against Arsenal.

"That's ridiculous," said Laura when I told her. She had fire in her eyes. "We're talking about one mistake, Tim. One."

I shrugged. "Yeah, well . . ."

She stood there, waiting for the end of that sentence.

"It was really big mistake," I said.

Ferguson put me back in for the final month of the season, including the FA Cup, a tournament that runs concurrently with the Premier League. We beat Arsenal in the semifinals.

Something had changed, though. I could feel it.

I could feel it in the way Tony Coton spoke to me during practice—or rather didn't. We went through our routines—our high volleys and low balls. Sometimes, if he didn't like how I went after one, he'd snap at me. Beyond that, though, I got almost no feedback. After training, he disappeared, scurrying off the field, almost as if he didn't want to be seen with me.

I always clear my throat before games—just another one of my tics. The closer to kickoff, the more I do it. Before one of the final games of the season, my phone rang.

"You okay?" Dan asked.

"Yeah, why?"

There was a pause. "Well, I got a call from Tony Coton. He said you're throwing up in the bathroom."

I scratched my head. Had Coton heard my throat-clearing and mistaken it for throwing up?

Dan added, "Tony's asking a lot of questions about your Tourette."

I felt my jaw harden. "Why?"

"It sounds as though he thinks it's affecting your play."

My TS had never been an issue in terms of my goalkeeping. Not here, not at the MetroStars, not even as a kid. But suddenly I felt like I was back in high school, like I had to hide my condition again.

The thing is, if that was in their head—that TS was behind my mistakes—that wasn't something I could overcome.

"You tell him he has nothing to worry about," I muttered into the phone.

Leaving Old Trafford that day, I kept my eyes fixed ahead. If Tony Coton or Alex Ferguson were somewhere in the vicinity, I didn't want to run into them, because I had no idea what I'd do.

At the very end of the season, Tony Coton approached me before practice.

He told me I'd won the Professional Footballers' Association goalkeeper of the year—the most prestigious award in England. He said it in such a matter-of-fact manner that it took a moment to sink in.

Each year, the PFA awards are given at an invitation-only gala dinner. It's held in London and staged like Oscars night for the

Premier League. Limos. Red carpet. Tuxedos. Paparazzi. If you're one of the 11 men to earn an award—for your position—you go. That's why it was so strange that Tony didn't say a word about the event. He simply informed me I was getting the award, and then—bizarrely—he walked away.

A few months earlier, Coton had paraded me around and patted himself on the back for discovering me. Now it was like he was embarrassed that I would be representing Manchester United at the awards banquet.

The event came and went, and neither of us spoke of it again. I suppose my name must have been announced and politely applauded at the dinner, but I wasn't there to hear it. A trophy arrived later, a silver symbol of where I hadn't been.

Laura and I went home to Memphis at the end of that season. We had a party to celebrate our marriage; my Poppa and three-year-olds danced while wearing Manchester United caps. Claudio and Danielle flew in from England with the kids. Eddie Lewis and Mari. Steve Senior and some of my other high school buddies were there. Mulch and Dan brought their families. *This is going to be my home someday*, I thought. *When all this soccer is done, I want to come right back here, to Memphis.*

Laura's mom approached me at our party. She gave me an enormous hug. "You two will always be married," she said. "Because you have God in your marriage." I hugged her back with gusto.

I believed it.

Roy and I spent the following season, 2004–2005, playing goalkeeping musical chairs. Roy was Ferguson's first choice for a while. Then, when he made a mistake, he put me in the game. I lasted until my next error. Then I was out, and Roy was back in.

Laura was furious on my behalf.

Shaking her head, she'd say, "I can't believe they ripped you out of the lineup like that."

When I didn't respond, she folded her arms over her chest, tapped her foot impatiently. "You do know it's because Tony Coton's afraid to stand up to Alex Ferguson, right? Because Ferguson is a big old bully and nobody stands up to him."

I loved her loyalty. But the truth is, it wasn't one mistake anymore. I was making many.

In October, we played Arsenal at Old Trafford. I didn't play, but I joined the fight, in a way.

Arsenal had swaggered in on the back of a 49-game unbeaten run. They skulked out with a one-match losing streak after we beat them 2–0. Ruud converted a penalty kick, and a 19-year-old prodigy named Wayne Rooney, who had come over from Everton, scored a stunning strike in stoppage time.

It was a physical game from the start and the bad blood flowed past the final whistle. We were in the locker room celebrating our victory when Ferguson walked in. He had this massive stain on his crisp white shirt—some kind of red splotch. He looked totally bewildered.

"Gaffer?" someone asked. "What happened?"

Ferguson said that as he walked past the Arsenal locker room, someone had hurled a slice of pizza at him. Outside the locker room, we could hear a commotion—loud, aggressive voices.

Some of our own teammates were out there, with several of the Arsenal players, and they were about to have a throw-down.

That was it. We leapt up and ran out into the hallway that separated the two locker rooms. It was a narrow space, and everyone was pushing and shoving, grabbing shirts, trying to swing at each other. It was like fighting inside a phone booth; nobody had the room to throw a punch; all we could do was push a palm in someone's face. A couple of police officers were trying to break up the fight, but they were no match for the out-of-control players. I watched as one of the police officer's hats got knocked off in the scuffle.

For whatever reason, Rio Ferdinand was late getting to the locker room—Rio's tall, and from where I stood, I could see him barging his way through the Arsenal players. When he reached our side, he turned around and starting whaling on anyone in a yellow jersey. He couldn't have even known what we were fighting about, but it didn't stop him.

When I got home that afternoon, I looked at Laura and shook my head.

"This is a weird job."

I'd started playing cautiously, tight. I knew I was on a short rope—a very short rope—and that everything I did was going to be scrutinized in a way it never had been before.

My game had changed.

I was focusing more on avoiding mistakes than on winning games. I was thinking, *Get through this game. Make sure that if a goal does go in, it's not your fault.*

As long as it wasn't my fault, I could stay on the team.

It was the worst possible mindset a keeper can have. A keeper needs to do everything in his power to stop the ball. Period.

In one game, I punched a ball out of the box. It was a weaker punch than I'd intended, and Rio admonished me, "Tim, you've got to catch the fucking thing."

So the next time the ball came toward me, in the same game, I caught it. But the catch was loose, just barely in my arms. Roy Keane looked at me ferociously. "Punch that fucking thing," Roy said. His voice was laced with venom. "Punch it next time."

Somehow, I needed to get back to a place where I had conviction, where I could take a risk. I needed to be Tony Meola, charging fearlessly out of his goal. Or Kasey Keller, unflappable in the face of uncertainty. And I'll give the guy credit where it's due: I could even have used a dose of Brad Friedel's bluster, his bullheadedness.

The fans noticed my timidity, every bit as much as my teammates and coaches had. One afternoon, a little old lady followed me around the grocery store. She was older than my mother, this woman. And I'm telling you: she glared at me. There she was in the dairy section as I put milk in the cart. Then again by the breads aisle.

Each time, I'd walked away, only to have her follow me to my next stop.

Finally, in the produce section, I looked right at her and spoke. "Hi," I said. "How are you?"

She glowered at me. "Well, I'd be doing a lot better," she said, "if you would stop dropping the bloody ball."

When we decided to have a baby, Laura paid the same meticulous attention to the details of her fertility that she had to every other aspect of our lives. She purchased an ovulation predictor kit. She mastered the art of peeing on sticks. She monitored her body temperature, the slightest change in her cycle.

"I mean, we might as well try to maximize our chances," she said. "I know so many people who tried to have a baby for so long."

In December, Laura and I flew to Marbella, Spain. I was so desperate for a break, even a short one. I needed to catch my breath before going back to the field.

"I'm going to sit on that beach," I said, "and do nothing at all."

Laura was changing in the bathroom. I walked around the room picking up everything we'd need by the water: sunscreen, Laura's sun hat, books, an extra T-shirt for me, a football for tossing in the sand. Extra towels. Beach chairs.

"Come on, girl," I called to her. "I want to get started with my doing nothing."

My arms were loaded by then with items in both hands and chairs wedged precariously under each arm.

Laura opened the bathroom door. "Tim?" Laura said. There was a glint in her eye. "I'm ovulating."

I dropped everything. I didn't even try to set it all down. Hats, chairs, sunscreen, football, went crashing to the floor.

I was by her side in two seconds flat.

The beach could wait.

Back home, 11 days later, Laura emerged from the bathroom waving a white stick in the air.

"Tim!" she exclaimed. She was laughing and glowing, the same way she had at the W hotel in Times Square. "Tim, guess what?! There are two lines."

A pregnancy test. Two lines.

Clayton ran over to her and danced around in circles. You could see him wondering what the fuss was about. A walk? A treat?

Laura didn't even look at him.

She wiggled the stick. "Look. The lines are really, really faint," she said, "but they're there."

I squinted. Sure enough, if I looked hard, I could see them. There were two blue lines.

I allowed that to sink in. Two lines meant baby. We were having a baby.

I hadn't felt this excited since our wedding day.

At that moment, nothing else mattered. Not Tony Coton, not Alex Ferguson, not Roy Keane's cursing at me, not whether I would play in the next game.

Laura and I were going to be parents. We had started our family.

I forgot all about my professional slump. With this news, everything on God's green earth suddenly seemed as good as it gets.

By now I was calling Mulch to ask him what he saw me doing wrong in my games. Since I wasn't getting any feedback from Coton, Mulch had become my go-to guy. He watched every match, and he was honest.

"You're not playing like yourself," he said. "You're stiff. Your face is tight. You look like you're not enjoying yourself."

He was right; I hated playing small like that. I hated feeling afraid.

"Just be Tim Howard," he said. "If you can get back to doing what you do, you'll be fine."

My mom visited.

I could feel her watching. I left for practice in the morning. Came home. Napped. When I got up, I didn't say much.

When the two of us were alone, Mom said, "Can I ask you something?"

"Sure."

"Do you still love soccer?"

I didn't even have to think about it. "No," I said. "I don't."

At the end of the 2004–2005 season, we met Arsenal again in the FA Cup final. Roy Carroll played. I watched from the sidelines.

By the end of 90 minutes, the game was tied, 0–0. We went into overtime, and still no goals.

About 15 minutes before the end of the game, it seemed clear: we were headed for a penalty kick shootout. Ferguson turned around.

"Tim," he said. "Go warm up."

Good, I thought. *He's going to put me in for the shootout, and I'm going to win this game for the team.*

I warmed up, then went back to the bench. Waited. The clock ticked by. Players ran up and down the field.

I stood again, jogged up and down the touchline. I stretched. I wanted to stay fresh.

When I sat down, I watched the back of Ferguson's head. Any minute, he was going to turn around and send me in.

The whistle blew. The teams started moving toward the goal for the shootout.

I waited, but Ferguson didn't turn around. He didn't say a word. He sat there watching as Roy Carroll took his place in the box.

I wanted to scream. *I can do this. I can handle penalty kick shootouts like no one else I know.*

Today I'd have spoken up. Today I'd have reminded him: I'm right here. I'm ready. But on that day, I didn't, and I never went in. We lost that shootout and the game.

Later, in the locker room, Ferguson ripped into the players one by one. Someone must have told Roy that I'd been warming up, because by the time Ferguson got to him, he snapped.

"Well," shouted Roy, staring right at Ferguson. "If you wanted to fucking put Tim in, you should have fucking put Tim in!" His face was red and his eyes burned like fire.

The stress of this season. I'm telling you. It was going to take us both down.

We finished the season third in the table. It was only the fourth time in 16 years that we hadn't earned a league trophy.

In June, Laura and I returned to Memphis—back to our house, back to our life there. We sat by the pool and watched her belly grow and waited for that baby to come.

Not long after we returned, my phone rang. Alex Ferguson was on the other end of the line. You know something's up when the club manager calls you at home, from another continent.

"Did Tony tell you?" he asked.

"Tell me what?" Tony hadn't talked to me since the season ended.

"We're releasing Roy Carroll. We've signed Edwin van der Sar."

Van der Sar was a highly regarded keeper from Fulham. He was long and lanky, cool under pressure. His nickname was "the Ice Rabbit."

"We need competition for this position," Ferguson said. "Nothing's set in stone. The first keeper job's up for grabs."

He was reassuring me, but I didn't buy it.

"Okay," I said. I hung up, then walked into the kitchen. Laura was there, her belly as round as a basketball now.

"Who was that?" she asked.

"Alex Ferguson."

She looked surprised.

"He just signed Edwin van der Sar," I said. I explained who Edwin was. I told her that Ferguson had said I might still be the starting keeper.

"But it's all a load of bullshit," I said. I knew the truth.

Sometimes a club's actions say it all. My platooning with Carroll made it obvious that they didn't believe in me as their regular keeper. Now they followed that up by acquiring someone who was a big star. Their intentions were clear.

In a few months, I'd have a child—a son, I was so sure of that. I didn't want my child to see his dad sitting on the bench. I didn't care how many millions of dollars I could earn watching from the sidelines. I was determined to play.

#24

Life as Edwin's backup was more or less what I expected. Tony fawned over him the way he once did over me. During trainings Edwin informed him what drills he wanted to do, and Tony did exactly as he was told.

"How's training going?" Mulch asked me.

"I don't know," I answered. "I don't get any feedback."

"What do you mean?"

"Tony talks to Edwin," I said. "That's it."

Mulch didn't say anything, but I could tell he was thinking, *That Tony Coton is a worm, and you need to get out from underneath him.*

Edwin, on the other hand, wasn't a bad guy; he was unfailingly polite, always a gentleman around me. But we were from different worlds, different cultures.

It was clear, too, that Edwin wasn't going to mentor me, or anybody else. He was focused on his own game, nothing more.

Edwin really was a terrific keeper, though. He had reach and agility, with an uncanny instinct for anticipating where the ball would land. At six feet six, he could stretch so far in goal that he made near-impossible saves look easy. Most of all, he was clear and direct with the defenders, positioning them with such authority and decisiveness that he often didn't even need to make those saves.

I can learn from this guy, I thought. *If I don't let my ego get in the way.*

Edwin can make me better.

We learned that the baby was breech. Laura and the doctor scheduled a C-section for September 5.

Laura's mom stayed with us in England, and my mom arrived two days before the procedure. Together, they fussed about the house. They folded and refolded baby onesies. They organized diapers, prepared heaps of food.

Our moms were so different—as different as night and day. Mine was a flower-power immigrant mom, quiet in demeanor, but a fierce political liberal. And Laura's mom was a friendly Southerner, a devout Baptist with conservative political views. Before, long, these two women would be grandmothers to the same child, providing both yin and yang in the baby's life.

When September 5 rolled around, I was a nervous wreck. I was jittery as we walked into the hospital, jittery as I put on scrubs and they prepped Laura for the procedure. And although I did my best to stay cool, I was completely off-the-charts terrified when they sliced into her.

But then the doctor said those three incredible words—*it's a boy*. We heard our baby boy cry, and a few minutes later a nurse handed him to me, all bundled up in a flannel blanket. And then I was holding him.

My son.

"Look at him," I said. "Just look." He'd been in the world mere minutes, but I was already completely head over heels in love.

"Yeah," said Laura. "I know exactly what you mean."

We sat there quietly for a while, then I turned to Laura. "You know, I think this is the first time I've ever held a baby."

She laughed. "Well, you look like a natural, Tim."

A while later, I threw open the double doors to the waiting room. There were the grandmothers. (The grandmothers! My mother was a grandmother now!)

They looked up hopefully. Nervously.

"It's a boy," I announced. Later, my mom would tell me that I was wearing the biggest grin she'd ever seen on me in my whole life. "His name is Jacob."

In an instant, they were out of their seats, hugging and kissing me.

"How can you be a father?" my mother said. She planted a kiss on my cheek. I felt wet tears on my skin. "How can you possibly be a father, when I can still remember holding *you*?"

The next morning I returned to training; the moments I spent with Laura on the day of the C-section would be all the paternity break I was going to get.

My teammates offered congratulations and clapped me on the back. Then Alex Ferguson approached.

"Is all well?" he asked.

"Yeah," I said. "It's a boy. We named him Jacob."

Ferguson looked like he approved.

"Good name," he said. "Jacob. That's a good, strong name for a boy."

Jacob was an easy, angelic baby. He took his morning nap and his afternoon nap on schedule. He ate well, he grew quickly,

When he was four weeks old, he slept four hours at a stretch. By six weeks, he was sleeping six hours.

His eyes were bright and curious. I made all kinds of moony faces at him.

"That's right," I'd say. "I'm your daddy, Jacob. And I love you forever and ever and ever."

I couldn't stop touching him. It was unconscious, almost primal, the way my fingers drifted over to the curve of his cheek, the downy wisps of his hair.

I rocked him to sleep, I burped him, I buttoned him into his little peanut onesie, I pulled miniature sports jerseys over his head. I lay down next to him and gazed at him.

When he napped, I peeked in on him just to make sure he was breathing. It was like I feared he'd be taken away from us somehow, whisked away as if he really *had* been too good to be true all along. We bought baby monitors to hear him at night. We bought a movement sensor, one that was capable of detecting the up-and-down motions of a baby's breath; if it didn't detect any motion for 20 seconds, an alarm sounded.

One afternoon, that alarm went off, and Laura and I dashed to the nursery as fast as our legs would carry us. I took the stairs two at a time, then bounded into his room.

There, standing at the center of the room, was my mom, rocking Jacob.

"I'm sorry," my mom said. She had this guilty look on her face. "I heard him wake up, so I came in to get him. I picked him up without turning off the alarm. I forgot all about that thing."

Laura and I took deep breaths. Everything was fine.

Just before I learned about Edwin coming to United, I'd signed an extension on my Manchester United contract.

Some keepers would surely have been content to remain the Man U backup. There's great fame, money, and royal treatment. And, like a backup quarterback in football, the backup keeper is rarely used, so all this would come without tremendous day-in, day-out pressure.

But it wasn't for me. I had things I wanted to accomplish.

Dan arranged a meeting with Manchester United chief executive David Gill. He told David what I wanted—respectfully, firmly, clearly.

"Man U is a great club," Dan said. "We respect your decision to sign a new starting keeper, but Tim doesn't want to be a backup. We'd like to find another place for him."

Gill said that they'd like me to stay at Man U. They needed a reliable number two keeper as cover for Edwin. He added, "Top goalkeepers are extremely tough to find," implying that I could be at Manchester United, at least as a backup, for years to come.

But he respected that I wanted to play and that I had been a good pro during my time at the club. David and Dan reached an understanding. If I gave them a good year as a backup, they would help me move to a place I could play regularly.

Clayton was the only one who didn't adore Jacob from the start. He sniffed the baby when we brought him home, was curious about this new plaything. But when Jacob didn't play back, Clayton took offense.

If Clayton was lounging on the sofa and we sat down with Jacob in our arms, Clayton would coolly get off the couch and head to a far corner of the room. He'd sulk at us, as if saying, *Make your choice, people: it's going to be me, or that baby.*

"It's not going to be you, Clayton," I'd grumble.

"You be nice to Clayton," Laura would scold me. "That poor dog's whole world has been turned upside down."

That season was one of stark contrasts. On the one hand, there was the warmth of my home life. Every day, I fell in love with Jacob all over again. It was as if every new thing he mastered—smiling, then cooing, then laughing; making fists and picking up toys; pushing himself up, then rolling over; sitting up, then pulling up on furniture—gave me a whole new way to love him.

Then there was work—the coolness of Edwin, the aloofness of Tony Coton, the chill that came over me whenever I was in that locker room. I wanted to get out of there. Go home to my wife and my baby.

But I kept watching Edwin and making mental notes.

When I dove, I caught the ball with my hands. But when Edwin dove, he cradled it with his wrists, his forearms, the curve of his shoulders and back. I imitated what Edwin did, and once I got it down, I made it my own.

Edwin also had this way of fielding those tricky low balls that sometimes come in so close to your body that you can't quite catch them with your hands. They're easy to fumble or let roll under you. But Edwin threw his body on the ground so quickly that the ball bounced off his chest. Only then would he try to grab it with his hands.

I made that one my own, too.

Most of all, I observed Edwin's confidence. Nobody ever yelled at Edwin to catch or to parry a shot.

I watched. I learned. I sat on the bench. Sometimes Ferguson put me in reserve games.

But there was that voice again: *You're never going to become great playing in reserve games. Go somewhere that you can become the best.*

As it became clear which teams would need a new goalkeeper for the following season, Dan began to explore the marketplace. The club that I was most interested in was Everton. My former United defender Phil Neville had transferred to Everton at the start of this season, and his brother, Gary, said he was quite happy.

They played in a great old-time stadium, Goodison Park. I'd always loved the feel of the place when Man U visited—it felt like going back in time in all the best ways.

Dan described his discussions with Everton's manager, David Moyes. "It's a really good club. I like Moyes, and I think you'll like him, too. And, Tim, they seem to really want you."

The morning after another match that I watched from the bench, I punched the address of the Everton training ground into my car's satellite navigation system and headed out to meet Moyes. He was waiting when I arrived. Lanky guy. Taller and younger than Ferguson. Red hair, firm jaw, Christopher Walken eyes. He had a scar above his eyebrows—reminders of wounds from his own days as a player.

We shook hands, then he cut right to the chase. "Look, Tim," Moyes said. "We could use a keeper like you."

He told me about Everton. The club wasn't Manchester United, he explained; they didn't have the massive budgets to buy any player they wanted. They had a fraction of the staff that Man U had. They didn't have the worldwide brand, the built-in cachet. They didn't have the same level of corporate sponsorships. Or, frankly, the winning record.

But, he explained, they had their own rich history. They'd competed in the top flight of English soccer for over a hundred seasons. And they had plans. When Moyes came on as manager late in the 2001–2002 season, the club was dangerously close to relegation. Yet he'd guided them to safety, in fifteenth place. The next year, they'd risen to seventh. In the most recent season, they'd gotten to fourth place and qualified for the Champions League.

"We're ambitious," he said. "And I know you're ambitious, too."

Moyes had been working with a crop of homegrown players— like Alan Stubbs, Leon Osman, and Tony Hibbert—guys who were raised in Liverpool, and who had supported Everton since they were kids, later moving up through the ranks of the club's academy. Moyes was trying to round out that core group with shrewd transfers. The Australian Tim Cahill, for example, who scored 12 goals in his first season with Everton. The Spaniard Mikel Arteta, a smooth midfield general. And my old teammate Phil Neville.

"We're hungry," said Moyes, "but I don't tolerate egos. We're a family club. An old-school working-class club, through and through. It's a great playing environment."

While we were sitting there, it dawned on me. *He's selling me.*

And that felt so good after being shunted aside for the past year at United.

Moyes told me that if I was interested, he'd try to work out a deal where I'd come on loan as Everton's starting keeper.

Then I asked the make-or-break question: "And what if I have a bad game?"

He didn't blink. "Tim, you're young and I want you to learn," he said. "Learning requires risk. So I'm going to encourage you to take some risks. Sometimes you'll make mistakes. When you do, I'm going to be honest. I might even scream and snarl from time to time. But I'm not going to take you out of the game. In the end, I know you'll win us more games than you'll lose us."

I'm not going to take you out of the game.

In that moment, it was as if somebody had opened up a window for me, let a blast of fresh air in.

Dan arranged a meeting with Alex Ferguson. Ferguson held the meeting in his office with a view of the training ground. A chef wheeled in a steak dinner on a white tablecloth. They made polite small talk; when Dan mentioned his Oxford history degree, Ferguson spent close to an hour talking about his cache of rare documents.

It was only toward the end of the meal that the conversation rolled around to my transfer.

"Tim's a good lad," said Ferguson. "He's held true to his part of the deal. He can go on loan to Everton."

Truth is, I'm not sure Ferguson cared much. I wasn't really a part of his plans by now.

Everton called to ask what number I wanted to wear.

Call it OCD, or call it a personality quirk, but I've always liked even numbers better than odds, 2's and 4's best of all.

Number 24, I said. I want 24.

Laura ordered a custom Everton jersey in Jacob's size. The morning I left for my final Manchester United game, Jacob was crawling around the house in that shirt with the number 24 on his tiny back.

I scooped him up. "Looks good on you, little man." I kissed his cheek, his neck, the top of his head.

Oh, man, how I adored this kid.

I hugged him and set him down. Then I walked out the door.

My deal with Everton was just a loan; there was no guarantee of anything. It was certainly possible that after a year, I'd return to the Old Trafford bench.

But that's not what I believed.

From that first day with David Moyes, I felt I'd be at Everton for a long, long time.

Poppa, my mother, and Momma, at home in Hungary, before they had to escape under cover of night.

With big brother Chris and my mom, looking sharp in our '80s attire.

As a kid I hated sitting still. . . . I suspect I could barely sit still for this photo!

Chris was my fierce protector when I was young.

Photos are courtesy of the author unless otherwise noted.

As a child, I always stood head and shoulders above the other soccer players.

Being named one of the captains for the '96 high school soccer season by my legendary coach, Stan Williston.

To my mom's great relief, I managed to stay in school long enough to take this high school graduation photo!

Tim Mulqueen: the man who made me the keeper I am today. He's been a coach, a mentor, and is now a dear friend.

(Brad Smith/isiphotos.com)

The dream started at the MetroStars! Here I am, 21 years old . . . with still so much to learn. *(Courtesy of Major League Soccer)*

Meeting Sir Alex Ferguson for the first time . . . naively wearing Manchester City colors. *(John Peters/Manchester United/Getty Images)*

I couldn't have dreamed up a better start to my Manchester United career. We beat Arsenal in a shootout to win the 2003 Community Shield and I made the decisive save. Here I am with the guys accepting the silverware (*from left to right*): Ryan Giggs, Rio Ferdinand, Eric Djemba-Djemba, Nicky Butt, Ruud van Nistelrooy, Paul Scholes and Darren Fletcher. *(John Peters/Manchester United/Getty Images)*

The perfect wedding was planned in only three days.

Nana in her Sunday Best at my wedding in Central Park.

Everyone adored sweet baby Jacob . . . everyone but Clayton!

Ali was a live wire right from the start.

Two things Ali likes most: the ocean and her big brother, Jacob.

My Everton mates celebrating with me after we beat Manchester United on PKs. *(Javier Garcia/BPI/isiphotos.com)*

Nothing was more rewarding than a handshake from my goalkeeping coach, Chris Woods, after a big win. *(Chris Brunskill/BPI/isiphotos.com)*

I'd run into a burning building for this man, David Moyes. *(Jamie McDonald/Getty Images)*

My day job on a Saturday morning. *(Matt West/ isiphotos.com)*

"Before" shot: throwing the ball to Landon near the end of the 2010 World Cup game against Algeria. *(Perry McIntyre/ isiphotos.com)*

"After" shot: celebrating Landon's game-winning goal against Algeria.
(Phil Cole/Getty Images)

Me and my pal Carlos after the last qualification game vs. Costa Rica, 2009. Thanks to the fan who threw me this hat! *(John Todd/isiphotos.com)*

In our 2014 World Cup game against Portugal, I changed direction mid-dive to scoop Eder's point-blank shot over the crossbar. It's one of my all-time favorite saves. *(Elsa/Getty Images)*

One of my 15 saves against Belgium. *(Yves Herman/ Reuters/Corbis)*

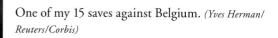

Brotherhood transcends even the toughest moments on the field: with Romelu Lukaku after the 2014 World Cup game against Belgium. *(Kieran McManus/isiphotos.com)*

Tess and Paige Kowalski, two of the many incredible kids I've met with Tourette Syndrome. *(Courtesy of the Kowalski family)*

Mom, Dad, and the kids sharing my proudest moment with me: my 100th cap for the U.S. national team.

I am calmest, most at peace, when my children are close.

LIKE COMING HOME

On Saturdays, they come streaming toward Goodison Park, a parade of blue. Blue scarves, blue hats, blue jerseys, blue jackets. They crowd into pubs—the Thomas Frost, the Brick, the Leigh Arms, the Lisbon—to knock back pints before the match. Some remain in the pubs through the game; others depart for the stadium—pass through Goodison's turnstiles and take their seat in the bright blue stadium chairs.

If they're loud and rowdy, they head for the lower Gladwys section, behind the goal at the north end. That's where the hardcore fans, the true nutters, congregate—the boisterous heart and soul of the home crowd. It's in Gladwys that the madness of the stadium reaches its fever pitch. It's where the songs echo loudest, where the ebb and flow of the game, the despair and the ecstasy, are felt most deeply.

Not that there's a single inch of Goodison where the fans stay quiet. Their cheers and groans and chants mirror precisely the action on the field. I swear, there are days when it feels like cause and effect have merged into one, as if those supporters are no longer reacting, but are instead dictating the tempo of the game.

Looking back, I think it was those fans, above all else, who saved me.

I loved Everton from the start. I loved that in this funny old stadium, I felt closer to the fans than I'd been since my Imperials days. Goodison Park is so compact there's not even room for a security gate between fans and the field. When I took my place in goal, I didn't simply hear the roar of the crowd, I heard individual fans calling out, "Come on, blue boys!"

This was English "football" the way it used to be, from the rowdy fans right up to its Liverpool born-and-bred owner, Bill Kenwright, an Everton fan from boyhood.

Even the locker room felt so much more down-to-earth than at United. On one wall was an image of Alan Ball, one of the Everton greats, with his quote: ONCE EVERTON HAS TOUCHED YOU, NOTHING WILL BE THE SAME.

It was true: I was welcomed with open arms. Somehow it didn't matter to my new teammates that I'd been warming the bench. I'd been at Manchester United, the holy grail of English clubs. They were ready to listen to what I had to say.

I felt like a leader for the first time since arriving in England.

My new goalkeeping coach, Chris Woods, was confident enough to trust me, to ask what I needed. On our very first day of training together, he set up a bunch of drills, but added, evenly, "If you feel like you need something specific, something I'm not doing, let me know."

Those were words I never heard at Manchester United. Not when I was playing well, not when I was playing poorly. Nobody once asked me what I needed to be comfortable. Somehow, it had never occurred to anyone at United that perhaps the key to working with an OCD goalkeeper might just be to give him a sense of control.

Chris Woods let me be my own man from the start. It was clear how sharp his eye was, how instinctively he understood the position. He challenged me, too. He pushed me to do some new footwork drills that required dexterity and balance.

I couldn't find a rhythm with that footwork. I'm a perfectionist, so when I can't grasp something, it's infuriating.

"Let's stop this," I snapped when I started getting frustrated.

"Sure, Tim," Woods said. "We can come back to that one."

I got aggravated again the next day—and I cut it short again. But after a while, I was more exasperated by my inability to grasp it than I was by the drill itself. Eventually, I came to training and said, "Let's try that footwork drill again."

Chris was taking me to the next level. Yet he was comfortable enough in his own skin, his own success, that he didn't need to micromanage me.

Whereas Tony Coton had walked around like a used car salesman, chest all puffed out, and always looking to cut a deal, Chris's demeanor was both calm and calming.

Coton had been a good goalkeeper, but not at Chris's level. Chris had been capped 43 times for England. Maybe that accounted for the gulf between them. Or maybe they simply had different relationships with the manager—Alex Ferguson versus David Moyes. Coton was never close to Ferguson, not really a member of his inner circle. Chris, like the rest of Moyes's staff, was a core part of the coaching team.

Whatever the difference was, it was profound. I've since played with Chris for hundreds of games—at Everton, and later, too, on the U.S. Men's National Team. His confidence to see our relationship as a collaboration has never wavered.

Every single game, win or lose, he shakes my hand, pats me on the back.

Then we get back to work.

There was a lot to like about Everton. But it was the Merseyside derby that really sold me.

The city of Liverpool has two Premier League teams—Everton and Liverpool—and the rivalry between them pits neighbor against neighbor, family member against family member. Driving through Liverpool's streets, you'll see blue Everton flags hanging mere feet from red Liverpool ones. Were you to walk inside those homes, you might see half of a household in red, the other half in blue, all of them "winding each other up"—trash-talking.

Liverpool is a port town, built on the bank of the Mersey River, and the folks who live there—these "Scousers," as they're known colloquially, after the traditional Liverpudlian stew—are the dockworkers, the steelworkers. They are hard people, and they're fierce in their loyalties. Liverpudlians are so passionate about their respective teams that the trash bins ("wheelie bins") can't be either red or blue, lest they risk vandalism by a devoted fan of the other color. The trash bins are all purple.

Twice a year, Everton and Liverpool meet in a derby (pronounced "darby")—once at Goodison, and once at Anfield, Liverpool's stadium. While there are plenty of other crosstown rivalries—Arsenal versus Tottenham, for example, or Manchester United versus Manchester City—the Merseyside derby is the most combative of all, complete with more red cards than any other in the Premier League.

My fourth game with Everton, September 9, 2006, would be my first Merseyside derby. I could feel the tension grow as we got closer to the match. Half of Liverpool shouted to me from the streets, "You beat those Reds this weekend." The other half—those dressed in red—shouted, well, different things entirely.

Inside our training complex, the halls buzzed. Not just the players, either. The cooks in the kitchen, all the support staff.

"You make sure you get those Reds!" called a laundry lady to me as we passed in the hallway.

"Gonna take 'em down, are ya?" said a woman who cleared my plate after breakfast.

Jimmy Martin, Everton's curmudgeonly "kit man"—the guy who's in charge of all the clothing we need for every training session, every warm-up, every game—regaled me with stories of past derbies.

"Ninety-one was the greatest of them all," said Jimmy. He was in his sixties, with a thick Scouser's accent, a short temper, and a fondness for profanity. "Fuckin' eight goals! One of 'em a last-second equalizer. A brilliant FA Cup comeback. We might have drawn 'em 4–4, but we showed the Blues spirit that day, I'll tell ya. Then we came back to beat 'em in the replay. . . ."

Jimmy narrowed his eyes. He challenged me: "I know you're on loan, but you're going to play it like a real Blue, aren't 'cha?"

"Yeah, Jimmy," I answered. "I sure am."

And I meant it.

There's a lot to remember about that first derby. I recall, for example, the moments before the game: lining up in the tunnel with my new team against our historic rivals. Neither side looked at the other. There were no hands shaken, no half hugs or fist bumps or friendly claps on the back. All eyes were fixed forward. I remember the flood of pride I felt when the theme from *Z-Cars* (an old British television show), today the Everton fight song, started up, the crowd going wild. I remember the walk out to the field, all my new teammates touching the Everton sign, HOME OF THE BLUES.

I didn't touch it; I was only on loan, and I hadn't earned that honor. Not yet.

But what I remember most are those fans. They reminded me, in many ways, of my own family: they were roll-up-your-sleeve, blue-collar fighters who'd had to scrap for everything they had. In the same way that I once wanted to give my mom that Mother's Day goal, I wanted to give these guys something to cheer about. I wanted them to be able to walk into work on Monday morning with their heads held high.

I made my first save inside of ten seconds, and I made every one after that. We won the game 3–0. We crushed Liverpool. It was Everton's biggest victory over their neighbors for 42 years. The crowd went absolutely bonkers.

Later that afternoon, I was back home with Laura and Jacob. Jacob and I were playing peekaboo—every time I pulled my hands away from my face and cried, "Peekaboo!" he burst into fits of giggles.

Laura sat beside us. "You know what, Tim?" she said. "You haven't once wondered what David Moyes thinks about you."

I glanced at her. "I'm not worried."

Jacob kicked out his chubby feet, so I did another peekaboo.

She was right: I hadn't felt insecure around Moyes or doubted that he was behind me. Although I'd noticed him during the game and hugged him proudly at the end of it, I hadn't been concerned about what he thought. For me, it was all about those fans.

I swept Jacob up in my arms then and buried my face in his belly. I gave him some raspberry kisses and he squealed happily.

"Bedtime for you now, little man," I said.

As I walked up the stairs I called back to Laura. "I love this team!"

At the same time that Chris Woods allowed me to take charge of my own training regimen, I began to cement my own series of personal rituals, those tiny motions that made me feel prepared. It was all coming together for me: my confidence, my control.

I'll admit up front that the line between superstition and preparation—maybe even superstition and OCD—can be very blurry. But the things I did before those early Everton games felt right. So I did them the next time. And the time after that. For example, I didn't touch the Everton sign in the tunnel before the derby. Although by now I've earned the honor, I have never touched it since. Hundreds and hundreds of games later, I still won't do it.

When I taped my hands for those early games, I did it in a specific order—left index, left pinkie, right index, right middle, right pinkie, left ring. I've never done it differently.

My own rituals quickly blended with my teammates'. When Leon Osman and I shook hands before an early game, we bumped shoulders. To this day, if we don't follow the handshake with a shoulder tap, I'll say, "That doesn't feel right."

And Leon will agree. "Let's do it again."

Same thing with Chris Woods. When he fired balls at me in warm-ups, I had to deal with them in a way that felt exactly right.

I could see that he didn't know what constituted "exactly right." But he listened when I said, "That's good, no more."

Poor Jimmy Martin, too. I quickly started to drive that man crazy.

Before games, Jimmy set out my warm-up clothes, all in a size large. But one day I tried them on and they felt . . . wrong. Wrong in the same way that packing my bags before youth league games in New Jersey felt wrong. Wrong as in, *it had to be changed right now.*

I sent for him, and he came in grumbling. "What's the matter? I know I set it out right for ya, Tim. I check and double-check your kits, you know."

"I need a medium," I said.

"You're a large."

I shook my head. "I need a medium *today*, Jimmy."

It didn't take long for Jimmy to start setting out two complete outfits, one large, one medium.

But I'm telling you: it helped. It was important that I was wearing the exact right-feeling shirt on the exact right day; it gave me a sense of control. And if I was going to succeed, I needed to feel in control.

The Everton players had their own rituals, too. I learned pretty quickly that you don't close the door to the bathroom stall. Ever. Not even when you need to—to put it euphemistically—*sit down.*

Mind you, these bathrooms are tiny. The whole locker area is small, no clubby chairs, no frills. Some hooks and stools, a refrigerator, and maybe a massage table crammed in a corner. When you're sitting there with the door open, there's no one who doesn't see you.

But that's the superstition. And by now I'd learned: you honor rituals when you have them.

If Moyes walked in while I sat on the pot, pants at my ankles, I'd shrug, like, *Yeah, I know this is weird, but what can you do?* He shook his head and averted his eyes, as he did for every player.

Whatever, he seemed to be saying. Whatever we needed to do to feel prepared out there.

At Christmas, I joined the team for their hospital visits, followed by the Everton Santa Claus—dressed only in blue and white, because of course he can't wear any red—and handed out presents to children. After our hospital visits, one of our defenders, Alan Stubbs, walked over to me. Alan was a Scouser through and through; he'd grown up in Kirkby, one of Liverpool's hardscrabble neighborhoods. Stubbs was stubborn, blunt, and tough. The guy had battled cancer and came back even harder than before.

Alan placed his hand on my back. "Tim," he said, "I wanted to tell you that you've done brilliant for us so far."

I was about to say thanks, but he held up his hand. "Don't get me wrong," he added. "You've got a long way to go. But the fans have really taken a liking to you. It feels . . ."

He paused for a moment. "Feels like you've become one of us, really."

I said only one word: "Thanks." Inside, though, I swelled with pride.

Alan shrugged. "Don't let it go to your head, mate."

One of Moyes's strengths was his ability to recognize "Everton" players, guys with very little ego and a high degree of loyalty.

Once in a rare while, a player would fall into his lap—maybe at a cut-rate price or in a position he needed—who perhaps had a bit of a question mark about his character. But Moyes would straighten him out quickly.

There was one player who was an unmitigated screw-up, forever causing drama around the team. He'd exhausted plenty of chances, and not just second or third chances, either.

After one game, we were in the locker room. Music was playing, a few of the guys had started showering. The atmosphere was loose. The fitness coach walked in.

"Right, listen up," he said. "Substitutes and guys who didn't get to play, come with me. Let's do our running drills."

This player, the screw-up, shook his head and didn't get up. The fitness coach left with the rest of the reserves. Next thing I knew, David Moyes barged into the locker room, his blue eyes flashing.

He pointed his finger at the player who'd refused to run. "You're going to get your ass out there," he said, "and you're going to run."

Moyes grabbed him by the scruff of his shirt and started shaking the kid, banging him against the wall.

The music clicked off.

"You're going to run," rumbled Moyes. Bang.

"You're going to run." Bang.

Suddenly the tough guy didn't seem so tough. "I'm going to call the police," he cried out.

"You do that," snarled Moyes. "In fact, I'll go get them myself." Moyes knew they would probably be Everton fans anyway.

Lo and behold, that kid went outside and ran. You didn't cross Moyes.

Moyes was true to his word with me. I could have a bad game, and he'd put me in the next one . . . and in the 200 games after that.

We'd go on that season to finish in sixth place. Not exactly a Manchester United–level success, but there's something to be said for ambition as a driving force, instead of fear. And that's the thing I was starting to understand about United. The players were afraid. They feared losing. They feared Ferguson. They feared, above all, falling from their perch.

In the spring, Moyes made me a permanent offer, for more money than I'd ever earned at Manchester United. I felt like I'd hit the jackpot in every way. Bigger salary. Supportive teammates. A goalkeeping coach whom I trusted completely. A manager who trusted me completely. The confidence that I could keep playing no matter what. And those fans—those crazy die-hards who made me smile again and again.

Before long, I had the number 24 tattooed over my right rib.

PART THREE

USA VS. BELGIUM: NOTHING GETS THROUGH
ARENA FONTE NOVA
SALVADOR, BRAZIL
JULY 1, 2014

In the 28th minute, I make my second save of the game, a right-footed shot from Eden Hazard. It's a routine save for me.

I feel good so far. Belgium is dominating—we're spending too much time in our own box—but our defense has been solid. They've made some strong clearances, blocked crosses from the flanks.

We're holding our own.

This is how we've won a lot of games. It's become a kind of blueprint for us: hold a high line, don't drop too deep, don't let them get behind us. Wear them down.

Then, when they're frustrated, smarting from their inability to finish off their chances, they'll change their tactics, try to find a new way to break us down.

That's when we'll seize our moment. Hit them on the counter.

We've won games where the ball barely got out of our end. We've done it by grinding down our opponents, then when they least expect it, we come flying up the field to score the goal that sees us through.

It's how we beat Spain, Algeria. It's how we beat Mexico at home and Mexico in Azteca.

We've won more games than I can count that way. It doesn't matter who dominates possession if no one can score.

Ninety seconds after I make my second save, Fabien Johnson, our right back, goes down with an injury: it's his hamstring, the same thing that felled Jozy for the last few games. Jürgen sends on DeAndre Yedlin of the Seattle Sounders. DeAndre's a kid, 20 years old, one of Klinsmann's surprise picks for this tournament. He's a relative rookie on the national team, just seven appearances under his belt. Now he's going toe-to-toe against Eden Hazard, the star man at Chelsea—one of the most dynamic midfielders in the Premier League.

Get in close, I holler at DeAndre, *stay tight.*

Got it.

And he does have it. When Hazard makes a blazing run toward goal, DeAndre throws his body in front of him. It's the kind of fearless play you expect from a veteran, but DeAndre is on a steep learning curve. There's no time for baby steps.

Good job, I call out.

I've been talking to my defenders throughout the half. *Watch over your left shoulder. A runner behind you.* I want to make sure the defenders are hearing my voice, that my directions are as urgent in the first half as they are in the final minutes. If you suddenly amplify your tone late in the game you can startle your players, which is why I keep the decibels loud from the start.

Just before halftime, DeBruyne finds a pocket of space and lashes a right-footed shot toward the center of the goal. I save it comfortably.

The half ends 0–0.

We head for the locker room. We've got strategy to discuss, one or two tactical tweaks that will tighten things up defensively.

We have at least 45 minutes to go, and I intend to hold them back.

GOLD CUP

Jacob was almost two when his sister, Alivia—Ali—was born in Memphis on May 17, 2007.

So far she has been silent for exactly five seconds of her life: the very first five.

She arrived halfway through my six-day break between the end of the Premier League season and the start of a month's training for the Gold Cup—the continental championship—with the U.S. Men's National Team. Bob Bradley, now the national team coach, had already told me I'd definitely be playing, possibly even starting.

So the timing of Ali's birth could be considered ideal (days after my season ended), or a complete disaster (just days before leaving for another month). Given that I had a maximum of two to three weeks off a year, total, I guess there wouldn't have been a "right" time.

Like her brother, Ali was delivered by C-section. This time it was less nerve-racking. I was relaxed on the way to the hospital, relaxed as they prepped Laura, and as relaxed as any man can be while watching a doctor slice into his wife's belly.

Which is to say, I was not completely and utterly terrified.

Newborns tend to emerge screaming, but not Ali. She didn't make a peep. No sound came out of her at all. I turned to the doctor. It was like being on a plane when you hit strong turbulence and your first instinct is to glance at the flight attendants to see if they seem rattled. But the doctor, nurses, and the rest of the medical staff behaved calmly, normally. The room was eerily silent for what felt like an eternity. It was probably a few seconds, but when you're waiting to hear your child's first cry, and your wife is lying on an operating table with fear in her eyes, those seconds might as well be forever.

And then our baby girl let loose with an earsplitting wail, an unmistakably assertive cry of "I'm here and I mean it." I pressed my forehead against Laura's as we laughed with relief.

"She's here," said Laura. "Listen to her, she's here."

That she was for sure. Our second child, every bit as miraculous as the first, already waving her tiny limbs as her face turned beet red from her screaming. After that initial scare, she was making quite the entrance. Within her first minute of life, Ali had convinced us all that she was a force to be reckoned with.

I really wish you didn't have to go," Laura sighed the next day.

"Me, too," I said, holding Ali in my lap. She was all wrapped up in a flannel blanket like a miniature burrito. Had Jacob ever really been this small? Had his nose ever been this tiny, his fingers this delicate?

"No," said Laura. "I really, *really* wish you didn't have to."

I didn't expect to see such sadness in her eyes. Laura seemed deflated, hollowed out somehow.

"It won't be long," I said.

Laura nodded.

The next day, she said it a few more times.

"I just hate that you're leaving."

Or: "I just had this baby. I wish you could stick around."

Or: "It stinks that you have to go."

These comments were so unlike Laura. She was always so up-beat, so vivacious.

I reminded her that she wouldn't be on her own. Laura had arranged for help from an all-star roster—her mother, father, brother, sister-in-law, cousins, and aunts and uncles, neighbors, and friends. She had people to back them up, and even backup for the backup. Armies of people would be on call around the clock, to pitch in with feeding and diapering, to do laundry, cook, and clean.

"You're going to be great," I said, and I knew it was true. Laura and Jacob and Ali were going to be surrounded by love.

As the clock ticked off the hours before I'd have to walk out the door, Laura grew increasingly uncomfortable. By the morning of my departure, she was in full-blown panic.

"I can't do this," she said. Her eyes darted all over my face, seeking some kind of assurance. But what could I possibly give her? My job didn't come with paternity leave. You had to go to training and you had to go to the games. You were either on the team, or you were not. It really was that simple.

"Tim," she said, sounding more shaken than I'd ever heard her. "I'm not going to be able to do this." Tears spilling out of her eyes, she began shaking her head back and forth.

This wasn't the Laura I thought I knew, the take-charge Laura who handled our finances and household help, and who sched-uled aqua-babies classes and oil changes for the cars. Laura ran our lives. She had everything under control, always.

Yet here she was, anxious and distressed. And here I was, knowing that any minute a taxi driver would pull up and I'd have to get in the car and go to the airport and be gone for the next month.

I felt so helpless. My wife was sobbing, and I wanted so badly to comfort her. I wanted her to know that she'd be okay. I wanted her to know that I'd be thinking of her, and of Ali and Jacob, every moment of every day.

I understood then: this *wasn't* actually her. Something chemical was happening, some flood of postpartum chemicals. If anyone could understand that, it was me—after all, my job came with a dose of adrenaline every single week.

But if this was truly a shift in hormones, then nothing I could do or say would provide any solace.

At this moment, I felt that my job—a good job, an enviable job, one that I'm blessed to have each and every day—could break me.

It could break *us*.

Week after week, in this job, you kiss your wife on the forehead and walk out the door. Week after week, you're on the road. Week after week, you have that anxiety, that absolute single-minded focus. You prepare for your games physically, mentally, and emotionally. You give everything you have. You do your best to be there for your family, to spoon mashed bananas into your kid's mouth, pick up Thomas the Tank Engine toys, feed the dog.

But the games keep coming. Every seven days, you play the most important match you've ever had. Every time you do, 50,000 people watch live. Another couple million watch on television. Pundits and commentators criticize. All those guys in the online forums. Drunk guys in bars, and little old ladies who follow you around stores, glaring.

It's hard to juggle it all week after week. It's hard to go seamlessly between Family Man and Professional Athlete, back and forth, without missing a beat. Sometimes, you just want to lock yourself up in a room somewhere, get your head into the space that pushes you to win. Or—if you lose—allows you to snap out of your funk.

And that's hard enough to keep up every week straight for nine months.

Then you get a break. Just a few days off, long enough to fly home in time to watch your wife give birth to your second child and get them both home from the hospital before you walk out the door again. Because you have to. Because your manager might make you the starting keeper. Because you're pushing 30, and you've got five years left—maybe ten if you're incredibly lucky—before it's over.

Five to ten years. To accomplish everything I've ever wanted. And then—well, frankly, I had no idea what would happen then.

"Laura, I—"

But how could I finish a sentence that had no end? There was no way to do both jobs. To do one, I'd be absent for the other. I wanted to do brilliantly at both, but it didn't work that way.

I pulled my phone from my pocket and held it in my hand for a while.

I could call Bob Bradley and tell him—what? That I couldn't make training for personal reasons, even though every one of my teammates surely had similar issues that they were dealing with at this very second?

I needed to go, and I needed to stay. At the same time.

Finally, I said, "I don't know what to do."

But Laura's brother would.

"Laura, can I call Jerry?" He lived next door. He'd know how to make this better. Or he'd tell me how I could.

Laura nodded, not looking at me.

I called Jerry and explained the situation. Laura's really upset . . . the car's going to be here soon . . . don't know what to do.

He was over within minutes, walking through the back door and into the kitchen.

"Hey, sis," he said. Laura's face was swollen from crying. She didn't, or couldn't, speak.

Jerry knelt on the floor next to her chair. "Listen, Laura," he said. "I'm here and I'm not going anywhere. You hear me?"

The phone rang. My mother.

"Mom, this isn't a great time," I said, in the understatement of the year. A few feet away, my brother-in-law was on his knees, whispering to my wife. So I took the opportunity to fill my mom in about what was going on.

"Tim," Mom said, "will you please put Laura on the phone?"

"I don't know, Mom, she's really—"

"Tim, if she'll talk to me, I'd like to speak with Laura."

I handed the phone to Laura. "Hello?" she sniffled.

I could hear only Laura's end of the conversation.

"Yeah," she said. "Yeah, I'm pretty sad."

There was a pause, then Laura started sobbing again. "Would you?" she said into the phone. "Would you really? Okay."

She looked at me, then at Jerry. "She's going to come. She's getting on the next plane from Jersey." She sounded so relieved.

"You see there?" Jerry said. "Everybody's going to take care of you. You're going to be fine."

Good ol' Jerry. So earnest. So good.

My taxi pulled into the driveway.

Jerry turned to me. "It's okay, Tim," he said. "We've got this."

I kissed Laura, took her hands in my own. We sat like that for a long time. The taxi sounded its horn.

"Go on," Jerry said. "Go win for the red, white, and blue," he said.

So I got into that taxi.

By the time I came home, Ali would be four weeks old. Jacob would have been a big brother for a month. My mom would have come and gone.

And Laura—I believed, deep down, that she'd be okay. But I hated that I couldn't be by her side.

Bob had put together an unbelievable team of guts-and-glory guys—hard workers, collegial, not an overstuffed ego in the bunch. It was clear during training that these players would run until they dropped, if that's what it took.

Shortly after becoming the coach, Bob had selected Carlos Bocanegra—my old buddy from the Youth National Team—to be the captain.

By now Carlos was one of my best friends in the world. He was still the same, steady presence he'd been as a teenager— hard-driving, self-deprecating, and utterly without drama. Bob couldn't have made a better choice.

Bob also had another piece of good news. He told me that I would be the starting goalkeeper for the U.S., with Kasey Keller as the team's number two.

This had to have been a hard moment for Kasey. I'd been there with Carroll, and with van der Sar. I knew exactly how much it smarted.

But Kasey was unbelievably classy. He shook my hand and

said he'd do whatever I needed during training; he just hoped he'd be able to get ten or 15 minutes one-on-one with the goal-keeping coach at the end of practice.

"Of course, man," I said. "Of course."

I loved how tough the U.S. team was, how inexhaustible the players were during training. Landon Donovan was there—and man that kid was amazing. By this point, he was the all-time leading goal scorer and the leader in career assists. Yet he didn't care about glory or kudos; Landon simply loved playing the game. Our team had a melting-pot feel. Carlos was of Mexican descent. Clint Dempsey, a down-home Texas guy, grew up in a Nacog-doches trailer park. Benny Feilhaber's grandfather had been an Austrian Jew who fled Europe and Hitler before it was too late. And me, half black, half Hungarian, married to a Southern girl. We had the sons of oil executives and the sons of military men. We were black and white and every shade in between.

None of our differences mattered one whit.

We played in Group B, achieving the best first-round record in the group. We beat all the teams we played: Ecuador, Trinidad and Tobago, then El Salvador. We scored seven goals in total, and conceded none.

We made it to the finals, a sold-out match at Chicago's Sol-dier Field against our archrivals, Mexico. I'll be honest: the way I feel about Mexico's national team borders on hatred, but a hatred born out of respect. I hate that their team is so damn good. I hate that they've beaten us so many times, for so many years. I hate that their fans turn out in such huge numbers—once again, the crowd was overwhelmingly pro-Mexico—allowing them to cre-ate a hostile environment even on our home turf.

I hate that the Mexican players dive—that when challenged,

they're likely to fall to the ground, roll around, appear to be on death's door in hopes of getting the referee to call a foul against us and award them with a free kick or penalty kick. Diving isn't part of our ethos, our culture. When a U.S. player gets tackled, he dusts himself off and keeps playing. Whenever Mexico dives, it fuels my already burning desire to beat them.

Walking out onto the field the day of the final, I'd say that every one of us felt that rivalry deep in our guts. We knew it would be a physical battle and sure enough before the game was ten minutes old, Carlos had earned a yellow card for a late challenge. Before the half, Mexico scored on a close-range shot. I dove for it and missed, landing on the ground, hard.

In the second half, Brian Ching was taken down in the box. Penalty. Landon stepped up to take the kick and coolly slotted it home.

1–1.

With 20 minutes left on the clock, Landon's corner kick was cleared, but only to the edge of the box, where Benny Feilhaber was lurking, all alone.

From my vantage point, it was both too far out and there were too many Mexican players packing the penalty area for Benny to take the shot. A couple of our guys were even screaming at Benny: *Don't do it!*

Benny paid them no mind. One touch and he sent the ball screaming toward the goal, past a cluster of Mexican defenders and their stunned keeper. It was one of the most amazing volleys I've ever seen. It almost tore the net off the goal. Later, the *New York Times* would call it "perhaps the greatest, the best, the most technically impressive goal scored in the long, long history of soccer in the United States."

About a second and a half earlier we'd been shouting, "Don't shoot," and now we were running toward Benny, waving our arms like a bunch of crazed banshees, and lifting him off the ground.

After that, El Tri ramped up the pressure on us. In the 89th minute, Adolfo Bautista was three, maybe four yards away from me when the ball landed on his right foot. A large part of the goal was wide open.

I had a split second to guess as to where he would try to place his shot and when he pulled his foot back, I knew he was going to shoot across my body and to my right. I dove and stopped that thing cold to preserve our lead.

But Mexico kept on attacking. Even as the final whistle blew, Carlos was deflecting a ball away from our goal.

We'd won the Gold Cup. Best team in North America!

Then came a shower of confetti and the soaring notes of our national anthem. Dignitaries shaking our hands, placing medals around our necks. The cup itself, to be handed to the team captain, was enormous. As Carlos lifted it, we were all jumping up and down, every one of us, giddy like eight-year-olds on a trampoline.

I was so happy for Carlos. I'd known him since we were teenagers, since he was just a kid in baggy jeans and earrings. He'd always had outstanding character; now he was the captain of a team that had beaten Mexico. I was as proud of him as I'd have been for my own brother.

I didn't get to celebrate in the locker room. It was my turn for random drug testing, so I was stuck in the doping room while the guys poured beer into the Gold Cup and drank from it. I missed the music, the dancing, the backslapping, and Bob Bradley beaming with pride.

By the time I finally got to the locker room, it was almost empty. I showered quickly and headed to the airport. From the cab, I called Laura. We'd spoken almost every night since I left a month ago. She was recovering nicely, in body and spirit. In fact, she'd bounced back so quickly that she'd even flown out to Boston for one of our knockout games, bringing the kids along for the ride. Ali was thriving, Jacob was as sweet as ever, and Laura was herself again.

"Oh my goodness," Laura said when she answered the phone. "That was amazing!"

I could hear baby noises in the background, soft little grunts.

"That her?"

"Yeah," whispered Laura. "She's finally quieting down. I think she might even fall asleep right here on my shoulder."

"And Jacob?"

"Napping. He can't wait to see you."

"I'll be there soon."

I passed the time waiting for my flight in an airport restaurant. I ordered myself a margarita—my own private celebration. Carlos texted to tell me they'd taken the cup on a bar crawl. Strangers kept coming up to them asking, *What is that thing? Who are you guys?*

I leaned back in my chair and looked around. Near me, a businessman barked into his phone. A middle-aged couple in matching white sneakers strolled past. A beleaguered-looking mom tried to get her daughter, who was dragging a rolling princess backpack behind her, to hurry.

Not one person recognized me. Nobody here had any idea that on this very day, the U.S. had established itself as the best soccer team on the continent.

I took a sip of my drink. Another text came through from Carlos: *Bartender can't believe we won this cup. Wish you could be here.*

And it would have been nice to have been there with them . . . but not nice enough. It had been too long since I'd seen my wife and children. My baby girl was sleeping in my wife's arms at this very minute. My boy was napping.

I was heading home.

SLAYING DRAGONS

By the 2008–2009 Premier League season, things were going well on all fronts. Ali had become a toddler, and boy did that kid keep us on our toes. She was animated and opinionated, constantly on the go. She fidgeted and fussed, struggled to sleep, could switch from laughter to howling in a split second. You never had to wonder whether Ali was happy or sad—whichever she was, she was all in.

But man, that girl could light up a room. Her eyes danced. By the time she was one year old, she was already throwing herself headfirst into everything. She carried the spark of life inside her, and it was pretty dazzling to see.

On Sundays, Laura and I took the kids to Tatton Park, a thousand-acre recreation area with acres of flowers and a painted carousel and jungle gyms. Every 20 minutes or so, a tiny red train drove past; we paid one pound to ride through the park on that thing, stopping at a working farm. The kids fed pigs and goats and cows, delighted by the animals taking the food from their hands. Then we paid another pound to ride the tiny train back to where we started.

Those were blissful days—more precious even than I could

understand. The kids were so young. So happy. And we were all together in the same place.

We had a strong defense at Everton that year. Our communication was excellent. We found an easy rhythm. As a result, we developed a kind of confidence that in every game we stood a good chance of earning a clean sheet. At the end of each shutout, I looked up at Bill Kenwright, the team's owner, applauding in the stands with all those good souls in blue around him, and it stoked my desire to do it again the next time.

And, with the help of my defenders, I often did. In fact, that season I had 17 shutouts—the highest number in Everton's history.

That year, we started our run for the FA Cup with a game against Macclesfield, one of the lower league teams. We'd be playing on their turf, tiny Moss Rose stadium, which they've called home for over 100 years. When I say tiny, I mean *tiny*. While we'd grown accustomed to playing in Premier League stadiums that hold 60,000 or more, the total capacity of Moss Rose, including standing room, was one-tenth of that. There were only 2,600 seats—barely more than my high school gymnasium, and fewer than the basketball arena where I'd once battled Jay Williams my senior year of high school.

The Macclesfield locker rooms are so small that players had to make a choice. You could either sit on the bench or put your bag on it, but not both.

Moyes didn't want us to be distracted by the snug conditions, so on the eve of the game, he took us out to the field. It had been snowing and sleeting for days, and, naturally, this matchbox of a stadium had no high-tech drainage or heating system (by contrast, Manchester United had recently installed a multimillion-dollar field, complete with 23 miles of heating pipes below ground). To protect the surface, they'd covered the entire place with tarps, weighted down by sandbags. Now they had to remove them. Whom did they enlist to do the work? The fans. The day we visited, the field was overflowing with Macclesfield supporters who'd come to shovel snow, carry tarps, do anything necessary to make sure the game could be played.

We stood there and marveled at all those guys who had taken time off work to slog around in the sleet, protected by only the thinnest of layers. Thanks to them, the game went on as scheduled the next day. Macclesfield fought hard. And although we beat them, 1–0, they earned our respect with their phenomenal team spirit.

After that, our FA Cup run saw us face only Premier League teams—and some pretty decent ones, too.

We tied Liverpool in the fourth round, then beat them 1–0 in a replay.

We defeated Aston Villa next, winning handily, 3–1.

In the quarters we knocked off Middlesbrough 2–1 to advance to the semifinals.

There, waiting for us, was none other than Manchester United.

It's hard to describe how high the stakes felt before the United match. If we could get past them, it would be the first time Everton had made it to the FA Cup final since 1995, 14 years ago. Since Moyes had arrived, he'd steadily moved the team forward, player by player, practice by practice, with a fraction of the budget of the big clubs. Meanwhile, three of us—me, Phil Neville, and Saha—were former United players. We didn't say it, but I know we were all thinking the same thing: how sweet would it be to beat the manager who had deemed us expendable?

Jimmy?" I said.

Jimmy grumbled. "What now?"

"I need another pair of white socks." I wear white athletic socks under my soccer socks, but the ones that I put on today felt wrong. Completely wrong.

"All our socks are the same," he said, sighing. But he knew me well enough by now. He handed me another pair of identical white socks. I tried them on, but they were still not right.

"Sorry, Jimmy."

He set out another pair. Then another.

It was only the fifth pair that felt right.

Jimmy shook his head at me. "You just shut those guys out today."

"You got it, Jimmy," I said. "I'll do it, or I'll go down trying."

Before I left for the game, which would be in London, I was packing my bag in the bedroom when Laura walked in there.

"I'm going to miss you," she said. "We all are."

She wrapped her arms around me, and I stood there—but the truth is, I just wanted to be left alone. I wanted to mentally prepare for the game. At the moment, that meant packing my bag without distraction.

I'd gotten better at packing through the years—it was no longer an all-night process as it had been when I was a kid. But still: I wanted to do it right, so I could feel prepared.

I wanted to be in game mode. Not husband mode. They were two completely different things.

The game, held at Wembley Stadium, was the highest-attended FA Cup semifinal in history—more than 88,000 fans. As tradition dictates, half the stadium is given over to Manchester United fans, half to Everton fans. One side red. The other side blue.

I felt sure that Manchester United, and all their supporters, thought they knew exactly what was going to happen in that game. Somehow, they didn't seem to expect much of a fight.

We gave them one anyway.

They had few chances in the first half and the ones they did have, I stopped. It was scoreless after 45 minutes. Then again at the end of regulation. Extra time came and went, and still nobody scored.

We were heading for a penalty kick shootout.

I flashed back to the 2005 FA Cup final when Ferguson had told me to warm up before the shootout and never put me in.

Well, I was in the game now. I was more confident than I'd been at Man U. I'd spent the last few years playing almost every match, and I had developed skills I never could have by sitting on the bench. I was determined to prove it.

The shootout would take place on Manchester United's side, awash in red jerseys. We were to kick first.

Tim Cahill took the first penalty. Their keeper Ben Foster didn't need to do a thing; the ball sailed right over the bar. Devastated, Cahill dropped to his knees. Around him, the United fans erupted. In that moment, I think they truly thought they had this.

My turn. I stopped a weak effort from Dimitar Berbatov. Still 0–0.

Our Leighton Baines smashed the ball slightly to Foster's left. He absolutely drilled it home. 1–0.

Then I faced Rio Ferdinand, my old teammate. Somehow I sensed he was going right and dove that way. Rio hit his shot with power, but I was able to stop it.

Phil Neville didn't flinch as he knocked one in against his former team. He sent the ball to the lower left corner as Ben dove toward the right-hand side. 2–0.

Nemanja Vidić added an unusual stutter step to his run up. It threw me. 2–1

Our James Vaughan sent a perfect shot to the upper right corner. Ben guessed correctly, but he had no chance on that one. 3–1.

Manchester United's Anderson kicked one way. I dove the other: 3–2.

Then our center-back Phil Jagielka stepped up. I made a cross and waited.

Jags had a fast run up to the ball, and nailed it.

The blue side of Wembley went wild then. I sprinted toward my teammates. I made it about 15 yards from the goal area before I was wrestled to the ground by my teammates: Joleon Lescott and Steven Pienaar and Tony Hibbert, then everyone else. It was the best kind of mayhem—guys throwing themselves on top of me. Tugging and hugging, and piling on.

The *Z-Cars* song started playing, our anthem. Up in the stands, Bill Kenwright looked as if half of his 65 years had fallen away in that moment of triumph.

Someone tossed an Everton scarf onto the field. I don't know who threw it, don't know anything about that person's life— where they worked, or what their family was like, or what challenges they faced as they walked through this world. I will never know what they sacrificed to be at Wembley that day.

But I knew this: they'd sent that scarf flying down to the

field out of gratitude. I picked it up and raised it high over my head.

Later, in the locker room, I sat down next to Tony Hibbert. I tossed my towel over my head to wipe the sweat from my face. But instead of removing the towel, I left it there. I sat for a moment in the dark, amid all the cheers and whoops of my celebrating teammates.

And before I understood what was happening, I clutched the towel to my face and began sobbing.

I didn't care that my teammates could see my shoulders shake. Didn't worry if my cries could be heard over the sounds of their laughter.

Jags noticed. "Hey, Tim? You all right?"

Then Hibbert's voice. "Yeah. He's all right." I felt his hand on my back. "He just needs a minute."

Hibbo understood. He understood without my telling him. He realized exactly what this game meant for me.

We hadn't won the final, mind you. In fact, we wouldn't. We'd lose to Chelsea 2–1, despite taking a 1–0 lead 25 seconds into the game. And that loss would hurt.

But as I sat in the Wembley locker room with that towel pressed against my face, I wasn't thinking about the game ahead.

Right now all I heard in my head was a single line on endless repeat: *I slayed the dragon.*

Faith Rice called me in England around that time.

"Listen, Tim," she said. "I've got a great idea. I need your help."

Faith had been working away back in New Jersey. The non-profit she'd started, now called the New Jersey Center for Tourette Syndrome, NJCTS, was doing everything it could to provide support and education.

"But we need to do more," she said. She explained that one of the great cruelties of TS is that the symptoms tend to peak in adolescence, precisely when kids are most vulnerable.

"I want to create a leadership academy for teens," she said. The Academy, as she envisioned it, would teach them the skills they'd need to navigate adult life. It would help them cope with the added social stress of being a kid with TS.

"Most of all," she added, "we'll give them the tools to find their own strengths."

Maybe if I'd had that kind of support, I could have slayed another kind of dragon even sooner: maybe I could have conquered the shame I'd felt about my TS.

In 2009, as a result of our Gold Cup victory, we automatically qualified for the Confederations Cup, a tournament contested by the six FIFA Confederations Champions, as well as the most recent World Cup winners and the upcoming World Cup host country.

It was going to be an uphill fight, but also an opportunity to prove ourselves against some formidable opponents—Brazil, Spain, and Italy. As a national team, although we'd been steadily gaining credibility, we weren't yet peers with the elite squads.

Our first couple of games were . . . well . . . they were pretty much disasters.

First we lost to Italy, 3–1. Then we got pounded 3–0 by Brazil. We were overmatched and outclassed in every way. I made a couple of tough saves in each of those games, but I'd let in six.

It shook me. With two losses behind us, we entered our game against Egypt, with zero points—dead last in the tournament. Even if we could beat them, we'd only get three points, maximum, and it's very rare that a team can advance to the next round out of a four-team group with only three points.

We were, for all intents and purposes, out of the tournament.

Since it was likely our last game of the tournament before going home, Bob Bradley decided to give some playing time to a bunch of the players who hadn't gotten any so far, among them Brad Guzan, another U.S. goalkeeper. Brad played well and we beat Egypt 3–0.

Through some miracle of the scoreboard—a combination of results that I still don't fully understand—that win advanced us to the semifinal.

Our next opponent was Spain, the world's top-ranked team. Not only had Spain conquered all of Europe in the UEFA Cup, but they were unbeaten in their last 35 games. Spain hadn't conceded a goal yet in this tournament. I doubt they lost much sleep over the prospect of playing us in the semis.

I got word that Bob Bradley was thinking about starting Brad Guzan against Spain.

The very idea of warming the bench during a semifinal of a major tournament against Spain made me absolutely crazy.

There was this voice in my head: *What if we can beat Spain?* The closer we got to the game, the louder that voice became. *What if we can make history, and you're sitting on the sidelines?*

After training one day, I found Bob.

"Look," I said. "I know you're thinking about starting Brad. But I need you to hear this from me: I want to play."

Bob looked at me evenly. "Tim, you're coming off of a long season, a great season. But we obviously didn't play well in those first two games." He paused, then added, "The truth is, I think you might be tired."

"Bob," I said, "you know me. You know I compete if I can, and you know I compete hard. And frankly, although we got peppered in those first two games, I can't think of one mistake I made that should keep me out of the semifinals."

I didn't actually believe that I'd sway Bob, because he doesn't cave to pressure. The man never lets himself get backed into a corner.

"I'll think about it," he replied. That's all he said.

The following day, he announced the starting lineup. I was in goal.

Bob prepared us tirelessly for Spain.

"You need to clog their midfield," he said. "Force them wide, make sure their attacks come from the flanks."

He clenched his jaw. "They can move backwards or sideways," he added, "but you can't let them move forward," Bob repeated.

We listened. We practiced. We ran drills. We were ready.

We took the lead in the 27th minute; Dempsey sent the ball to Jozy Altidore, who lashed a powerful shot from 25 yards. Their keeper, Iker Casillas, got a hand on it, but not enough of one. 1–0.

That was the first goal Spain had conceded in 451 minutes of play, and it was a 19-year-old American kid who'd done it.

After that, Spain's danger men—Fernando Torres, David Villa, and Cesc Fàbregas—attacked nonstop. I was barraged in a way I wouldn't be again until I was standing on a field in Salvador, Brazil.

But our defense was in lockdown mode. Bob's strategy had been absolutely perfect: every time they tried to move the ball forward, one of our guys was right there to intercept it. Our back line of Carlos, Jay DeMerit, Oguchi Onyewu, and Jonathan Spector was brave and inexhaustible.

We held on to our lead. Then late in the game we got another breakaway. The ball deflected off one of their defenders. Clint took a single touch, and put that thing away.

At 2–0, we knew the game was over.

We had won.

It wasn't supposed to happen that way. Few people believed that we were capable of beating these soccer titans, let alone shutting them out. A few days ago, we'd been on the verge of elimination. As recently as 90 minutes ago, the whole world had been waiting for Spain to annihilate us.

Yet somehow, inexplicably, here we were, with a win so big it was jaw-dropping. *Thank God*, I thought. *Thank God I went to Bob Bradley and asked him to put me in the game. Thank God he did so I could be a part of this historic occasion.*

And I did thank God. I literally dropped to my knees at the end of that game. I looked up to the heavens and I spoke out loud.

"I don't know why," I said. "And I don't know why me." I took a deep breath, drank in everything about the moment—the vuvuzelas buzzing in the stands, my giddy teammates at the other end of the field, the floodlights and the understanding that we'd actually done this huge, amazing thing. I kissed my gloves and gazed up again at that night sky.

"But thank you."

We played Brazil in the final. Though we took an early 2–0 lead, Brazil came back with a vengeance. We lost 3–2.

But here was something curious: we'd later learn that the match was the most-watched non–World Cup game in the team's history. Worldwide, nearly 60 million viewers tuned in. Four million of those were in the U.S.

When I'd started playing this sport professionally, nobody gave a damn about it. The MLS was barely considered a pro league. Soccer was a game kids played; it wasn't a sport that adults paid attention to.

You had to leave the country to play in any serious way.

But look: we'd beaten the number one team in the world. We'd taken second place in one of the major tournaments. We were playing well, and for the first time in my professional life, people cared.

Could it be that soccer was finally gaining a foothold in the last outpost on earth that had resisted it all these years?

Around that time Kasey Keller called me.

"Tim," he said. His voice was funny somehow—he didn't sound like the Kasey I remembered, the always easy, unflappable guy who'd seen everything before.

"What's up?"

"Jack Reyna's not well." Jack Reyna, son of Claudio and Danielle, Laura and my first friends in Manchester. Laura had slept in Jack's room during so many of my away games.

Claudio had left England for the U.S. a few years ago; he was playing for my old team, the MetroStars, now renamed the Red Bulls. I hadn't seen Jack for a while. God, the kid must be ten years old by now.

Not well, Kasey had said. As I tried to process those words—not well—Kasey spoke again. "He has a brain tumor."

Oh, God.

My heart sank. I could still picture little Jack pushing his toy cars along the floor in his pajamas as the adults sat around laughing. I could remember Claudio scooping him up and carrying him up to his room when his eyelids grew heavy.

Jack Reyna. Sweet Jack with his dark, cherubic eyes. Ten years old now. With a brain tumor.

"You want to give Claudio a call?" Kasey asked.

"Just pass on my love, okay?" Claudio didn't need to hear from me. Not right now. He and Danielle had enough going on without having to answer phone calls.

"Yeah," said Kasey. "I will."

"And keep me posted."

That night, I stood in my children's rooms for a long time. I watched them sleep, and I prayed.

"LOOK AT ME NOW, POPPA"

Well, this is surreal.

I was standing in the West Wing of the White House. Everything around me was exactly like I'd seen it a hundred times before—in movies, on television, in textbooks, and in news reports. There were the battle flags, the heavily framed portraits of past presidents, the round eagle carpet in the middle of the Oval Office.

But the angles had gone all funny; somehow I was in the middle of the picture, as if I'd unzipped a television screen and walked right onto the set.

It was 2010. Tomorrow we'd be heading to South Africa. Our destination was the World Cup.

We'd spent the last month training at Princeton University, Bob Bradley's old stomping grounds. We'd worked our butts off, running up and down the field as Bob stood there with his arms folded, giving us simple one-word commands. *Sharp. Punch. Good. Now. Play.*

Then we'd driven down together to Washington, D.C. And here I was, Timmy Howard, the kid who hadn't been able sit still in his classroom once upon a time, now an invited guest at the White House.

Our team wasn't getting any old tour, either. Vice President Joe Biden had given us a full 30 minutes. Former president Bill Clinton had come in and shaken our hands. Clinton would be attending the World Cup as part of the U.S. delegation that was making a bid to host the 2022 World Cup.

Now we were shaking hands with President Obama himself.

"This is incredible," Carlos whispered to me. On the bus ride down here, Carlos had probably told us 40 times how excited he was to meet Clinton—*my favorite president ever*, he'd say. *I love that guy.*

A crisply dressed woman clapped her hands at us. "We're going to take a photograph now," she said. "Please follow us outside to the steps."

We opened the doors and stepped out into the D.C. summer. It was sweltering out there—93 degrees and humid. We were all dressed alike, in khakis and precisely matched brown leather shoes, dress shirts, and heavy warm-up jackets emblazoned with the U.S. Soccer logo. Clinton and Obama and Biden mingled with the team—*those are some sharp shoes*, said Clinton, when he realized we all were wearing the exact same ones. We wiped sweat off our brows, trying not to look like we were melting in the heat.

Standing there, I kept thinking about my Poppa.

Poppa had passed away last September. Because I was in England, I hadn't been able to go to the funeral. I wished he were still around so I could share this moment with him.

What would he have thought if someone could have told him, on the night he was fleeing Hungary for his life, that I'd be here someday. *You will escape*, they might have said. *And you will succeed in your new country. And one day, your grandson, the child of the little girl whom you're trying so desperately to hush, will stand at the White House flanked by the most important leaders in the world.*

President Obama spoke.

"I just wanted to say how incredibly proud we are of the team," he said. "Everybody's going to be rooting for you. Although sometimes we don't remember it here in the United States, this is going to be the biggest world stage there is. You're going to be representing all of us."

I'd been 11 years old back in 1990, when the U.S. qualified for the World Cup for the first time in 40 years. I'd watched us play in that tournament on a grainy television in my mother's living room, no earthly idea what might lie ahead. Since then, I'd marched steadily toward this moment. I'd been in the stands in '94, with Mulch pointing down to the field saying, "That should be you." By '98, I'd been playing side-by-side on the MetroStars with Tony Meola, the U.S. World Cup goalkeeper. By 2002, I was friends with a bunch of guys on the team, and I'd earned a spot as the number four keeper—not enough to attend the tournament, but getting closer. Then in 2006, I'd sat on the bench watching Kasey.

Now it was my turn.

President Obama finished speaking: "We are incredibly proud of what you've done already, and we are going to be proud of what you do when you get to South Africa."

The camera shutters clicked as sweat trickled down my neck. Bill Clinton was so close to me that I could have reached over and patted him on the back.

In the photograph that was published later that day, I'm beaming like a little kid.

Back when we were training in Princeton, I'd managed to get away a couple of times. I'd seen my brother, some of my friends. One night, my old basketball teammate Steve Senior organized a steak dinner, complete with players and coaches alike. We'd talked about the good old days, all those trips to away games on school buses, the hundreds of pounds of pizza we'd devoured afterward.

We hadn't been all together like this since high school; it simultaneously felt like no time had passed, and like three whole lifetimes had gone by. *New Jersey will always be inside of me*, I thought.

Laura called after dinner that night. I knew the kids must be asleep in their beds, that it would be just Laura on the other end. For some reason I hadn't picked it up. Instead I texted her back.

Heading to bed. Tired.

I don't know. Maybe I was already thinking about the next morning's training. Maybe I was nervous about what was coming up—the most important competition I'd ever been in. Maybe it was that I'd spent several hours with the guys who had known me long before I was anybody's husband, and I wasn't quite ready to be a husband again.

But somehow, in that moment, there wasn't room for Laura.

Landon had come on loan to Everton earlier that year. He'd stayed in a hotel near my house, and every day I picked him up, and we drove to training together. I loved having him there, loved introducing him to everyone—and I mean everyone: players, the youth academy players, the office workers, the physios. I wanted all of them to know Landon.

"Listen," I said to him on his first game day. "If there's one thing you need to know to be successful here, it's this: leave the bathroom door open when you go."

"What? That's crazy!"

"Trust me, Landon."

He did, even though he didn't understand why. Until one day, someone new entered the stall and shut the door. The guys got a giant bucket of water and doused him while he was going.

Landon fit right in. He was lighthearted enough to leave the bathroom stall door open, and he could dump buckets of ice over guys who were getting rehab in the hot and cold tubs like the rest of us. But he was also a straight-up professional, who played great for us. The fans sensed a real Evertonian. They took to him instantly.

In the evenings he came to the house, and hung out with Laura and the kids. Sometimes we watched American football together. Nothing with Landon was ever forced. We had been friends and teammates for a long time. Things went unspoken between us now, the way they once had with my mom. I could sense how relaxed he was with the Everton guys, how much he liked Laura and the kids. It was just easy.

Now we were headed to South Africa together—it would be Landon's third World Cup, and my first as a starter. I was so psyched we were going to get to share this together.

We flew through night and day, 17 hours in all, then climbed aboard a bus and rode for hours more. By the time the bus rolled to a stop at the lodge where we'd be spending the next month, I had no idea how long we'd been traveling, or even what time zone we were in. As the bus doors opened, we heard the sounds of a traditional South African choir rising up into the night sky. They sang in a language I didn't understand, but their tone said *Welcome. Welcome to our home at the far southern tip of this continent. Welcome to everything that is about to happen.*

When I woke up in the morning, I stepped out onto the balcony. Wow, this place was lush, built around a grand lake. Across the water I could see Clint Dempsey sitting perfectly still, fishing rod in his hand. The guy might have traveled the world as a member of the national team, but he was the perennial Texas country boy at heart.

We were isolated there—far from the rest of the world, lots of time on our hands. Everything was taken care of for us—our meals, our lodging, our schedule. Our sole responsibilities were to show up to practice, train until we had nothing left, then rest so we could do it again.

Something happens when you're in that kind of setting—you fall into a kind of suspended reality.

We retreated back into a kind of grade school mentality. On the bus rides to and from the gym, guys threw gum wrappers at each other, mocked each other about their haircuts. We laughed often, ribbed each other endlessly. Jay DeMerit and Stuart Holden belted out Justin Bieber songs at the top of their lungs. Brad Guzan was an easy target. The guy was a lovable teddy bear. He had a missing front tooth and size 14 shoes and always looked like a kid dressed up in his dad's clothes. But Brad gave as good as he got.

"Well," he'd say when I teased him, eyeballing my backward baseball cap, "at least I'm not a grown man dressed as a sixteen-year-old."

We didn't see much of Bob Bradley during our downtime. Every so often, though, we'd glimpse him walking around with a portable DVD player—the kind that parents might hand to kids for a long car trip. It didn't matter where we were—on the bus, in our hotel rooms, eating dinner—we'd see Bob hauling that thing around, and we'd know he had something new to show us.

"Uh-oh," Carlos might say when he saw Bob coming. "Better hide in the bushes. Bob's got his DVD player out again."

"Shh. Don't make eye contact," I'd respond.

But Bob would walk up, grab one of us, and press play.

"You see where you are here," he might say, pointing at a clip from a recent game. "Next time, I want you to get five yards over so their winger can't make that pass." Whomever he was talking to would agree . . . because of course Bob was right.

Once, Bob tried to bring the action to the big screen. He called us all into a conference room to show us highlights from a recent game against Turkey.

"See, here, the way their striker veers to the left . . ."

He picked up the remote control and pressed a button. It didn't work. He tried a few more times.

"But you're closing him down a little too quickly," Bob continued. He adjusted his angle, holding his thumb down. The television blanked out completely. "Shit," he muttered. Then he stood there, pressing it again and again, until finally the screen popped back to life.

"Anyhow, if you watch that play again, you'll see . . ."

He held the rewind button and it didn't work. He moved closer to the television, then attempted to hit the rewind button a few more times. The television kicked in at too high a gear, rewinding too quickly, to a different moment in the game altogether.

"Come on," he muttered to the television. He hit fast-forward, but again, nothing happened.

It went on for a while, this battle with the remote. He changed position, then pressed. Nothing. He moved closer to the television. We sat there quietly waiting, when suddenly Bob slammed the remote on the conference table.

"Fuck you!" he screamed at the remote. "Fuck you, you fucking piece-of-shit garbage!" Then he banged the remote down with every word: "Why-Won't-You-Fucking-Work?"

I had known Bob since I was a kid in New Jersey. Had played for him in some very high-pressure games. In all that time, I had literally never seen him lose it like this. Bob was Mr. Control. He was the guy who took ten minutes to answer a single question from a reporter, because he never, ever wanted to say anything he hadn't carefully thought through.

Bob snapped off the television. He closed his eyes, took a long, deep breath. Then he turned to us.

We sat perfectly upright. We didn't dare move a muscle.

His eyes flicked from me to Jay to Carlos to Steve Cherundolo, and on around the room.

"Damn it," he finally said. "Can't one of you crack a joke right now or something?"

And just like that, we burst out laughing.

Bob was howling, too.

I'd seen my brother in New Jersey. Over the years, he'd gotten deeply involved with martial arts training. He loved how it blended the physical and the mental.

The last time I saw him before leaving for South Africa, he'd given me a book, *A Fighter's Heart*, by Sam Sheridan.

On the inside flap, Chris had written a quote from Heraclitus, along with a note of his own.

"A WARRIOR"

Out of 100 men, 10 shouldn't even be there,
80 are just targets,
9 are the real fighters,
and we are lucky to have them,
for they make the battle.

All, but the one,
One is a warrior,
And he will bring the others back

—HERACLITUS

Good luck in WC 2010!!
You will bring them back.

I read that note again and again.
Good luck in WC 2010!!
You will bring them back.
And I wanted to. Oh, man, I wanted to so badly.

I spent a lot of time alone in South Africa. During those moments, I wanted to stay focused on my game, but other thoughts kept creeping in—thoughts I didn't want to have. I thought about Jack Reyna a lot, fighting for his life.

I thought about how quickly everything could disappear.

And I thought about Laura. I thought about all those times I'd headed off to games, and Laura had come toward me smiling. All those times she wrapped her arms around me, when the only thing I wanted to think about was the game.

What was wrong with me in those moments? Wasn't she supposed to be the one who would save me from my single-minded focus on winning and losing?

When my kids hugged me, I felt so much warmth, so much love.

When Laura did the same, I felt like a fake.

In the evenings I called home to speak to the kids. I made kissing noises into the phone and heard their sweet voices. They were still so little they didn't have much patience for the telephone, even to talk to their daddy, who was at the bottom of the world. They'd quickly hand the phone back to their mom.

Laura asked me questions, and I tried to answer them, tried to be a good sport, a communicative husband.

And when she talked, I listened. I listened to her tell me about how Jacob had mastered the backstroke in the pool. How Ali fell asleep facedown on the living room floor, as if her batteries had, in a single instant, run out.

I loved those stories about the kids.

And I told Laura that I loved her, too. That I missed her and couldn't wait to see her.

But then after hung up, I'd have to pray.

Because I knew that what I'd just said was a lie.

I didn't miss her. Not the way I should.

You'd think that spending that much time with the same group of guys, in one location that's nearly 10,000 miles from home, might present some challenges. You'd think, for example, we might start getting on each other's nerves. But that was the thing about this team. We dined together and played together, and in the afternoons we'd get together to talk about nothing whatsoever, or everything. Music would waft across campus—John Mellencamp or Guns N' Roses, or classic Springsteen or Eminem. Once in a while, some jokester might throw water on another player while he sat out on his balcony reading.

We were like a bunch of rowdy puppies—we'd tumble all over each other, roughhouse together, always playful. Then we'd retreat to our separate rooms and wake up ready to start all over again.

Maybe there's something about soccer being a team sport, the fact that we had to work together and trust each other to accomplish anything meaningful on the field.

Maybe it's something about the fact that we weren't just soccer players, we were *American* soccer players—mostly unknown to our nation, fighting for respect both home and abroad.

Maybe it was something about this group of guys in particular. It's hard to imagine that any other collection of pro athletes would ever be so easy to be around for so long. So relaxed, so humble. So damned much fun.

The closer we got to our first game, the more I could feel myself turning inward, trying to get mentally to that place where I felt ready. We'd be playing England, then upstart Slovenia, then Algeria.

When the England match was a few days away, I sat on the bus on the way to training jiggling my leg nervously. Stuart and Jay were two rows ahead of me. Naturally, those clowns were singing again.

Baby, baby, baby, oh . . .

Landon threw half a granola bar at them. The bar landed on the seat; Jay leaned over, picked it up, and popped it in his mouth, still singing, now with crumbs falling out of his mouth.

Like, baby, baby, baby no . . .

I watched them, but my mind kept drifting toward the game.

It wasn't enough to be here. I wanted to advance. I wanted to go as far as we possibly could. Something big was in our grasp. I could feel it, and I wanted to reach out and grab it.

Our game against England proved that no one should write this team off. Ever.

England was the clear favorite, and they took control of the game almost immediately. With vuvuzelas in the stands buzzing like bees, England's Emile Heskey sent a reverse pass to Steven Gerrard, who slotted it past me with ease.

Four minutes in, we were down by one.

And then it got worse.

Twenty-nine minutes into my World Cup debut, I was injured.

I made a diving save, parrying the ball at exactly the moment Heskey came sliding toward it. His foot was extended, studs up. He was stretching to slam the ball into the net, not to meet flesh and bone.

Even in that split second as he came toward me, I thought, *This is bad.*

Heskey crashed into my rib cage so hard it sent me flying backward. As our Steve Cherundolo cleared the ball, I lay there on the ground, my hand on my chest.

When I didn't get up, doctors ran onto the field.

"Is something broken?" I asked. It was all I could do to speak. "I don't know what's going on, is something broken?"

"You want to come off, Tim?"

Oh, God. No. No, I didn't. Not after 29 minutes. Not when I'd waited so long to get here. But the pain was blinding.

I'd been playing long enough to know that adrenaline is the world's greatest painkiller. Adrenaline is the medicine that no doctor can give you. Only the game can give it to you. If you let adrenaline run its course, sometimes even extreme pain disappears.

I managed to stand.

"Let me see how I do."

In the 40th minute Clint Dempsey sent an innocuous shot rolling toward England's goal. It looked like their keeper Robert Green was scooping it up. But wait, hold on—he wasn't! The ball went beneath him, right through his legs. We watched it crawl across the line in a kind of disbelief.

A goalkeeper's worst nightmare . . . and on the biggest stage possible.

Now we were even.

The second half of the match was thrilling. England had plenty of chances, but we held the line. It ended in a 1–1 draw.

And my trusted friend adrenaline worked its magic. I didn't even need the cortisone shot that the team doctor had prepared for me. And I managed to make enough strong saves that I earned Budweiser's Man of the Match.

Slovenia was another come-from-behind draw—one of those hard-fought, back-and-forth dramas that highlight exactly how exciting this sport can be. And also how infuriating.

We dug a hole for ourselves in the first half. A 2–0 hole. But we knew we were a better team than we had shown in those first 45 minutes and in the second half we took the game to Slovenia.

Five minutes in, Landon surged down the right flank and dribbled into their box. A Slovenian defender slid into his path, forcing him to shoot from, what looked to me, like an impossible angle. But Landon blasted the ball with such force at their keeper that had he not ducked at the last instant, his head might have gone into the goal along with the ball.

You could feel the game turn in that moment. Cries of "USA! USA!" rang out over the din of all those vuvuzelas. We were back in it.

And then in the 82nd minute, we were all square. Jozy headed Landon's cross directly into Michael's path as he charged in on goal. When the Slovenian keeper came out, Michael stabbed the ball over him.

2–2.

And now came the infuriating part.

In the 85th minute, Landon floated a perfect free kick into the box. Maurice Edu, who had come on as a substitute, ran onto the ball and redirected it into the net. The scoreboard was about to change to 3–2 and I was ready to go tearing up the field to give Maurice the biggest hug of his life.

But wait. Why was the referee suddenly waving his arm? Wasn't that the signal that a goal is disallowed?

I thought maybe my eyes were playing tricks on me. There was no infraction on the play. No offsides. No foul. A bunch of our guys surrounded the referee and demanded to know why he'd made the call.

The referee didn't answer. He didn't answer then and later, FIFA would restrict him from ever answering questions about it: the call was the call. But since that moment, Edu's non-goal has been replayed tens of thousands of times. It's been slowed down frame by frame. Every split second has been analyzed and to this day no one can tell me why the goal didn't count.

Here's what I see when I look at freeze frames of the action: I see a Slovenian defender holding his arm out, forcefully blocking Edu's run toward the ball. I see another Slovenian defender bear-hugging Michael from behind—pinning Michael's arms. I see Carlos being smothered by one of the Slovenians, Jozy being gripped from the side, Jay being held.

In fact, in this whole melee of grabbing and shoving, I see a single American—Clint—holding on to any Slovenian player at all, and that guy's not even near the ball.

There had been no foul. We'd been hosed, that's all.

The game ended in a 2–2 draw. Which meant if we were going to advance to the round of 16, we *had* to beat Algeria.

I will never forget our bus ride to the Loftus Versfeld, the Pretoria stadium where we'd play our win-or-go-home match against Algeria. All along the route, American fans stood on the road, waving and cheering. By the time Loftus came into view, the bus had to roll to a stop. A sea of supporters stretched out in all directions. Some wrapped themselves in American flags, others had painted stars and stripes on their faces, and everyone rocked the national colors—red, white, and blue. They held up scarves like one might see at a Premier League match except these said LAND OF THE FREE. They held up signs proclaiming ONE NATION. ONE TEAM, and DIVERSE. HUNGRY. UNITED. AMERICA. Fans were rapping on the windows screaming "USA!" They also held up our bus—not that anyone minded. We were so far from home, and yet all these fans made us feel like *were* home.

"Holy crap," said Carlos. "This is awesome."

The game was scoreless for 90 minutes. A draw wouldn't be good enough for us; to advance we had to win.

At a certain point, tactics went out the window. Defensive principles? Gone. The notion that a soccer game might be a chess match? Forget about it.

With the clock ticking down and the prospect of our World Cup ending, there was no time for rhyme or reason. If we had a strategy, it was this: throw everything we have at them and hope they break.

We attacked with three strikers and a midfield that marauded forward with only one thing on its mind: putting the ball in the back of their net. Algeria massed as many as nine players in front of their goal. Still we had chance after chance. We hit the post. We had a goal called back for offsides. We did everything but score.

I watched on full alert, thinking, *All we need is one play, one moment of inspiration where we catch them on their heels.* And then, a minute into stoppage time, it arrived.

Algeria's Rafik Saïfi had a clear header at goal but it was weak and straight at me. The ball bounced and I caught it. I had to move fast. There was no time to survey the field and pick out a safe outlet. There wasn't even time to even look up. I had to operate on instinct.

My instincts were formed on the fields of New Jersey with Mulch hammering certain lessons into my brain. *When the ball comes in from the left, look to the right.*

A split second after catching that ball, I knew—I just knew—that Landon would be tearing down the right flank. And because the game had been stretched wide open in those final frantic minutes, all those players abandoning their positions in their desperation to score, I also knew there'd be acres of green grass in front of him.

So I hurled that ball as far as I could to where Landon would be by the time it landed. It came to rest at his feet, like Mulch always insisted it would.

Landon set off toward the Algeria goal, 10 yards, 20 yards, 30 yards, chewing up the space as he searched for an open teammate. He pushed the ball ahead to Jozy, who picked out Clint across the box. I thought Clint would finish it but at the exact moment that he reached Jozy's pass, the Algerian goalkeeper Raïs M'Bolhi threw himself bravely at Dempsey's feet.

The ball ricocheted off their keeper and away from goal. For a moment, it looked to most of the world like we were going home.

But my eyes were on Landon. He was still running, accelerating as he moved closer to the ball. I'm not even sure the Algerian defenders knew he was there.

That's the thing about Landon. He doesn't broadcast his presence like some of the flashier players. He glides in, cool-as-you-like, and no matter how high the stakes, no matter how pressurized the situation is, he does what Landon always does—executes the finish with flawless precision.

There were 92 minutes on the clock. The ball had traveled from goal line to goal line in a few historic seconds before Landon buried it in the back of the net.

Landon raced toward the corner flag. He stretched out his arms and dove, bodysurfing along the grass.

Benny Feilhaber slid behind him. Then everyone got in on it. All the guys on the field. All the guys on the bench. The coaches.

The staff. Everyone. They ran toward Landon and threw themselves on top of him, one after another. Jozy flew onto the pileup like he was Superman. Jay DeMerit finished it off with a rolling somersault over the whole delirious gang.

I watched the jubilation from the far end of the field. I kneeled down and touched the grass, five precise touches.

I stood. I kissed my goalkeeper's gloves, and raised my arms toward the sky.

"Thank you," I said, looking up. "Thank you."

Someone brought a bunch of Budweisers into the locker room. We cracked them open.

When we learned that President Clinton was waiting outside to congratulate us, Carlos turned to me.

"I want to invite him in," he said.

"Do it," I said. "That'd be sweet."

So Carlos, shirtless and sweaty, walked up to the former president of the United States, his favorite commander in chief of all time, and said, "Sir? These guys are going to drink a few beers here. We'd be honored if you'd join us."

So that's exactly what President Clinton did. He rolled up his sleeves and popped open a beer and stayed for half an hour.

Laura and I often vacationed at a lake house in Hot Springs, Arkansas, and I sat there talking to one of the most influential men in history about his home state, about books, about this incredible match we'd just played.

And again, my thoughts returned to my Poppa. *Look at me now, Poppa. I'm not just talking to a former president, but I'm hanging out and drinking a beer with him. I hope you're enjoying watching this up there.*

We played Ghana in the round of 16. After winning our group in such dramatic fashion, we felt confident and strong, genuinely believed we could keep going in the tournament. But there's only so much adversity that a team can overcome before the odds catch up to them and we had ridden our grit and resilience for three straight games.

Once again, we gave up an early goal. Once again we let an opponent dominate us in the first half. And once again, we emerged from the locker room a different team—full of creativity, precision, and attacking dynamism. We took our time equalizing with Landon converting a late penalty, but we looked like the fitter and more dangerous side as the game entered extra-time.

Only it was Ghana who scored. Asamoah Gyan scooped the ball over me at the near post. I took a lot of criticism for that one. There are very few things worse that a keeper can do than getting beat at his near post.

And it's hard to know what to say about that. What I can say for sure is I gave my heart and soul to the game, and once in a while, a keeper gets beaten to the near post.

The game is beautiful, and it's cruel. That was a cruel, cruel day.

In the locker room, heads were down, eyes staring at the floor—such a stark contrast to the euphoric mood after the Algeria game.

President Clinton walked in. He shook hands with everyone. And then he addressed us as a group.

"Guys," he said, "it's never fun getting your ass kicked."

I glanced over at Carlos. His eyes were red.

"It's happened to me again and again," Clinton continued.

"This won't be the last time it happens to you. But you're going to keep picking yourself up."

Somehow, his words were exactly right.

He spoke the hardest truth—we had gotten our asses kicked, and we would get our asses kicked again. It would feel just as terrible next time as it did right now.

We thanked him, and he left quietly.

We showered off. Then we got out of there as soon as we could.

"CAN WE GET BEYOND THIS?"

Relentless striving comes with a price. For me, the price was my marriage.

Laura and I had been a great team from the beginning. We agreed on money, never overspending on houses or cars. When we had kids, we agreed on schools and on discipline. We enjoyed the same things—jet-skiing in summer, quiet family dinners in winter. We were good parents and good partners.

But a good marriage, a happy one, needs more than that.

It was the month in South Africa—all that time at the isolated lodge, alone in my hotel room—when I began to understand.

At first, I'd felt only a vague gnawing, a sense not yet articulated, that things at home weren't right.

Then the vagueness began to take shape, growing more and more defined, like a figure emerging from fog, until it became a fully formed thought.

And after that, I knew.

I didn't want to be married to Laura anymore.

I was addicted to my job. That's no metaphor; I was an addict in all the tangible, physical ways that signify true addiction, regardless of the substance.

My substance is winning, the pursuit of greatness. I was addicted to the adrenaline rush of victory, that beautiful flood of endorphins, of dopamine, of norepinephrine, every time we won.

I've read that cocaine floods a person's system with dopamine. Speed floods it with norepinephrine. A great save, a win, does both of those things at once.

The feeling is clean and pure. It makes you feel invincible, but only for a while. Within a day the flood recedes, and the game becomes part of your past, like all the others you've already played.

Every single week, from August to the end of May, I went looking for my fix.

Roy Keane once said that the only thing winning does is put off the fear of losing for a few days. Roy had put into words the very thing I'd been experiencing for decades.

I could remember all those years ago, watching the athletes around me and thinking, *I don't want my comfort to come from winning or losing. I want to be connected to something bigger than myself.*

I'd done better than many—maybe even better than most—at staying grounded.

But I hadn't succeeded completely.

My whole career was so front-loaded. I had friends who were getting PhDs, who were attending law school. Their careers would be just getting started when they hit their 30s. For me, turning 30 marked the beginning of the end.

There could be no putting work on hold to focus on my marriage.

I had no time to spare.

If I was going to achieve—if I was going to be great—it had to be right now. Or never.

When I walked through the door in Memphis after the 2010 World Cup, Laura threw her arms around me.

In response I felt . . . nothing. I was numb.

I hugged the children, kissing their hair, their cheeks, their ears, their arms. Laura watched, smiling. I could not meet her eyes.

I'd be home for a few weeks, not quite a month, before reporting to Everton for preseason. I couldn't imagine how I'd even begin to talk to her about what I was feeling.

Are you okay?" she asked me later that night.

"I'm tired," I said.

We spoke little to each other, busied ourselves with the kids. We read to them and brushed their teeth and put them to bed and picked up their toys. We swam in the pool. We ate out.

One evening, after the children had fallen asleep, I sat in an armchair, flipping through a magazine. Laura sat down on the sofa. She patted it, not unlike the way she had all those years ago when we watched *Remember the Titans* together in Dallas.

"Tim?" she said. "You want to come watch TV with me?"

This could be the end of my marriage, I thought.

"Not now."

I was terrified to say it out loud. As soon as I did, everything would change. I wasn't ready for that.

As the weeks went by and we got closer and closer to preseason, Laura tried to connect with me, to make things better. "Tim?" she asked. "What's going on with you?"

I can be a good father, Laura.

I can be a good provider.

I can be a good partner when it comes to raising kids and running a household. But I'm no longer sure I can be a good husband.

Every time I try, I feel like I'm faking it.

"Tim?" she repeated, still waiting. "Can you talk to me?"

This could be the end of my marriage.

"I'm tired."

What if we went away, Tim? Just you and me."

I'm not sure there is a you and me anymore. There is me and the kids, and you and the kids, and us as a family. But you and me might be gone.

"Nah, I don't want to go anywhere."

This is about us, isn't it?" she asked.

I met you when I was a kid. I married you so quickly.

And I don't think I want to be married anymore.

"Maybe," I answered. "I don't know."

Could you talk to our pastor," she asked. "Or a friend?"

Maybe it's because I sensed it back then, sensed the change that was coming. Maybe some part of me already understood, deep down, that I was mere months away from having money and cars and a home and hangers-on, not all of whom could be trusted. Maybe I'd been looking, most of all, for some sort of stability amid that flurry. And if that's true, I'm so sorry.

I shook my head. "I don't want to talk about it with anyone."

We could go to marriage counseling."

No. I already know what will make you happy. But I don't

think I'm capable of doing it. Not for real. Not with authenticity or integrity.

"No counseling," I said.

"Tim, tell me what I can do."

There is nothing you can do. Nothing you could have done. You've done it all brilliantly.

"I don't know. I really don't know."

Tim?" she asked. It was almost August—I'd be flying back to England for preseason soon. She and the kids were to follow me a few weeks later. "Do you still want to be married?"

No.

No, I do not want to be married.

But these children sleeping upstairs are my heartbeat. They are everything. And I know that if I answer this question, I will lose them; I will lose the family as we know it. I cannot imagine living apart from those kids, not having Ali crawl into bed and lay her little head on my chest in the mornings, not laughing with Jacob in the kitchen. I cannot imagine it, and I am scared to death to set this into motion.

The day I left for preseason, I knew. I knew that the next time I came back to this house it would be her house—hers and the kids. Not mine.

We had a goodbye group hug in the kitchen, all four of us. Then I started to walk out of the room, but rushed back instead to cover Ali's mop of hair, her neck and her ears, with kisses. She squealed with delight, clutching her dog security blanket to her chest. Then I did the same for Jacob. He was quieter than his sister, and I knew he was sad, even though he laughed.

"See you in a few weeks," I said.

Laura walked with me to the car that was waiting in the driveway.

We hugged and kissed.

Goodbyes might be my life, but they're one thing I've never gotten good at. This was the saddest one I've ever had.

When I got to my home in Manchester, the phone rang. Laura.

"Tim, can we get beyond this?" she asked.

That Southern lilt. The girl who once sat in a hotel room in a black dress repeating, over and over again, "I can't believe it, I can't believe it," as the lights of Times Square flashed through the windows behind her. All that exuberance: gone.

I had made her so sad.

I knew that the problem was me, my job, my addiction to the game, my unavailability, but knowing that changed nothing.

"No," I answered, finally honest for once. "We can't."

Many conversations lay ahead—about kids, about schools, about the fact that it would be best for them to stay in Memphis and I'd live in Manchester, alone. There would be conversations about assets and properties, depositions and signings, lawyers and mediators and affidavits. The conversations would be difficult, then divisive, and ultimately deeply bitter.

But all of that was in the future.

For the moment, we sat, silently, in separate houses, with an ocean—literally and figuratively—between us.

PART FOUR

USA VS. BELGIUM: STILL ALIVE
ARENA FONTE NOVA
SALVADOR, BRAZIL
JULY 1, 2014

There's a moment that lies suspended between the shot and the result. If you can stop time in this instant—somehow press pause, allowing the ball to hover in the air, the players frozen mid-run—you straddle two worlds.

In one world, the shot goes in. In the other, it does not.

The second half of this game has been a siege of shots from Belgium. I don't know how many I've stopped. I don't even have time to wonder.

All that's come before has disappeared into the blunt staccato of shots on goal.

Bam. Bam bam. Bam bam bam.

One upon the next, they've rained down so fast there's no time for a chess match, no time to reflect on what's broken down, or how we might fix things.

We're too busy defending for our lives.

But here's the thing: we are alive.

The number of corner kicks doesn't matter, attempts on goal don't matter. Possession stats? Irrelevant.

All that matters is that we're entering the 92nd minute and the score is still 0–0. Belgium has dominated everywhere but the scoreboard.

One goal. That's all it will take.

And look—at the other end of the field, Jermaine is rising in the box. He heads the ball toward the far post. Chris Wondolowski is right there.

The goal in front of Chris is gaping.

Wondo is the consummate poacher, a guy who makes a habit of the late winner.

As the ball flies off his foot, I can almost picture in my mind's eye what will come next: the net bulging, the delirious run to the corner flag, the jubilant ten-man pileup.

It will be like Landon's Algeria moment four years ago.

In that world, I lift my arms heavenward, and say with heart and soul, "Thank you."

But, of course, the world that flashes in my mind is only one of the two possible outcomes.

There is another world, and it is that second world we enter in the 92nd minute.

If I could choose, I'd put the ball in front of Wondo today. He's money in the box.

It's just that this time, his shot goes high and wide.

We may still be alive, but we have 30 minutes of play still ahead of us.

We are heading into extra-time.

DIVORCE

On August 14, three days after Laura filed for divorce, Everton played its first Premier League match of the season, against the Blackburn Rovers.

I'll never forget that game.

In the 14th minute, Blackburn headed the ball into my box. Three of us charged toward it at the same time: me, Everton's center-back Sylvain Distin, and Blackburn forward Nikola Kalinić. There was nothing unusual about the way the ball was moving, or how we went for it—I'd lived a thousand moments like this one already.

Sylvain saw me coming and got out of the way so I could grab the ball. Kalinić was still barreling toward me, as any good striker would, but the ball was secure. Safe. I had it in my hands.

My plan was to roll it out to Leighton Baines, let him take it down the left flank. But as I went to roll the ball, I dropped it right at Kalinić's feet. The striker couldn't believe his luck as he slotted the ball into the wide-open net.

That proved to be the only goal of the game; we lost 1–0.

Opening day of the season—and I'd made a spectacular blunder.

As I walked off the field, Chris Woods shook my hand and patted me on the back as he always does. But I knew there would be hell to pay with Moyes.

There was. "I don't understand," he hissed. "What were you doing? What were you *thinking?*"

On Sunday, I was too depressed to get out of bed, much less go anywhere. I lay there, thinking, *I can't take it. I can't handle letting down my team like that. I can't bear my life right now.*

I didn't feel any better the next day, but I couldn't miss practice. I also needed to talk to Moyes, not to justify my howler against Blackburn, but to explain what was going on in my personal life. If anyone needed—and deserved—to know that, it would be him. So I dragged myself out of bed on Monday and drove to the training ground early.

From Everton's parking lot you can see into Moyes's glass-walled corner office. I saw Moyes already there, sitting upright at his desk.

I entered the building and I knocked on his door. "David?" I asked. "Can I come in?"

Moyes looked up. "Sure, Tim, sit down."

So I did. But when I tried to speak, the words wouldn't come. I opened my mouth, closed it, stared at the floor. Right here, in front of me, was a man who put his faith and trust in me, unconditionally, and I'd let him down.

It felt like I'd let everyone in my life down recently.

"Tim?" he asked, gently. "What's going on?"

As my eyes welled up with tears, I managed to speak.

"I need you to know where I'm at personally," I began. "Laura and I are getting a divorce. The kids are going to stay with her in Memphis."

"Tim," he said, concern and empathy suddenly etched into his face, "Look, I had no idea. If I'd known I never would have reacted—"

I held my hands up. "Stop," I said. "You had every right to react that way. I'm a big boy, and I made a big mistake. I can handle it. I just wanted you to know."

"If you need anything," Moyes said, "you tell me."

I said nothing.

"I mean it. Come around to my house anytime. Day or night. Nothing's off-limits, you hear me? We'll sit. We'll talk."

Discreetly, David let Chris Woods and some of the senior players in on the news. One by one, they approached me, telling me how sorry they were, inviting me to dinner, insisting that whenever I felt like talking, they'd be around to listen.

After a while, everyone at Everton knew. Even cranky Jimmy Martin shook my hand. "I'm sorry about your personal trouble," he said. Then he handed me three sets of white socks. "You let me know if you need any more, okay?"

I called Dan and Mulch, talked to them together. I told them what was happening. Divorce . . . kids in Memphis. It upset them. Both of these guys loved Laura; everyone did. They were both family men, and they'd seen me around the kids. They knew how much it would pain me to be apart from Jacob and Ali.

Dan in particular pushed me hard to make sure I'd thought through every angle.

"Dan," I said, "it comes down to this: I don't want to feel like a fake in my own life."

"Okay," he replied. "And you're ready for this, for all that comes next?"

I took a deep breath.

"As ready as I'll ever be."

I called my mom. She mostly listened, the same way she always does. If she was thinking, *You got married too young*, she didn't say it. If, on the other hand, she was thinking, *This divorce is a mistake*, she didn't say that, either.

She asked a single question: "How are you going to be apart from the kids?"

I'd already thought through all the possible ways I could stay close to the kids. I'd wracked my brains trying to figure out how we could live on the same continent. I could return to the States, try to play for an MLS team. There was no MLS team in Memphis, though, and I'd still have training all week, games every weekend. I'd still see them only occasionally. Besides, playing in the Premier League, I could retire comfortably and live permanently in Memphis by the time I was 40. If I joined an MLS team, I'd have to play far longer to earn enough to retire.

So I told my mom the only thing I knew for sure.

"Mom," I replied, "it's on me to be the kind of father I want to be."

In my next life, I want to be a divorce lawyer. It seems like the easiest job in the world: pit one spouse against the other when both are at their most vulnerable and, hopefully, most ignorant about the process. Then they'll believe whatever you tell them.

Actually, scratch that idea: I'd rather clean toilets. The whole divorce business is too damned dirty.

Maybe there really is such a thing as an "easy" divorce, but I wouldn't know. All I can tell you is that Laura and I didn't have one. Instead, it turned out to be an extended, outrageous, stupid fight.

Each of us hired a lawyer. The lawyers told us what to expect. In theory, it was all about material things—money, homes, cars—that could be easily settled. Assign a monetary value to each item and split that number down the middle. Done.

But that was in theory. The reality was anything but easy.

Part of the problem was the nature of my job. I was making a lot of money now, but sometime in the future, possibly the very near future given the potential for injury, I would no longer be able to play soccer, and there was no certainty about what I could do after that.

There are plenty of Premier League players who have declared bankruptcy in the wake of bad investments, bad luck in the real estate market, and, yes, bad divorces; I'd played with a few of them. But Laura's attorney insisted my career would remain lucrative indefinitely—guaranteed—even long after I was too old to play anymore.

"Yeah?" I said to my own lawyer. "Is she offering me a job?"

But the real fight and the real ugliness wasn't over money or property or anything you could put a price tag on. The financial issues were stand-ins for the emotional ones. We were fighting, because Laura felt angry, because I felt guilty, and because both of us felt broken and shaken to the core.

When we said our vows, it was with the mutual belief that we'd be married 'til death do us part. I remembered Laura's mom saying just that. "You'll be married forever because you have God in your marriage."

I believed it then.

If you want your faith to be shattered, enter marriage trusting in that faith to protect you from divorce. Then go through the hell of having your marriage crumble.

Laura hadn't given me any cause for anger during the marriage. She'd been a good, faithful, loving wife, a sweetheart in every way. But still, I was angry. I was angry at the world, angry at how hard it was to do the right thing, angry that I couldn't stay true to myself, and have what felt like integrity in this world, without hurting the people I most cared about.

Mostly, I was angry that doing the right thing for my kids—providing for them, protecting their future, our future as a family—meant I had to live apart from them.

A few weeks after talking to David Moyes in his office, I hit the wall.

Ali and Jacob lived 4,200 miles away on a different continent. In Memphis, the school year had started. They had teachers and friends I'd never met.

There's no scheduled time off for Premier League teams. By tradition, we'll get the day after a game, usually Sunday, one other day that week, typically Wednesday—but not two consecutive days off when I'd be able to travel. But frankly I didn't know how much longer I could go on without seeing my kids.

I went back to David Moyes and asked for permission to fly home after the upcoming Saturday match. I'd arrive in Memphis on Sunday evening. I'd spend all day Monday with Ali and Jacob, then drive them to school Tuesday morning. After dropping them off, I'd go straight to the Memphis airport for a plane to Atlanta; from there I'd take a connecting flight to England, arriving Wednesday morning. I'd head straight to the field and train as long and as hard as I could to make up for the time I'd missed.

It was an almost unheard-of arrangement, but Moyes fixed those flinty eyes on me and said, "Absolutely, Tim. You go see your kids."

I did.

During that trip, I held Ali in my lap as Clayton tried to scramble up onto the sofa with us. I got to listen to Jacob tell me about his new school friends, listen to the sound of his laughter.

It filled me up, gave me the energy to keep moving forward. It kept me going.

We broke the news to the kids that we were splitting up. We said all the usual things—*Mommy and Daddy aren't going to be living together anymore . . . we both love you guys very much*—words that try and fail to convey the depth of regret in your heart.

Ali was three years old at the time. I don't think she sat down the whole time we talked. She climbed off and on the furniture, turned lights on and off, asked if she could watch cartoons. Jacob had just turned five. Did he understand what we were saying? Even a little bit? He said he did, but honestly, it was hard to tell.

When we stopped talking, Laura and I looked at each other—maybe the first time we'd locked eyes the whole trip—and both of us shrugged, as if to say, *Well, that's done.* Her eyes were so sad that I wanted to take everything back.

Maybe I should have faked it, I thought. *Maybe I should have gone through the motions instead of ripping this family apart.*

In early November, Moyes approached me. I'd been feeling dark and jittery, easily frustrated on the field. "You need to see your kids again?" he asked.

"Yeah," I said. "I really do."

So he let me make the trip again.

And again. Every few weeks for the rest of that season and most of the next, I'd fly back to Memphis on the same schedule: Leave England on Sunday, chasing the setting sun. Spend a little time with the kids that night and all day Monday. Then reverse course on Tuesday, flying through the night, then arriving in time for training on Wednesday. However sore and tired I was on those Sunday flights—the games rip you apart—I'd return feeling refreshed.

The trips were worth every one of the hundreds of thousands of miles traveled, worth the jet lag and the discomfort and the solitary nights in a hotel room.

I wouldn't fly halfway around the world and back to spend 36 hours with the pope himself. But my kids? Yes, I would. And I did. Every chance I got.

Divorce is complicated no matter what. But it becomes a nightmare when you and your wife live on different continents and you need to be present for depositions, mediation, hearings.

In March 2011, I had to leave U.S. National Team training to attend mediation.

The session was held at my attorney's office. He and I took one room, Laura and her attorney another, and the mediator went back and forth between us all day.

Still, we got nowhere. Laura remained furious with me, and by now I was furious with her. Neither side would bend even an inch. I'd say it was the biggest waste of my time in 35 years of existence. The only people who benefited were our lawyers.

At the end of the day, the mediator called us into a room together. Laura walked in with her head high. Not once did she even glance at me. I jiggled my leg under the table and wouldn't look at her, either. The mediator addressed both of us in turn. "Guys," he said, "I could literally solve this in five minutes. You think it's complicated. It's not. Eventually, one of you is going to have to budge."

I thought then, *Nobody's ever going to budge here. This is going to go on for 20 more years.*

I believe divorce comes down to who can endure the longest beating. You poke and punch away at each other, piling up one bad feeling on top of another—all while shelling out hundreds of dollars an hour in legal fees. It doesn't matter what's on the table or how much it's worth. In the end, nobody wins.

I was on a bus in Scotland with Everton when the phone rang. It was nighttime, and I saw Kasey's name light up on my phone.

I knew it couldn't be good.

"Jack Reyna died," he said.

I held the phone against my ear and didn't speak. Outside my window, the landscape was dark and shadowy.

Jack Reyna, my friend Claudio's son, was gone. He'd been a beautiful, happy boy, beloved by his parents.

I thanked Kasey for calling, then I pressed my hands against my forehead.

I dialed Laura's number. Somehow I had to tell her this unfathomable thing.

God, it was all so fucking precious. The time we have with our kids—with anyone—was so fleeting. In the best of circumstances, it would be gone in the blink of an eye.

It was a blessing, every bit of it—the skinned knees, the temper tantrums, the sleepless nights. I recalled my mom's words when Jacob was born: *How can you be a father, when I can still remember holding you?*

I wanted to grab my kids, breathe deep, and inhale the smell of their skin. I wanted to protect them, throw myself between them and every terrible thing that could happen on this earth.

But they were in Memphis, and I was in England.

I stayed in Memphis for the summer of 2011, and bought a three-bedroom town home so Jacob and Ali could have their own bedrooms—Ali decorated hers with butterflies while Jacob opted for a surfer theme. It was Daddy's house, but theirs, too. Jacob sat on the sofa watching *SportsCenter* until he fell asleep. In the morning, Ali padded into my bedroom on her tiny bare feet, ready to curl up and snuggle.

I covered them with kisses every chance I got, and at night I lay in bed, thanking God for this moment, when our three hearts could beat in sync under a single roof . . . at least for a while.

There is a favorite photograph of my kids from before the divorce: Ali's lips are parted slightly, a wisp of hair falling onto her forehead. Jacob looks intently forward—eager, calm. I love this photograph: it captures them exactly—their innocence, the joy that's ready to burst out of them.

I wanted them with me all the time, so I took the photograph with me to my favorite tattoo artist, Alex Rodriguez, who works in Liverpool.

"Can you tattoo this image?" I asked.

He studied it closely. "Sure can," he said. "But it's going to take some time on the table."

Around the same time, I got another tattoo, this one on my lower ribs. There were lyrics I couldn't seem to get out of my head—the lyrics to James Taylor's "Fire and Rain," a song that my mom had played endlessly when I was a child.

> *Won't you look down upon me, Jesus . . .*
> *I won't make it any other way.*

The divorce proceedings needed to be over. It had to end, and fast. I couldn't stand it anymore. Couldn't stand the lawyers talking in circles. Couldn't stand going around and around until we were dizzy and our wallets were falling out of our pockets yet again. *Life is too short for this*, I thought.

Finally, Dan made an offer: "What if I spoke to Laura? Would that help?"

"At this point," I told him, "I have no idea what would help."

But I phoned her.

"Laura, none of us trust each other. I don't trust your lawyer and you don't trust mine, and quite frankly, I don't trust him myself. But we both trust Dan."

Dan spent the better part of a month talking with us one at a time. One by one, the issues narrowed.

Through these conversations, he was helping us settle a lot more than the terms of our contract; he was also enabling us to trust each other again, and to envision a future without animosity as we developed separate lives.

Bit by bit, he guided us out of the pit and into the light.

Then, at last, it was done. We brought a finished deal to our own lawyers.

Tada! we said. *It's over.*

Honestly, I don't know how any couple anywhere manages to get divorced without Dan's help.

MOVING FORWARD

In July 2011, U.S. Soccer announced that they'd fired Bob Bradley and hired Jürgen Klinsmann as head coach. Jürgen had once been a world-class German striker; now he was regarded as a successful, if controversial, coach. He'd taken over the German national team after they'd had a poor showing at Euro 2004. He'd shaken things up, replaced older players with younger ones, brought in new coaches, changed formations, and even rotated goalkeepers during the 2005 Confederations Cup. He hired sports psychologists and motivational speakers and nutritionists. But he must have done something right on the field as well. By the time the Germans got to the 2006 World Cup, they swept their group and advanced all the way to the semifinals.

When you play professionally, you get accustomed to turnover. Players come and go—they get injured, they get transferred, they get cut from the team. Coaches are hired, and coaches are fired. It's just part of the world you live in.

But that doesn't mean everybody likes it.

I'd been lucky; I'd had remarkable continuity since my MetroStars days—I'd had a decade of training with Mulch, five years with Bruce Arena in my early days on the U.S. team, five years with Bob Bradley, all three of my Manchester United years with Ferguson, and now five years under David Moyes.

But that kind of consistency is the exception, not the rule.

I had always admired Bob, both as a person and a coach. He was driven and competitive and thoughtful and good. I was sad to see him go.

Jürgen was different from Bob in so many ways. Whereas Bob had been closed off to the media, with a steely, quiet demeanor, Jürgen was charismatic and telegenic, quick to flash a smile or make an off-the-cuff remark in front of the cameras.

Whereas Bob had been focused on tactical adjustments, modifying each game plan according to the strengths of our opponents, Jürgen talked about a broader vision for American soccer. He wanted to instill a more proactive philosophy throughout all levels of the sport—from youth clubs to the national team.

In Jürgen's view, we needed to create our own opportunities, instead of reacting to our opponents. And he wasn't shy about changing the way we did things under Bob, starting with our training regimen. With Bob, we'd generally had one long session each day, often filling the afternoon with discussions of tactics and video sessions. Jürgen had us training twice a day. Sometimes three times.

Bob was an American, through and through: he had always allowed us to dress the way we wanted in our free time. If we had a craving for a chicken fajita every so often, Bob was cool with it. As long as we were at training on time, he didn't care when we woke up, or even when we went to sleep.

Jürgen was an Americanized German . . . but the man was still a German at heart. He managed every action of the players—some even said he micromanaged them.

Jürgen dictated when we woke and when we slept. He insisted

we wear USA track suits during training, and even when we hung around the hotel. Sugary snacks were replaced by leaner, high-protein bars, "Performance nutrition," he called it. I'd spent my whole life eating PB&Js; somehow, under Jürgen, the sandwich morphed into a natural version of the staple that was practically unrecognizable . . . and to my taste buds, inedible.

We had earlier curfews. Less time to sit around after meals shooting the breeze.

Jürgen was even determined to change our breathing.

Some of our training sessions became two hours of yoga exercises. If there is a less likely sight on this earth than Clint Dempsey, the Texas trailer-park kid, doing downward-facing dog poses, or the stalwart Michael Bradley deep breathing through a tree pose, I have yet to see it.

Jürgen banned cell phones from the locker room. He insisted that the team administrator was on call 24/7. We began bringing our own gym equipment to hotels, to ensure we always used state-of-the-art machines. Each dawn, we took "empty stomach runs," 30 minutes of sprints designed to pull energy from body fats. He took us on field trips—to Versailles, to the 9/11 Memorial—to inspire us as human beings.

Even as he advocated for a creative game, personal expression on the field, he left nothing to chance when it came to the players. We were his now, and he wanted to mold us, shape us, push us further than we could imagine.

As an OCD guy, I find change difficult. But it's possible Jürgen's innovations were easier for me than some of the others. After all, I'd had over a decade of playing in Europe. I recognized Jürgen's approach. I understood, at least, the context of where he was coming from.

None of the players argued with Jürgen, but you could sense misgivings from their body language, a kind of tension when they were around him. Or I might glimpse one player's eyes flick to another's as Jürgen explained the way things were going to look from now on—a tiny moment of "what exactly is happening here?"

It wasn't an easy transition. Maybe if we were a club, training together daily, week after week, we would have settled in faster.

But Jürgen kept at it. He wasn't going to modify his system for us. He believed in his methods. He was planning to usher in a new era of American soccer, and he wasn't afraid to let the world know.

I couldn't have been more thrilled with one of his changes: he announced he was hiring Chris Woods, my Everton goalkeeping coach, to work with the U.S. keepers.

To me, this was ideal: I'd have Chris's steady, calm, expertise guiding me both at Everton, and on the national team. And I knew Chris would be a great fit for the other keepers, Brad Guzan and Nick Rimando, too.

Back in New Jersey, the New Jersey Center for Tourette Syndrome was becoming increasingly influential. Under Faith Rice's leadership, the NJCTS educated schools and hospital staffs, counseled families, and organized antibullying programs. Its expanding library had become one of the best resources in the country. They'd teamed up with Rutgers University to establish a first-of-its kind clinic, offering therapy, testing, and skills training for TS kids and their families.

And then there was the Leadership Academy that Faith was planning. If she could pull that off, the lives of people with TS would dramatically change.

During the 2010 season, I'd helped the NJCTS earn $50,000 in grant funding from Pepsi; it was a promotion they'd run as a part of their U.S. Soccer sponsorship. Several players had picked a favorite charity, and fans had voted online for where the money would go. I'd chosen NJCTS, and won. All the money would support the Leadership Academy.

More recently, Faith had created a fund-raiser in the form of a raffle called "Team Up with Tim Howard." The winners were from Plainsboro, New Jersey: Tim and Leslie Kowalski and their two daughters, 12-year-old Tess and 8-year-old Paige, both of whom had been diagnosed with TS. The four of them would fly to England with my mom, we'd all have lunch together, and they'd be my guests at the upcoming Everton game.

"Just so you know," Mom said, "Tess in particular has a pretty severe case."

The lunch took place at a Thai restaurant in Liverpool. I got there first, and when I spotted the Kowalskis I thought, *This family seems really in sync with each other.* I liked how gently Tim nudged the girls forward, encouraging them to shake my hand, and how warm Leslie's voice was whenever she spoke to one or the other; you could sense that Tess and Paige trusted their parents, and that the trust worked both ways. *Sort of like Mom and me,* I thought.

Mom and I sat on one side of the table, the Kowalskis on the other. Both Leslie and Tim urged the girls to come sit near me, but they shook their heads; they were sticking close to mom and dad.

Tess and Paige were lovely, both with Leslie's dark hair and sparkling eyes. Did they fidget more than other kids their age, make more noise? Sure. But that didn't change who they were. Sweet, shy, young girls.

"You know, I really want to thank you for this," Leslie said to me.
I shrugged, as if to say no big deal.

"No. I mean it," Leslie said. "It's been a really tough year for our family. Tess has been dealing with the strongest tics she's ever had, and it's been hard for her."

She turned to Tess. "Okay if I tell him about your TS?" When Tess nodded, her mom added, "Do you want to tell him yourself?" Tess looked alarmed; her eyes said no. Mom and I exchanged a quick glance of recognition.

Leslie explained that Tess's symptoms had shown up in kindergarten. Grunting and sniffing and throat-clearing and shoulder jerks, all drawing attention in the classroom. After a while, she resisted going to school at all and there were tears every morning. By the end of her kindergarten year, the crying had turned to screaming. The boys in the class were making faces at her, Tess said. She couldn't stand being there. Her parents were bewildered, but they could see from the pictures Tess had been drawing—sad faces with dark gray shadows—that they needed to know what was going on.

Eventually, they got a diagnosis: Tourette Syndrome.

Her symptoms had hardened since then. She spat or blew in people's faces.

"And sometimes I poked them in the eye," Tess suddenly blurted out. Immediately, she clammed up, looking down at the table.

Leslie reached over to rub her daughter's back. "That's true," she said. "But you can't help it."

"I know," Tess said. "But I wish I could."

My mom reached over to me then and touched my forearm almost unconsciously.

Tess's next symptom, Leslie said, was muttering curses under her breath.

Tim Kowalski flashed a warm smile at his daughter. "I thought, oh boy," he said. "What's coming next?"

Tess didn't seem to be ashamed by the conversation; she didn't mind her parents' comments. These were simply the facts of Kowalski family life. They talked about the trials of TS matter-of-factly, as other families might talk about hiring a math tutor. Their openness and ease seemed really healthy to me.

Tess found a way to mask the curses, sort of. She'd figured out that if she mumbled her words and strung them together as fast as she could—*shittybitchfuck*—people might not understand what she was saying. If she added the word *pie* to the end of a string of curses—*shittybitchfuckPIE*—it obscured the curses even further.

My mom and I were impressed.

"That's pretty smart, Tess," Mom said.

Paige had been diagnosed with TS more recently. So far, the disorder manifested as grunting, whistling, and throwing her shoulder so far forward that she often dislocated it. Her symptoms weren't as severe as her sister's, but I remembered how I felt when my mom labeled my own symptoms "mild."

When you're living inside TS, there's no such thing as mild. Whatever your symptoms, it's damn hard to cope.

I told the Kowalskis about my own experience, especially the battle to suppress my tics, and being unable to focus on anything going on in the classroom.

"I don't try to hide them anymore," I said. "I just let them pass through me. As you get older, you stop worrying as much about hiding it, you know?"

"And it seems like it's never held you back," said Leslie.

"Right," I responded. "The only thing that ever held me back was attempting to hide it." And that, I knew now, was the truth.

The Kowalskis came to Goodison Park the next day, watching as Everton beat Wolverhampton 2–1. I met them after the game and introduced them around. This is Marouane Fellaini. Leighton Baines. Phil Jagielka. We snapped some photos of the family as they posed with players.

The four of them returned to New Jersey, and to navigating their lives with TS, a process that few people understood. I couldn't stop thinking about them after they left, remembering what Faith Rice had told me the first time we met. *These kids are going to have to stand up for themselves every day of their lives.*

A few months later, I got a package from the Kowalskis. Each of the girls had written a thank-you note, and there was a hand-knitted scarf, perfect for the bitter Manchester winters, from Leslie, who also included a card of her own:

> Tim—
> Tess recently decided to give a presentation to 100 people at
> our temple about TS. She explained what TS was, and what
> it felt like to have it. She used you as a model of someone
> who lives successfully with TS.
> I don't know that she would have done that if she hadn't
> met you. I wish every child with TS could have the chance
> to sit with someone who understands them.
> Leslie

Funny. I'd spent the last few months wishing that every child with TS could have a family like the Kowalskis surrounding them.

CHANGING THE SCOREBOARD

Here is what it's like to arrive at the Estadio Azteca in Mexico City.

You're wheezing, first of all. The Azteca is 7,349 feet above sea level. But it's hard to tell what makes it harder to breathe: the altitude, or the city's blanket of smog. Forget about playing a game: simply walking up a flight of stairs makes you feel like you've just climbed Kilimanjaro.

It's the greatest home-field advantage I've ever encountered.

The moment the bus pulls off the highway, you can see Azteca in the distance. It's huge—114,000 seats in steep risers—and it looms like a concrete Colosseum rising over the City of Hope. You have police escorts, sirens flashing all around your bus, because of course, you're American. On game day, you *need* those escorts. But for the moment, all you can do is look at that stadium in the distance. There's standstill traffic everywhere, in all directions. Nobody's going anywhere for a while.

You inch toward it. With each passing minute, the stadium grows bigger and bigger.

When you do finally get there, you head downstairs. Far downstairs; the visitors' locker room is so deep inside the stadium it might as well be a dungeon. You change into your warm-up gear and walk through dingy corridors looking for a stairwell. It's poorly lit down there, dank and cold. And since you're the away team, your locker room is at the far end of the tunnel. Those corridors go on forever, and you don't have any idea where you are, or how much distance remains before you get to the stadium entrance.

By the time you jog out to the field to warm up, you're already out of breath. All around you are stands that climb straight toward the sky.

They're filled with people who hate you. They hiss and boo and jeer.

All this, and you haven't even touched the ball yet.

It's daunting. It's intimidating. And the more times you go down there without winning, the more ingrained that feeling becomes. After nine games and zero wins in that stadium, you begin to believe you can't possibly win. Not there.

On August 15, 2012, when we arrived at Azteca, our record there was 0–8–1. We were 0–23–1 in all games against Mexico on their soil.

We'd gone down for a "friendly"—a misnomer if I've ever heard one. We're talking about a rivalry so toxic that Mexican fans launch missiles—entire beers, bags of urine, rocks—down onto the field in the middle of the game. In 2004 fans chanted, "Osama! Osama!" at U.S. players. At Azteca, the "away" fans sit protected by barbed wire fences and police in riot gear. Even reporters and commentators require armed escorts to leave the stadium safely.

Jürgen had made me captain for this game. Down in that

locker room, in the bowels of the Azteca, I moved from one player to the next, reminding them of their responsibilities. I watched as Landon laced up his cleats. He looked like he was a gladiator, about to face the lion. I slid on my captain's armband.

Then the locker room bell rang, signaling that it was time to head up to the tunnel, start lining up.

I held up my hand to the team. "No," I said. "Hold up."

No one moved.

I delayed to make the Mexico players wait. I wanted them to stand there, not sure where we were, and not see us coming. I wanted *them* to have to turn around to look at *us*.

We waited just long enough to be confident they would have lined up already. Then I led our team out into the hallway, that long, dark walk beneath the stadium, and up the concrete ramp to where the Mexican players stood.

Our voices in those corridors were deep and loud.

Come on, boys!

This is our night!

We lined up next to El Tri, stared straight ahead.

I held my chin high. Tightened my jaw. Behind me, I knew all the other guys were doing the same.

If any of us felt fear, we weren't going to show it.

The first half was like a tennis match; we sent the ball back and forth, back and forth. Neither side accomplished much. Mexico created some good chances, forced us on our heels a couple of times, but our back line held steady.

At halftime, it was 0–0.

Mexico came on strong in the second half. They attacked in waves and Geoff Cameron had to bail us out time and again.

Then in the 80th minute, three of our second-half substitutes—Brek Shea, Terrence Boyd, and Michael Orozco Fiscal—changed the game. Kyle Beckerman passed to Brek, who hit a low cross to the top of the six-yard box. Terrence got in front of his marker and back heeled the ball toward the right post.

Michael Orozco Fiscal—in only his fifth appearance for the national team—slotted it home.

Holy shit, I thought. *We're winning.*

We needed to hold that 1–0 lead for ten more minutes.

Those final minutes were as tough as any I've ever faced. The back line fought hard and I had to make a sprawling save in the 84th minute. Five minutes later, I had to make another diving save.

But we held them.

When the final whistle blew, the crowd was stunned into almost complete silence. The U.S. had beaten Mexico at Azteca—something that had never happened in decades of competing against them.

Coming off the field, Chris Woods gave me the traditional handshake and pat on the back. This time, though, it was accompanied by an enormous grin. Chris may have been English, and new to the USA-Mexico matchup, but he knew all about massive rivalries. And whatever he didn't know before today, the atmosphere at Azteca made clear.

We'd lost both the 2009 and 2011 Gold Cup finals to Mexico. In 2009, we'd been embarrassed 5–0. Then in 2011, I'd caused a bit of a controversy. I'd been frustrated that even in California, the pro-Mexico crowd had blared air horns during our national anthem. I'd been infuriated that we'd blown a two-goal lead and ended up losing 4–2. The last of those goals—a brilliant piece of improvisation by Giovanni dos Santos—had been especially maddening. Then, when the postgame ceremony was conducted almost entirely in Spanish, I'd lost my cool. After the match I told the media that it was a "fucking disgrace" that even in Pasadena, California, I'd felt like a visitor in my own country—I'd later release a statement apologizing for my language.

Now, in Azteca, those Gold Cup losses made this victory feel even sweeter. Our locker room was as celebratory as I've ever seen it. Even though this was a technically a "friendly," the victory felt as important as any we'd ever had—as big as Spain. Or Algeria.

I remember looking across the room at Landon. He had this huge, wide smile plastered across his face, but there was something about his eyes. He looked almost bewildered in his joy, as if some part of him was still wondering, *Is this even real? Did this really happen?*

Landon caught my eye then, and for a long, great moment we grinned at each other.

Yeah, it's real. It happened.

On the way out of the stadium, there's a long ramp toward where the bus—and all those police escorts, more important now than ever—sat waiting. Each team that's ever played in Azteca has a plaque with their record in the stadium. We found ours, and we stared at it for a little while. In the wins column was a zero.

They were going to have to change it, as a result of what we'd done here today.

I took a picture of myself with that sign, then I looked around. "Hey, does somebody have a Sharpie?"

Nobody did; if they had, I swear I would have changed it then and there.

On the bus ride home, a text popped up from Mulch: WAY TO REPRESENT THE 732.

I laughed. But I didn't reply to him right away. Instead, as we rolled slowly through Mexico City, I dialed a Memphis number.

"Hi, Tim," Laura said when she picked up.

We'd come through the divorce intact. We'd moved forward. We hadn't been able to do it until the ink was dry on that stupid contract. But once we'd signed it, we'd started seeing each other as teammates again, instead of opponents. We were on the same side, trying to raise good, strong, loving children in this world.

Even as we were living separate lives, we were still managing to be a family.

"Hey," I said. "Guess what? We beat Mexico. At the Azteca."

She gasped.

"Oh my goodness," she exclaimed.

Then I heard her calling out into the house, "Jacob! Ali! Come to the phone! Your daddy just made history!"

We would meet Mexico again. We'd draw 0–0 with them at Azteca in March 2013, and six months later, we'd beat them 2–0 at a World Cup qualifier in Columbus, Ohio.

Actually, in that game, we would do more than beat them; we would break them. I saw it in their eyes that day; by the end of the match, those El Tri players looked empty, scooped out. We had crushed their spirit.

BROKEN

Near the end of the 2012–2013 Premier League season, Everton played Oldham Athletic in the FA Cup. Actually, it was a replay; we'd drawn with Oldham 2–2 the week before. We should never have tied them—Oldham plays two full divisions below us, but that, of course, is the beauty of the FA Cup: you never know what plucky upstart will ambush one of the big dogs.

In this game, we were winning comfortably 3–1. Toward the end, Oldham brought on a substitute whom I'll call Bonehead. From the moment Bonehead came on, he ran around that field, making stupid, rash challenges and kicking people. He was the worst sort of idiot . . . the dangerous kind. It was as if he'd decided, "This a Premier League team, so I'm going to make a name for myself." I wanted to shout at him, "That isn't how it's done in the top tier, mate!"

We might be rough-and-tumble, but the game is played fairly.

At one point, the ball came toward me, swerving in the air to the left-hand side of the box. It was a nothing play: jump, catch it, come down.

But while I was up in the air—the ball was high over my head—Bonehead barged straight into me. He had no intent to play the ball.

When Bonehead and I collided, he swept my legs out from underneath me. Ordinarily, I'd try to land on my side, shoulder, hip, or stomach. But because of my positioning, and his, I couldn't. My back and tailbone hit the ground first.

I've had plenty of injuries in my career. I've been bumped and bruised and kicked and elbowed and knocked down again and again. This was different. I tried to roll over, but I kept getting a sharp, shooting pain.

Everton's head of medicine, Danny Donachie, rushed onto the field.

I lay flat, looking at the sky. "Danny," I said. Oh, God. That pain. "I'm really hurt, I'm really hurt. It's my back. Danny, I'm not okay."

He asked if I could get up, and I tried. I couldn't step too hard on my left side; if I did, I doubled over, put my hands on my knees.

"Can you play?" Danny asked.

No, I can't.

"Maybe," I said.

I should have limped off the field and gone straight to the training room. But I couldn't. I wouldn't. I wasn't finished. I hadn't seen this game out yet.

The adrenaline, I rationalized. *Surely that adrenaline will numb this.*

The ref had called a foul, awarding us a free kick from deep in our end. It would normally be mine to take, but I was thinking, *I don't actually know if I can even kick.*

When the referee blew his whistle, I hobbled backwards. I took a few very ginger steps toward the ball, planted my left foot.

Suddenly, I felt this searing pain up the left side of my back.

I kicked anyway.

In that moment, I thought of Bill Kenwright, Everton's owner. He's a good, honorable man, an Evertonian to the core. Every 30 days, Bill signs my checks. If I were in his position, if I were signing all those checks, I wouldn't want to hear about a nagging hip injury, or an elbow bruise. I wouldn't want to hear about a ruptured back.

I try to remember that this game is a gift, and Bill Kenwright is the one who gives it to me. For his sake, and for the sake of the team and our incredible fans, I'm always going to choose to play. I play when I'm sick, I play when I'm hurt.

The next morning, I couldn't get out of bed. It took me five full minutes to go from my back to a sitting position on the edge of the bed.

On Saturday, we were scheduled to play Reading. But by Friday, I couldn't bend down. I caught a couple of balls standing still, and that's about it.

The game's not for twenty-four hours, I said to myself. *Twenty-four hours is enough time to heal.*

It wasn't. Before the game, I went out to the field with Chris Woods and Danny and some other members of the medical team. I jogged across the box. I tried to stretch. I caught a couple of balls.

It hurt like hell.

"Want to try some diving?" Chris asked. He didn't look optimistic. When I tried, I was wild with pain.

"Let me warm up some more." The process went on longer than it should have. Chris and Danny were going to let me decide. The decision—and any consequence of that decision—would be my own.

Everything in my body screamed *Don't play! Don't play!* Everything in my mind screamed *Play!*

But how could I protect Everton's goal if I couldn't dive?

Finally, I took off my gloves and set them down.

Later, I'd learn that I'd been just two games shy of breaking Neville Southall's record of the most number of consecutive games played for Everton. Neville was a club legend, and it killed me to have come so close to his record, and then not make it.

I tried to watch the game in the stands that day. I tried. But I couldn't stand seeing all the action and not being able to control any of it. I lasted maybe 15 minutes before heading inside, down below the stands.

I watched the rest of the match on television with Jimmy. Amid the pain of my back and the frustration of not playing, Jimmy's grousing was a welcome balm.

Later that week, I learned I had two broken vertebrae. I was in the training room with Danny when the results came back. I heard his side of the conversation only.

"Okay, two vertebrae . . . fractured . . . right . . . and how much time should he . . . four to six . . ."

That's when I panicked. *Four to six months?*

I couldn't afford to be out for that long. I'd miss important World Cup qualifiers. I'd miss the end of the season. I'd miss so much training. I'd miss, I felt sure, next year's World Cup.

I was 34 years old; if I missed this one, would I ever get another shot?

For a few moments, I wondered if this was the beginning of the end.

Danny hung up the phone. "Okay, Tim," he said. "You're going to need to stay off it for four to six weeks."

Weeks. Not months. Relief suddenly flooded over me. Weeks I could do.

Daddy, daddy, pick me up." Ali's arms stretched toward me. She was six years old, missing two of her front teeth, and with her untamed curls she looked every bit the wild child.

"He can't pick you up," said Laura, retrieving Ali's stuffed animals off the floor. "Remember? He's hurt."

I'd come home to Memphis to recover. Laura let me spend much of that time lying on the sofa of what was now her house. She served me food and beverages, and when I was well enough, she let me rummage through the refrigerator on my own.

I admired Laura. Even during the worst of our divorce, Laura had made sure that our kids saw only goodness and warmth within their family. Even at her angriest, she never stopped welcoming me into the house.

"Please, Daddy?" asked Ali. "Just for a minute?"

Jacob looked up from his book. "He *can't.*"

"Come on, Ali," said Laura, trying to distract her. "Help me feed Clayton." Clayton, an old man now, lifted his head and staggered to his feet at the sound of food in his bowl.

It was nice to be there. We were a different kind of family than we'd once been, but we were still a family.

"Hey, Tim," Laura said. "My mom's coming over tonight to watch the kids. You're welcome to hang around while she's here."

"Cool," I said. "Where are you going?"

Laura lifted an eyebrow. It had been nearly three years since we'd broken up.

"Out," she said. I noticed she had a twinkle in her eye.

When I returned to the field, I played my 300th game for Everton. We drew 0–0, and that shutout just happened to be my 100th clean sheet.

After that long month of not playing, it felt terrific to be back.

Thank God that injury wasn't worse, I thought. *Thank God I can keep doing this for a while longer.*

NEW FACES

A few weeks after I came back, Sir Alex Ferguson announced that he'd be leaving Manchester United after 27 years at the helm. You can imagine how nuts the media went with that news. In the time he'd been with Man U, Ferguson had won 13 league titles, five FA Cups, four League Cups, and two Champions League crowns. The man was an institution.

Manchester United is a publicly traded company. Stockholders hate uncertainty. While some Premier League teams might drag out a search, interviewing multiple candidates, Manchester United didn't have that luxury. They needed a replacement, and fast.

The English bookmakers placed their odds on David Moyes.

That week, David called me and five other senior Everton players—Phil Jagielka, Leighton Baines, Tony Hibbert, Leon Osman, and Phil Neville—to a secret meeting in a Liverpool hotel. It could be about only one thing.

I almost dreaded walking through that door. I knew that when I walked out, everything was going to be different.

"I've taken a job," David told us. "I've accepted the manager's position at Manchester United. Saturday will be my final game."

Hearing the news, I was at once devastated and happy. We were losing one hell of a manager, but I was thrilled for David. As I knew from experience, playing or coaching at United was a once-in-a-lifetime opportunity, and David possessed the qualities that I believed would make him a good fit. He had a history of nurturing young, talented players. He had a fierce work ethic. He had a progressive, analytical approach to the game. He was a tough son of a gun, another fiery Scot. Everton didn't have the glittering record that Man U did but neither did it have its vast resources. If David had done this well with Everton's kitty, who knew what he could accomplish with United's?

On May 12, his final game, we played West Ham at home. When David arrived at Goodison, he was met with applause and cheers by stadium stewards. The stands were filled with hand-made signs:

THANK YOU DAVID MOYES.

GOODBYE AND GOOD LUCK.

THANK YOU FOR 11 YEARS OF MEMORIES.

When he appeared on the touchline, every fan in the stadium stood. Throughout the game, they sang his name. After it was over—a satisfying 2–0 win, thanks to two great goals by Kevin Mirallas—the players lined up along the edge of the field so David could walk between us, honor guard style.

If anyone could ever fill Alex Ferguson's shoes at Manchester United, Moyes could. But I swear, I couldn't imagine Goodison without him.

During the summer Bill Kenwright announced that Roberto Martinez, who'd been at Wigan Athletic, would replace Moyes as

Everton's new manager. Although Wigan had been in the Premier League only since 2005—and some years barely escaped relegation to the second division—he'd taken them this year on a memorable FA Cup run, beating heavily favored Manchester City in the final.

Roberto had a reputation for being classy and confident, affable and intelligent. Officially, I was optimistic. But in truth I felt wary and defensive. Everton was *my* team. He was the newbie. He'd be bringing a different style with him, not to mention a new goalkeeping coach. He was going to have to earn the right to belong. He and his whole gang.

The U.S. National Team had seen some big changes, too.

After the 2012 season, I'd learned that Landon planned to take a break from playing soccer. He was exhausted, fried from a decade and a half of nonstop, all-consuming competition. Even if I understood, I worried.

I was concerned for the team, first of all. We had critical World Cup qualifiers coming up at the time and Landon was our best player. We needed him. I feared for Landon, too. He was already past 30, the age when many players retire . . . or are phased out.

Take time off when you're 31 years old, and you risk never getting your place back—even if you're Landon Donovan.

When I heard the news, I picked up the phone to call Landon. Maybe I could make one final push, convince him to reconsider. People sometimes just need a nudge from a friend. *Hang in there, remember how important these games are—to you, to your teammates, to the fans.*

I dialed his number but before I heard the phone ring on his end, I hung up.

Landon was a ferocious competitor. If he was making this choice, it's not because he hadn't thought it through. And if that was the case, then he certainly didn't need to hear my opinion on the matter.

The same spring, Jürgen had left Carlos off the roster for some key World Cup qualifying matches, moving in some less experienced defenders. These guys weren't better, but they were younger, and they would fight hard to establish themselves and their careers.

Carlos was getting phased out.

It's part of what goes on in every World Cup cycle, but it was difficult to watch it happening to a friend. To me, Carlos was one of the best team captains the U.S. has ever had, and he was still a strong defender.

But that's soccer: your position can disappear in an instant. Already, so many of the guys with whom I'd come up through the ranks were gone.

Carlos had a choice: he could sit on the bench, and maybe come in as a sub in the late stages of the game. Or he could step aside for the new generation.

He called me and I asked him what he planned to do.

"I don't know, Tim. I really don't."

We talked for a while. Then I said, "If you ask me, you've got a legacy to protect. Do you sacrifice it for a few more years of hoping you can play for twenty minutes?"

There was a long silence. Then Carlos said, "I know what I need to do."

And by the tone of his voice, I knew: Carlos wasn't going to be my captain anymore.

Between Landon's sabbatical and Carlos's departure from the team, I suddenly I felt like the last of a generation.

It wasn't just professionally that things were changing.

Laura called me up one afternoon. "Tim," she said. "I've met someone. His name is Trey."

There's the joy, I thought. *There's the joy in her voice that I remember so well.*

This was the Laura who had once called her mom from a Times Square hotel to tell her we were getting married. She sounded as excited as when she'd found her wedding dress, the one she never got to wear. This was the voice so bubbly that it broke through the Manchester gloom during my first weeks in England. "I'm here, I'm here, I'm here," she'd said, back when she and I were just beginning our new life together.

Her tone now was unmistakable: Laura had fallen in love again.

I was happy for her. She deserved better than being a professional athlete's ex-wife. She deserved someone who adored her completely, someone who wouldn't ignore her calls because he was too busy thinking about his next game.

"He doesn't play soccer, does he?"

She laughed. Of course he didn't. She knew better than to make the same mistake twice.

A few weeks later, I made one of my lightning-fast visits home. Laura had arranged for all of us—her, me, Trey, Jacob, Ali, and Trey's kids, 13-year-old Savannah, and 10-year-old Jake—to meet up at a Memphis Grizzlies basketball game.

I was nervous. What if this Trey and I didn't click? What if he didn't want me around? How was this guy going to affect my relationship with my kids?

Before tipoff Laura said, "Trey wanted to make sure you knew he didn't have to come tonight. He said if you preferred to spend time with the kids without him around, he understands."

That, right there, told me everything I needed to know. Trey understood exactly how important my time with the kids was. And he was making it clear that he wasn't going to get in the way of it.

"Of course he should come," I said.

When I met him—when I saw the way he smiled at Laura, the way he laughed so easily with his kids and my own—I knew Trey was going to be in all our lives for a long time.

The start of the 2013–2014 season, when Roberto Martinez came on as manager, was like an old-time high school dance, with the boys on one side of the wall and the girls on the other. Everyone was sizing each other up, but nobody knew who was who, or what to expect. I was determined to keep an open mind about Roberto and his crew. But the truth was, I didn't feel particularly receptive to new ideas; I had a set way of working and I didn't want anybody messing with it.

And Roberto did things differently. Our training sessions were shorter, but higher intensity than I was used to. Roberto was transforming our style of play, encouraging us to focus more on ball possession—and not just in attack. He wanted our defenders to pass the ball out from the back rather than hitting long clearances. It would take some getting used to.

During the transfer window, Roberto brought in some new players—James McCarthy from Wigan; Romelu Lukaku, a Belgian international from Chelsea; and Gareth Barry, an English international from Manchester City, the last two on one-year loans.

I liked them all, especially Romelu. At 21, Rom was already a major talent, as driven as any player I'd ever seen. Yet he was humble, too, easy to be around. He didn't party, didn't care for flashy cars or the nightclub scene. In his spare time, he studied tapes of the world's great strikers; he'd made a highlight reel of plays by Cristiano Ronaldo, Didier Drogba, Robin van Persie, and Wayne Rooney. He relaxed with video games—soccer video games, of course.

After practice, Rom fired shots at me the way Ruud once had, both of us honing our skills. He may have been on loan, but he *felt* like an Evertonian, and he immediately endeared himself to the fans. In his first Everton game, away to West Ham, he scored the winning goal. In his Goodison debut, he'd banged in two more. But it was the Merseyside derby that sealed the deal. Not only did he score twice against Liverpool, helping us draw 3–3, he later declared the whole event to be his favorite moment in club soccer.

It was a reinvigorating season for me. I was an old dog, and it was hard for me to learn new tricks. But I was learning that there was more than just one way of playing this game.

I thought I'd seen it all by now, like Kasey once had. I had played so many games, experienced so many emotions, I thought nothing could surprise me anymore. But I was amazed by how calm I felt with so much change swirling around me.

It was during that season, the one in which we hurtled toward the 2014 World Cup, that I lost my fear.

WORLD CUP TRAINING

Jürgen selected a 30-man roster for World Cup training camp; since only 23 of us could go to Brazil, it meant we'd practice together for a few weeks . . . then he'd send seven of us home.

I was glad to see Landon's name on the 30-man list.

He had come back from his sabbatical in time for the 2013 Gold Cup. There he had stolen the show, scoring five goals and adding seven assists.

To my mind, Landon proved—again—that he was still the best of the best.

Of course, Jürgen had made it clear all along, both in the media and to each of us, that nobody's job was safe—that just because someone had been to a previous World Cup, it didn't mean they were automatically qualified to play in the upcoming one. The media made a huge, stupid thing out of that, but frankly, it shouldn't have been news. I'd *always* understood that my job could be taken away in a moment. There's never a time when someone's not gunning for your position. It's true for every player on that field, and nobody ever forgets that.

So Jürgen's "nobody's job is safe" sound byte got the media in a lather. But for us it was business as usual.

We trained at Stanford University—a sprawling, lush, immaculate campus. We ran. We did our drills. We scrimmaged. We prepared.

Chris Woods fired volleys at me with increasing intensity.

Brazil was getting closer every day.

I grew a beard during training.

I'd had a beard just one other time—in the six-month period from January to August 2013. I'd loved it for a while. Sometimes it even felt like a secret source of strength.

Then one night, just before an Arsenal game, I decided to shave it off. It had nothing to do with Arsenal. There was something about the way my face felt that day. When I got to the stadium, though, my clean shave gave me the same sensation I have if Leon Osman and I don't bump shoulders when we shake hands. It felt . . . wrong. I tormented poor Jimmy Martin that day, making him give me probably half a dozen pairs of identical white socks until I found the pair that made up for the absence of facial hair.

Now, during training, the beard felt right again. "Nice scruff," Landon joked as it grew in. I had no idea just how much this beard would come to represent me—no clue that this beard would soon have a life of its own, including its own Twitter account, or that the president of the United States would suggest I shave it off.

A few weeks into training, Landon walked into the locker room.

I could tell immediately that something was wrong. Landon always had a loose-limbed gait, but now his steps were precise, almost rigid. It seemed unfathomable, yet I knew: Landon wasn't going to the World Cup.

I remembered seeing him when he scored his first professional goal against me in 2001. We'd grown up together, as players, and as men. I'd watched him handle the pressure of being a young prodigy, then a full-blown superstar. We'd been together when we beat Mexico in 2007 in the Gold Cup. We'd been together when we beat Mexico on their soil. We'd been together when we beat Spain in the Confederations Cup. We'd been together in South Africa, at Everton. We'd traveled the globe together, experienced wild highs and deep lows. Now he was going, and I was staying.

He said three words to the team.

"I'm going home."

Some of the guys spoke to him. They told him how sorry they were, told him that they couldn't believe it.

I didn't say a word.

No matter what I might have said, or how heartfelt my sentiments were, words themselves would have rung hollow. Besides, Landon knew exactly how I felt about him.

The media created a firestorm around Landon's having been cut. That story was dragged out for weeks and beaten to a pulp. And while I know that kind of thing keeps people watching *SportsCenter*, I kept thinking, *Cripes, leave the guy alone.*

More than that, I wanted to remind all those pundits that six other guys had been dropped, some of whom had tears in their eyes. Their dreams had been cut short, too. Yet there was barely a mention of them in any blog or newspaper story. Where were the articles about Brad Evans, or Maurice Edu, or Clarence Goodson, or Michael Parkhurst, or Joe Corona, or Terrence Boyd? Every single one of those guys had bled for this team. They'd sacrificed huge parts of their lives for a memory they wouldn't have.

I kept my mouth shut about it all. Here's why: Jürgen gets paid to make big, tough, hard decisions. I get paid to put myself in front of a ball. I get paid to organize a defense. I get paid to stand in that goal, scan the field, and anticipate danger.

But my opinion about the roster? That counts for nothing.

Jürgen felt that he had 23 players who would best suit this team in this World Cup. Frankly, at 35 years old, I was glad to be a part of it.

Only few of us had a lot of experience—DaMarcus and Clint had more than 100 caps. Michael Bradley and I had nearly the same number. But many on the team were basically rookies—Julian Green, who'd grown up in Germany, was still a teenager, and had only three caps. John Brooks, another young American raised in Germany, had five.

Scanning the roster, I realized that some of these guys were closer in age to my son Jacob than they were to me. Between us, only two players had ever scored in a World Cup: Clint had scored twice, and Michael Bradley once. Our leading World Cup scorer, Landon Donovan, was no longer here. Of the 23 guys who were going to Brazil, fully 17 players were heading to their first World Cup. Since goalie Brad Guzan, hadn't yet played, that meant only five of us had ever seen the field.

We'd been placed into the so-called "Group of Death"—the toughest of all eight groups. We'd open with Ghana, the team that had knocked us out of the round of 16 in the last World Cup. They had also helped send us home in 2006. We'd play Portugal, where we'd face the newly crowned World Player of the Year, Cristiano Ronaldo. We'd play Germany—the team I was betting would win the whole thing.

Plus, our matches would require nearly 9,000 miles of travel, including a visit to Manaus, Brazil, a city deep in the Amazonian jungle, which was known for its steamy and strength-sapping weather conditions.

Jürgen called our draw "the worst of the worst."

In the days between the roster cuts and the team heading to Brazil, our training tended to be light. We played beach volleyball. We turned a sandpit into a soccer tennis court. We spent a lot of time at the Aquatics Center. It's an amazing facility—four pools, all outdoors. There's a regulation Olympic diving platform—a tower with boards at 1, 3, 5, 7.5, and 10 meters. Brad Guzan was like a kid at an amusement park—he went right up to the 10-meter board and leapt off.

I don't know who got the brilliant idea, but someone decided it would be a good team-building exercise if every one of us jumped off that board.

If you've never bounded off a platform three stories high, let me tell you, it goes against every instinct a sane person has.

I'd done it once before—back when I was a teenager, visiting Mexico, the very first time I'd ever left the country for a youth national game. I'd been terrified when I'd gazed down at the water—it seemed a million miles away. But, of course, I wanted to look like a man, so I'd closed my eyes and jumped, all the while thinking *Oh shit, oh shit, oh shit.*

I did it again here—fast, because I wanted it over with. Clint and Michael approached it the same way: do it quickly and move on. Some of the guys stalled before jumping. A couple—Jozy and Jermaine—were genuinely afraid. As each of them hesitated, we waited 30 feet below, hooting at them.

We called them chicken. We chanted their names over and over—Jozy, Jozy, Jozy! Then, Jermaine, Jermaine, Jermaine!

We shamed them into it, and when they finally took that scary leap, we cheered.

Brad Guzan whooped loudly, then went back to the board and jumped again.

We were determined to make as big a splash in the World Cup.

Twelve years after I played my first senior game for the United States, I received my 100th cap, this one against Nigeria. The game was held in Jacksonville, Florida, on June 7. Laura brought the kids down. Friends and family from all over came to watch: Dan. Mulch. Some of my high school buddies. My brother, Chris, hadn't been able to make it—he and his girlfriend had recently had a baby girl—but aside from him, it was almost everybody who mattered in my life. I'd never had all of these people in the same place, at the same time.

I was only the 15th player in U.S. history to reach the 100-cap mark. I now held the team record for wins as a goalkeeper.

I was also the oldest player on the World Cup squad.

U.S. Soccer made me a jersey with the number 100, and there was a brief ceremony on the field.

I cherish the pictures from that day. The stands are filled. My teammates are off to my side. My dad is on my left, with his hand on Jacob. My mom is on my right, and my arm is around her, tight. And in front of all of us is Ali. She and her brother are holding up that commemorative jersey.

HOWARD
100

All those game I'd played. A century of them now. All those friends I'd made and kept along the way. All of them here now— well, almost all of them, minus Landon and Carlos—watching and cheering.

Even Laura—standing on the sidelines, but unmistakably still proud of me.

It was an extraordinary moment, but I couldn't bask in it for long.

Right after the game, we were flying to Brazil.

TEAM USA

There is a photograph I look at sometimes. It has nothing to do with soccer, yet for me, it's somehow intimately connected to what I do every day.

The picture was snapped at roughly 5 p.m., September 11, 2001. Three firefighters stand atop a mound of rubble. Behind them lies the vast, impossible destruction of splintered buildings. These men are working together to hoist an American flag. They are covered in ash, looking upward. They have surely witnessed unimaginable things.

When the planes hit the World Trade Center, I'd been driving on the New Jersey Turnpike. I was on my way to practice with the MetroStars. It was a crisp, clear morning, not a cloud in the sky— one of those spectacular days where even the weather forecasters on TV use the word *perfect*. Just a picture perfect day.

The turnpike runs due west of the Hudson River, parallel to Manhattan—maybe six miles from the World Trade Center. From the highway, I saw plumes of smoke, like dark cumulus clouds that made no sense against the blue sky.

I turned on the radio. I heard the news.

In the MetroStars locker room that day, we clustered around

a television. Our training ground was on the flight path of the Newark Airport, and as we sat together, numb from all we were seeing and hearing, we heard fighter jets flying overhead.

I knew all around us, here in my beloved Jersey, good people had gone to work on an ordinary day—account managers and messengers and receptionists and waiters, mothers, brothers, fathers, sisters, grandmothers, sons. Many would never come home again.

I play soccer. It's what I do. I'm not a firefighter or soldier. I catch balls. I play a game for a living.

But it means something to me when I put on that USA jersey. It sounds clichéd, but it's real: I believe I'm representing something that matters. I'm serving in the best way I know how—in a way that engages my heart and soul and mind and body completely—on behalf of the country that gave my family opportunity.

It is the country that my ultra-progressive immigrant mom has always told me is the greatest on earth. It is the nation that gave my poppa sanctuary after he'd fled Hungary for his life.

Soccer is the gift I was blessed with. On the U.S. National Team, I use that gift to represent all the things I see when I look at that photograph from 9/11: Unity. Spirit. Resilience.

Our team had players who weren't born in America, for whom English isn't their first language. Players whose club careers had taken them to Mexico, England, the Netherlands, Norway, France, Turkey, Germany, and England.

I realized that some of these guys—the Americans who'd been raised abroad—didn't know the national anthem. John Brooks, for example, a German American born in Berlin, had no idea what the words were.

I liked John. He was quiet and humble, and at 21, he was

already an assured defender. He understood positioning, he was composed, and he gave as good as he got. John and I spent a lot of time with each other on the field, and we often roomed together—the old man and the new kid on the block, just as Tony Meola and I had once been.

I felt comfortable giving him grief about the anthem.

"And you call yourself a U.S. National Team player?" I asked.

I got a hold of some printouts of the lyrics to "The Star-Spangled Banner." I handed them out during a team meal. "Learn this," I said. "You've got a few days, and then we'll all sing it together."

Occasionally I'd taunt my teammates: "Have you memorized the words yet? You ready to belt it out?"

And when we finally sang it together at the end of training, I suddenly understood how lucky it is that our voices are usually drowned out by the crowd. We sounded horrendous.

We trained in São Paulo, an enormous concrete jungle, amped up with energy and urgency. São Paulo has two and a half times the population of New York City, 20 million people spread out over 3,000 square miles, packed into modern high-rises, luxury mansions, and the endless shantytowns and slums.

São Paulo pulses. It feels alive.

We stayed in a downtown hotel famous for its chic lines and minimalist décor. In 2010, we'd been effectively quarantined, with little access to anyone else. Now we were in the beating heart of Brazil.

We'd crisscross the country for our games—which, given Brazil's enormous size, means traversing the continent.

Our first match against Ghana would be played in Natal, on

Brazil's northeastern coast. In the days before we arrived, the area had 13 inches of rain, more than the city typically receives in an entire month. There were sinkholes all over, along with suffocating humidity.

Although I was painfully aware of what happened in our previous World Cup matches against Ghana, some of the guys on the team were so young that they didn't even remember the 2006 game, and probably couldn't have told you the score. But I recall those games all too vividly. How they muscled us off the ball. How they counterattacked with speed and precision. How they sent us home in both 2006 and 2010.

I sure as hell didn't want to let it happen a third time.

Before the game, we sang the national anthem. I stood on the field, one hand on my heart, the other on Matt Besler's shoulder. I glanced over at the sidelines.

There was John Brooks, in full voice. He nailed every single word.

We couldn't have scripted a better start to the match. Thirty-one seconds in, Clint Dempsey settled the ball off a Jermaine Jones throw-in. He went on a surging run toward Ghana's goal. He blew by two defenders, then coolly steered a low shot inside the far post.

It was 1–0 and the game wasn't even a minute old. But whatever jolt of euphoria we felt was soon replaced by concern for three of our players who were injured in a physical first half. First, Jozy dropped to the ground clutching his hamstring—it would turn out to be a serious tear, one that would keep him out the rest of the tournament. I felt terrible for him—not only because he'd be missing this huge opportunity, but also because his goal-scoring form had been off coming into Brazil and he was hoping to have a big Cup to prove his critics wrong.

Midway through the half, Clint came down from an aerial collision. Blood poured from his nose. But leader and warrior that he is, Clint shrugged it off. He stuffed his nostrils with cotton and played with his usual edge. Then right before the half, Matt Besler pulled up, grabbing *his* hamstring. It didn't look as bad as Jozy's injury, but Matty was unable to continue. We still led 1–0.

In the second half, Ghana banged at our door for a long time. They finally forced their way through in the 82nd minute. That's when the always dangerous Asamoah Gyan sent a blind heel pass to André Ayew, who fired a left-footed shot right past me.

We weren't about to settle for a draw. We kept pushing for the winner. In the 86th minute, we won a corner and Graham Zusi sent in a perfectly weighted ball. John Brooks, our young anthem-singing, German-born defender who had come on for Matt Besler, soared above everyone else in the box and powered a perfect downward header into the net. It was a heart-stopping moment, one of those last-gasp miracles, like the kind Landon had pulled off against Algeria.

You could see that Brooks barely believed what had happened. He scrambled toward the edge of the field and lay still for a moment, facedown. Later, he'd reveal to the media that he'd dreamed that he'd score a game-winning goal in the 80th minute of the Ghana game. He was off by six minutes, but nobody was about to quibble.

USA 2, Ghana 1.

Portugal, our next opponent, had the look of a wounded animal. Not only had they been humiliated 4–0 by Germany in their opening match, but their hot-tempered central defender Pepe, had been sent off for head-butting Germany's Thomas Müller. This meant he would miss our game.

But Cristiano Ronaldo would be there, and even if he was reported to be carrying an injury, I knew he could still tear us apart. We worked long and hard on a game plan to funnel him into areas where he'd do the least damage.

Laura had brought the kids to cheer me on. We swam in the hotel pool and played video games. Jacob had World Cup fever, so he and I watched England play Uruguay and rooted for my Everton teammates, Leighton Baines and Phil Jagielka. Later, Laura would tell me that Jacob spent the whole flight home debating whether he should play for England when he grows up, or for the U.S.

Sometimes all the kids got together for a game of hallway soccer outside the media room. I played goalie on my knees, letting Michael Bradley's toddler son—like a mini-Michael, but with more hair—kick the ball past me. Ali was on my team, and she was endlessly frustrated with my goalkeeping in those matches.

"Daddy," she scolded. "You have to *stop* the ball!"

We felt good about our preparation as the match kicked off, but it's like what Mike Tyson used to say about his opponents: "Everybody has a plan until they get punched in the face."

What made Portugal's goal in the fifth minute so painful is that we basically punched ourselves in the face with a mistake in the box that allowed Nani to score from point-blank range.

But we're a resilient group, and history has taught us that we can fight back from early deficits. In the next 20 minutes, we found our rhythm and started playing our best soccer of the tournament, moving the ball crisply and to great effect. Clint and Michael were immense. Both of them forced the Portugal keeper into sprawling saves to preserve their lead. Meanwhile, you couldn't even tell Ronaldo was on the field, he was so quiet.

Instead, it was Nani who caused us problems. Before the half, he hammered a shot from outside the box that looked to be coming right at me until at the last minute, it dipped sharply. I managed to get a finger to the ball and tip it onto the post. It rebounded straight to Portugal's Éder, who had a wide-open goal from three yards out. I started to scramble right: I could see by the shape of his body that he was going to put it in the bottom far corner. I lunged flat out across the width of the goal.

If Éder had struck his shot cleanly it would have been 2–0, but he scuffed it and the ball bobbled right over my head. Mid-dive I had to change course. I arched backward and threw my left hand in the air. The ball was beneath the crossbar when I scooped it up and over to safety. Now that's a save I hope to tell my grandkids about one day.

Later, I'd observe to Chris Woods how surreal the moment was. "A few centimeters' difference," I said, "and they'd be calling it a horrendous mistake."

Chris gave me a knowing look, one battle-hardened veteran to another. "Goalkeeping margins are razor thin."

We were still down 1–0 at the half. It wasn't until the 64th minute that we busted through. Jermaine latched onto a poor clearance off a corner kick and unleashed a howitzer that flew through the packed box and into the far corner.

Game on.

We thought we had it won ten minutes from regulation when Zusi squared a pass across the goalmouth. Clint was first to the ball, knocking it in off his chest. Judging by the roar that shook the stadium, our fans believed the game was over.

You can never count out the great players, though. They are always capable of producing something special as long as there are still seconds on the clock.

And there were. Michael lost the ball in midfield and Cristiano pounced. The lob he floated over our defense was inch-perfect, far enough out of my reach that his teammate Silvestre Varela could run onto it. He headed in the equalizer as the last seconds ticked off the clock.

What a sucker punch by Cristiano that was! He was barely noticeable for ninety minutes and then on the last play of the game, he came up with a piece of artistry that only a few players in the world could have pulled off.

We were numb as we walked off the field. Truth is, 2–2 is not a bad result against a team of Portugal's pedigree, except when you think you've already beaten them. But as deflated as I felt, I couldn't let my disappointment get in the way of seeing my family. Ali, Jacob, and Laura would return to Memphis in a couple of hours.

In the locker room, I quickly stripped down to my shorts and T-shirt, put my running shoes on, and jogged back onto the field. I waved to Ali and Jacob, blew kisses, and pretended to catch their kisses back. We had as much fun as we could given the distance between their seats and the grass.

When it was time for them to head to the airport, I blew them one final kiss—just the latest in our countless goodbyes—and I began to think about Germany.

There were many intriguing subplots to our Germany game. For one thing, Jürgen had coached their national team two World Cups ago and some of the same players were still on the squad.

For another, Joachim Löw, the guy who had helped Klinsmann transform that 2006 German team into an attacking force, would now be matching wits with his old mentor. And then there's the number of German American players on our team. Five of them had been born and/or raised in Germany and had spent their careers in the country's top-tier Bundesliga, going head-to-head with many of the players we were about to compete against.

There wasn't a question in my mind that Germany was the best team in the tournament. They had physicality, skill, guile, and remarkable tactical awareness.

They were as close to the perfect side as there was in Brazil.

Fortunately, we didn't need to beat them to advance; a draw would automatically get us through. There was even a scenario by which we could qualify for the knockout round with a loss; we had a slim margin over Ghana based on goal differential. As long as we could maintain that, we could still advance. Ghana would play Portugal as we faced off against Germany.

"I need to know the Portugal-Ghana score," I told Chris Woods. Depending on what happened in that game, I could adjust our defensive strategy. If we absolutely needed a goal to advance, I could push one of my fullbacks forward, take more risks. But if we might get through even without a goal, I could tuck players in, hold them back, and concentrate on not letting Germany score on us.

"Okay, Tim," said Chris, "Got it."

Before the game, there had been some talk in the media about how Klinsmann and Löw might agree to take it easy on each other and have their teams play for a draw since that would be enough for both teams to advance. Whoever concocted that ridiculous scenario clearly doesn't know the competitive mind-set of the two coaches, let alone the 22 players who would be on the field.

On the contrary, this would be anything but a stroll in the park.

From the kickoff, Germany attacked relentlessly. Because they always seemed to have the ball, that meant I had a busy 45 minutes. I made a couple of tough saves but at halftime, the game remained scoreless.

Then in the 55th minute, I dove at full stretch to keep out a shot by the big German defender Per Mertesacker. I could only parry it to the edge of the box where Thomas Müller was lurking. Müller ripped a grass-cutter past me into the far corner. Germany was up 1–0.

I glanced at Chris Woods then. He held up both index fingers. He was telling me that a thousand miles away, Portugal and Ghana were tied, 1–1.

If Ghana got another goal, and if our score remained the same, we'd be going home.

In the 73rd minute, two of our players, Jermaine Jones and Alejandro Bedoya, collided with each other going for a high ball. I could hear the smack of their heads from where I stood, half a field away. They both crumpled to the ground. Jermaine lay there for two minutes. Later we'd learn that he'd fractured his nose, too—our second broken nose in three games.

With ten minutes left, Chris flashed me a 2–1 score with his fingers, without noting whether Ghana or Portugal was ahead. I glanced at Matt Besler, who gave a slight shake of his head, as if saying, "Don't ask me." I turned back to Chris. He gave the thumbs-up sign. Portugal was on top.

All we had to do now to advance was not to concede another goal. That is, if the Portugal-Ghana scoreboard didn't change.

We played it tight until the final whistle. There was the tiniest pause then, when no one was 100 percent sure of the Portugal result. Then suddenly the subs and coaches on the bench were sprinting toward us on the field. We'd lost this game, but it was clear from their faces that we had won something bigger.

Portugal 2, Ghana 1. We would advance.

Before the Belgium game, my mom and I went out to dinner at a landmark restaurant in the lush Jardins district of São Paulo.

Right away, I heard people whispering about me. *Tim Howard . . . goalie . . .*

U.S. keeper . . . Tim Howard . . . that's him.

Mom and I sat together for a long time. We talked about the tournament, the children, the Leadership Academy that would soon open in New Jersey; Faith had told me recently that it would bear my name.

We talked about Laura and Trey: they'd tied the knot last October.

"It's nice to see her so happy," I said.

My mom smiled. "It's funny," she mused. "My generation is the one that had bitter divorces. Maybe yours will find a kinder way of doing it."

We talked about the future—what my life might look like in a few years when I was done with soccer and finally able to move back to Memphis.

Dan was encouraging me to take advantage of opportunities right now, to sign endorsement and broadcasting deals.

Mom sighed. "It's hard to believe that you might retire someday," she said. "I can't imagine you doing anything else."

"I know. But I'm thirty-five now, Mom."

It was easy conversation, the most leisurely, undistracted time we'd had together—just the two of us—in years. Here we were at this exquisite restaurant, and all around us people were surreptitiously trying to snap my photo. But in a way, it was as if we were right back in one of those roadside motels in Jersey: just me and Mom, eating our PB&Js. It was like nothing had changed, even though everything had.

"How do you feel about Belgium?" my mom asked.

I gave her an honest answer.

"I think it's going to be a tough game," I said. "But they're certainly beatable."

MAKING HISTORY

So much has been said about the Belgium game. Every minute of play has been analyzed, every save I made has been dissected as if I were some kind of lab animal.

Since July 2, 2014, I've seen what feels like eight million images of the game as it was refracted through other people's eyes.

I've seen the images from packed stadiums and crowded living rooms and standing-room-only bars and city squares. I've seen still photos and video clips of people watching: the crowd in Soldier's Field, my family, even Landon. I've seen photographs of strangers clutching their heads in anguish. People peeking through their fingers as if they're afraid of what they might glimpse, yet they cannot look away.

It's hard to connect all those images to what I experienced on the field.

Here's what I would tell someone about the first 45 minutes of that game: We fought hard. We held our own. Nobody scored.

Then ten minutes into the second half, something shifted. It was like the Belgium players got a turbo boost during halftime. Suddenly every time I looked up, a ball hurtled toward me. Mertens took a shot. Then Fellaini. DeBruyne. Origi. Vertonghen. DeBruyne again. Vertonghen again.

By the end of regulation time, Belgium had 31 attempts on goal to our 7. They had 16 corners to our 4.

None of them got through. We went into extra time believing we would find a way.

Every game a person plays is a culmination of all his experiences leading up to that moment. That was as true for me in the Belgium game as it has ever been.

It was as if 20 years of learning from my role models had been distilled into that 120 minutes.

Take the first save I made, for example—the shot by Origi that I kicked away with my leg.

That one came from playing in all those New Jersey youth league games. That save made me feel like I was 15 again, working with Mulch. I had been a good athlete then, but I was still raw. To protect the goal, I had to make myself big, use every part of my body.

By the time I got to my fourth save—a leaping fingertip deflection over the crossbar—I was right back in my MetroStars days, knocking the ball away from the chaos and confusion in front of me. In fact, the entire second half reminded me of playing on the losing-est team in the MLS. We were pinned back, defending for our lives just like we'd been all those years in Giants Stadium.

In a way, it felt like Mulch was right there with me—all of those painful "blast drills" that he insisted upon, when the shots flew in at me so fast, I didn't have time to think. The times he made me get up and keep going, when I felt like I had nothing left to give.

But Mulch wasn't the only one on the field with me. Tony

Meola and Kasey Keller were out there, too—Tony with his brash, blue-collar courage and Kasey with his dogged refusal to get rattled under any circumstance.

And those footwork drills that I'd hated so much when I first came to Everton? Those helped me make my sixth save. A low, hard ball came skimming across the grass, headed straight down my throat. Using Chris Woods's balance drill, I killed it dead. Just like he always wanted me to.

Even Edwin van der Sar was in that game with me. My second and third saves required that I drop down and let my body cushion the ball as it pinged off my chest. That move? Classic Edwin; I learned it from watching him when I was his number two.

And the truth is, it wasn't just my soccer influences I channeled. My Nana and Poppa and Momma and Mom. Laura and my children. They were all present in the urgency I felt. There had been so much sacrifice, by so many people, so many nights and months and years we'd been apart. I'd given up everything—my marriage, my home, my role in the day-to-day lives of Ali and Jacob—to be here.

I'd be damned if, in this moment, on the world's biggest stage, those sacrifices weren't going to be worthwhile.

All through the match, I kept waiting to see Romelu Lukaku get off the Belgium bench and be summoned to the touchline as a replacement for Origi. Big Rom had been a game changer at Everton last season.

Now, as we headed into overtime, he was about to become one here as well.

Rom is so powerfully built, so deceptively quick, that he's tough enough for defenders to deal with at the start of a game when they're feeling fresh and energized. The last thing I wanted was for him to come on the field now, when we were running on fumes.

His impact was instantaneous. He muscled the ball off Matt Besler near midfield and burst down the right flank. Then he crossed the ball to DeBruyne, who was making a run into the middle of our penalty area.

Besler raced back to our box and did his damnedest to block DeBruyne's shot from one angle as I slid in from the other direction. Too late.

DeBruyne's shot flashed through the sliver of space between where Besler could stop it and where I could. 1–0, Belgium.

We pushed for the equalizer with everything we had. We had a great chance when Jermaine blasted a shot from the edge of the penalty area. The ball took a deflection off of Jan Vertonghen, and it bounced toward Clint in front of the goal.

A couple of inches to Clint's left or right, and he would have buried it. But the ball landed awkwardly under his feet. He couldn't get a shot off before Belgium cleared.

By this point, Rom was causing havoc down at our end of the field. Twice, I had to scramble the ball away from his low drives.

But I could do nothing about his third attempt, which came in the last minute of the extra-time half.

DeBruyne had torn down the left flank. He sent a defense-shredding pass between Cameron and Besler. It was right in Rom's flight path. Rom never even broke stride as he rifled the ball past me.

Now we were down 2–0, with just a single 15-minute half left in the game.

I glanced up at my mom in the stands. The look on her face was one I rarely saw. It was pure anguish. She'd been riding the crazy emotion of this game with me—hell, she'd been riding the crazy emotion of my life with me—that second goal had devastated her.

I flashed her a hint of a smile. I pumped my fist slightly. It's like I was saying to her, *It's okay, Mom. It's going to be alright.* It was as if we'd reversed roles since my days on the rec field.

The thing is, even if the rest of the world had given up hope, I still believed.

Back in November 2008, when I was still a fresh face at Everton, we played a game against West Ham. We'd trailed by a goal until the 83rd minute. Then, Everton's Louis Saha crossed to Joleon Lescott, who headed in an equalizer. Two minutes later, Saha drove the ball into the lower corner of the net. In the 87th minute, Saha scored again. Three goals in four minutes.

Games can turn around fast, especially when teams get nervous.

So I knew that if we could score one—take it from a comfortable lead to an uncomfortable lead—Belgium was going to feel the pressure.

Could we do it? Absolutely.

During the extra-time break that's all anyone talked about: one goal. One. Jürgen remained upbeat, full of positive energy. We were going to get one, and then we were going to keep fighting.

After all, if there's one defining characteristic of the U.S. team, it's that we don't know when to give up.

Two minutes after the restart, all that belief resulted in an incredible moment.

Julian Green, our German American teenaged sub, had come on the field as Jürgen's final roll of the dice. Michael Bradley dinked a ball over the top of the Belgian defense, and Julian took his first-ever World Cup touch.

Whoa baby! He scored on a gorgeous volley.

All we needed was one more.

I remember looking at Michael Bradley during those final minutes of the game. I don't think I've ever seen anyone battling harder. Michael's engine never stops. Not even when the gears have been stripped and ground down to shavings. He's Bob Bradley's son, through and through. Somehow, he'll open up into a sprint even when he's cramping. He'll push from one end of the field to the other, even when everyone around him is gasping for breath. In the group stage, Michael had logged more miles than any other player: nearly 24 miles in 3 games.

Now I saw him running, emptied out, yet still going, and I believed—not hoped, not prayed, *believed*—we were going to nail the equalizer.

When we did, this game was going to go to penalty kicks.

And when it went to PKs, I was going to do what I've done so many times before. I was going to save some. And we were going to win this thing.

We had two final chances. In the 114th minute, we won a free kick just outside Belgium's penalty area. In training, we'd worked on a clever set piece that could surprise a defense expecting one of our guys to curl the ball over or around the wall. To pull out that play now, with just a few minutes left in the game, required massive guts.

Michael ran up to the free kick as if he was going for glory but suddenly drew back his leg and passed the ball on the ground to Wondo, standing with his back to the goal on the edge of the area. As the Belgium defense converged on him, Wondo flicked the ball to his left and onto the foot of Clint, who never broke stride as he busted through the logjam of players in the box. At that moment, I started thinking about penalty kicks. But Thibaut Courtois, Belgium's towering keeper, reacted with world-class anticipation and threw his long body over the ball.

What a beautiful "almost" that was.

A minute later, we made our last charge up the field and DeAndre had a decent look at goal. How amazing would it have been if a kid who was only in his second year in MLS had tied the game in the final seconds? But we were flat out of miracles. Yedlin's shot was saved by Courtois.

And that was it. All around me, my teammates dropped to the turf, as if they'd been powered by hope alone. Now that the hope was gone, they had nothing left.

The first person to come up to me was Romelu. He hugged me. I've had a lot of bittersweet hugs in my life. This one topped them all.

As I left the field, a FIFA official told me that I'd been selected randomly for drug testing. He handed me a bottle of water and said I'd better start drinking.

Then another official approached me. He told me something that I couldn't quite make sense of in that moment.

He informed me I'd just made World Cup history. I was the first keeper to have made 15 saves in a single game.

Fifteen saves.

The number was meaningless, divorced completely from this hollowed-out moment in time.

History?

I'd have given up that history in a nanosecond if we could have made it through to the quarterfinals.

When I walked into the doping room, Romelu was sitting there, too, his own bottle of water in hand.

"Hey, man," I said.

I was so tired, I could barely speak.

I sat down. Rom and I'd already said everything we needed to say in that hug we'd shared on the field. We sat for a few moments in comfortable silence.

"Tim," Rom said, "how's the family?"

"Good, Rom. Thanks. They're great."

"Did the kids get down for any games?"

"Yeah, they did," I said. "Jacob's got World Cup fever big time."

We each took huge gulps of water, as much as we could possibly swallow. The sooner I could produce my urine sample, the sooner I could get home.

"You get any word about next season?" I asked. I knew he wanted to come back to Everton, but he still belonged to Chelsea, who had loaned him to us last season.

"Nothing for sure," he said. "I hope I can come back. It's a good club."

"It is," I said. "It's the best club in the league."

"There aren't a lot of . . ." He paused.

"Egos," I said.

"That's right, not a lot of egos or drama."

"Well," I said, "I hope you come back. You fit in well."

Our eyes met, and we smiled. Then we each knocked back a bunch more water.

I called the kids after leaving Salvador.

"Daddy?" Ali asked. "Are you sad?"

"Yeah," I said. "I am."

She thought about that for a bit, then responded, with more assurance than you'd think a child could have, "I'm proud of you, Daddy. And I'm really happy. Because now you're coming home."

Ali's words soothed the sting of the Belgium loss. Sometimes all it takes is the perspective of a 7-year-old.

GAME OF MY LIFE

Over the next few days, I received hundreds of texts, emails, and phone calls from all over the world.

From Steve Senior, my high school buddy: *OMG!!!! You were AMAZING!!!!!!!*

From Mulch: *You inspired a hell of a lot of kids out there today.*

I got texts from Landon and Carlos. From Kasey and Tony Meola. From my Everton teammates and friends.

I was too drained, and too down, to respond to more than a handful.

Steve got a two-word text: *thx man.*

For Mulch, there was only one: *Gutted.*

That night I slept for 16 hours straight. In the morning, I met up with Clint. We were told President Obama would be calling.

"You guys did us proud," Obama said. Then he said to me, specifically, "I don't know how you are going to survive the mobs when you come back home, man. You'll have to shave your beard so they don't know who you are."

Even before I left Brazil—and then for weeks after—I started getting media requests: *Jimmy Kimmel Live!*, *The Tonight Show*

Starring Jimmy Fallon, the *Today* show, *Dr. Oz*, *Access Hollywood*, the *Late Show with David Letterman*, the *Nickelodeon Kids' Choice Sports Awards*, *Good Morning America*, and the ESPYS, just to name a few.

Disney wanted to fly my family and me to Orlando. Nickelodeon was willing to send a private jet. Other companies offered staggering amounts of money for me to show up, sign autographs, and pose for photos.

"Nah," I told Dan.

"You sure?"

"Yeah. I just want to go home and be with my kids."

My assistant, Amber, showed me the "Things Tim Howard Could Save" memes that had been popping up all over the internet. There I was, saving the *Titanic*. Saving a swimmer from the shark in *Jaws*. Saving Janet Jackson from her Super Bowl wardrobe malfunction.

She also showed me a screen grab for the secretary of defense's Wikipedia page: some prankster had briefly substituted my name for the real one, Chuck Hagel. Then Chuck Hagel himself actually called to congratulate me.

It all seemed so surreal; I couldn't process what was going on.

Only when I saw a *New York Times* graphic showing all 15 saves superimposed onto a single image did the number itself make sense. I studied them in turn.

Oh yeah, I'd think. *I remember that one. And that one, too.*

My flight from Brazil back to the U.S. landed just as the summer sun began its rise above the horizon.

It didn't occur to me at the time that maybe President Obama had been right and I should have shaved off my beard when I had the chance. As soon as I arrived at the terminal, I was immediately swarmed by people of every age, every background, every shape and size.

They gave me high-fives. They crowded in for selfies—too many for me to count. They asked for my autograph on their boarding passes and coffee-shop receipts.

"Captain America!" shouted one middle-aged woman.

"I'm gonna grow a beard just like you!" shouted a college-aged kid, dressed in jeans and flip-flops. "You're the man!"

"Tim Howard!"

"Great game!"

"We're so proud of you!"

"Game of your life!"

I heard that phrase again and again: game of your life.

Was it?

What I did against Belgium is the same thing I've tried to do throughout my career: keep the ball from going into the net.

That's just my job. Some games, I barely touch the ball. I'll focus for 90 intense minutes, only to make one big save.

Other days, like when we played Belgium, I'm asked to deliver 15 of them.

Okay, so I made history on that field in Salvador. But it didn't feel like beating Mexico in Azteca, or defeating Spain in the Confederations Cup. It's not as if there were last-minute heroics like Landon's winner in South Africa.

Slowly, it dawned on me. Over the following days I began to understand that, somehow, people saw something that mattered to them in this game even more than winning.

They'd seen us fight. We'd been knocked down and battered and depleted. Yet we kept at it. Not just me but every one of my teammates. And every day all over America, people were fighting with similar intensity against their own opponents, internal and external, in their own way.

But our fight had been seen on TV by tens of millions, in the U.S. alone. And because I was the keeper—the last line of defense—I became the face of that battle.

That's when I understood: maybe, it really was the game of my life. Maybe "the game of your life" is simply the one that means the most to others.

I went to Destin, Florida, with Trey and Laura and the kids . . . and 50 members of Laura's extended family.

Laura and Trey got a bottom-floor condo, and so did I, so the kids moved back and forth easily between the two. We set our beach chairs next to one another and relaxed in the sun. At night, Trey and the kids came over to my condo, and we all watched baseball.

We ate all our meals together. Laura rolled her eyes as people surrounded our table asking for photographs and autographs. I caught her winking at Trey, as if to say, *See? What did I tell you?*

But I said no to requests when I was with my family. Soon after I'd gotten home, Ali had said, "I wish people didn't always have to come up to you, Daddy."

"Not while I'm with my family," I told people. "Sorry, but I'm with my family now."

It was a busy summer. I visited Carlos Bocanegra, my old team-mate and friend, in Los Angeles for the baptism of his baby boy. I was his son's godfather.

I was so honored to have been asked, first of all, that I had been rendered speechless. The godfathers to my children were my brother and Steve Senior—two people who I knew would be in my life forever.

And I was thrilled that I could be there for the baptism. I'd missed so many meaningful moments during the years— weddings and funerals and births and baptisms. But this one: this one I could attend.

The night before the baptism, Carlos and I split a bottle of wine from our birth year—1979. We smoked cigars. He told me that he was nearing the end of his MLS career; a few months later, he would announce his retirement. Carlos had been retired from the national team for over a year now. Already, he was staring at life beyond the soccer field. For a few days, I got a glimpse into what that life might look like.

My face was suddenly everywhere—newspapers, magazines, TV, and gossip-entertainment web sites. When I went on a date, or so much as talked to a woman, it was shown online for the whole world to see.

My mom called me.

"Tim," she said. "Who are these women, and why don't I know anything about them?"

I laughed.

"Mom, I promise you. When there's somebody in my life in a significant way, you'll know it."

Weeks after Belgium, I opened the door to Laura and Trey's house.

"Hey, is anybody here?"

My greeting committee—the four huge dogs that live with Laura and Trey and the kids—gave me a rousing reception. Clayton was among them, that old hound, wagging his tail in circles. The years were slowing him down and his muzzle was now covered in gray fur, but he was still unmistakably the creature who'd wreaked havoc all over that beautiful Man U house so many years ago.

"Okay, guys," I said, pushing my way through them. "Come on, let me through."

Trey's daughter, Savannah, hugged me first. "Hey, Tim," she said. "Dad's in the garage. Laura's in the kitchen."

Then Ali came charging into the room. She leapt into my arms. *God, she's getting so tall now.*

I carried her into the kitchen. Laura was loading dishes in the dishwasher—four hungry kids make an awful lot of dishes. "Hey, Tim."

Jacob ran into the kitchen from outside. At nine, he's already all limbs and angled muscles. "Hey, Dad. Can Jake sleep over tomorrow?"

Of course he could.

Then Trey came in. We clasped hands and came in for a friendly half hug.

Trey rumpled Ali's hair. "Hey, Ali. Get that picture for your dad, will you?"

Ali ran over to the table and picked up a picture she'd made. It was done in Magic Marker: a green field, with a crisscross net at one end. There were two players on the field—stick figures with different color uniforms, a ball between them. The player in front of the goal was about to kick the ball. Above his head, she'd written the words NO GOAL. All over the sky, she'd added the words USA! USA! USA!

"This one's going on my refrigerator for sure," I said.

And it did.

In August, the first-ever session of the Tim Howard NJCTS Leadership Academy kicked off in New Jersey. By then, I was already heading back to England.

I got updates about the Academy from my mom, from Faith, from people we knew in common.

Over four days, 23 kids with TS were led by eight coaches—all of whom also had TS. Later, Faith Rice described for me a single moment from the Academy—a five-minute period when 31 participants, both coaches and kids, all started having tics at the same time.

There was whirring and hooting and echoing and roaring. There was shoulder jerking and neck-rolling and eye-rolling. There were outbursts of laughter and yelps.

After a while, it began to feel like everyone was volleying their tics back and forth. The room was so loud, so fluttering with movement, that nobody could hear a word anyone was saying.

Faith looked around, at all these kids. *This*, she thought, *is the most glorious cacophony I have ever heard.*

She started laughing then—laughing about the absurdity of this disorder, and at the joy of seeing these kids be 100 percent themselves.

When the kids all noticed her cracking up, they burst out laughing, too.

I was happy for those kids, maybe even a little jealous. I wished that when I was a teenager I had been surrounded by people who understood me, who knew what I was going through. I wish we could have laughed together about our funny brains.

I've gotten letters and emails from kids with TS for many years. I've read them all. Sometimes I can't respond personally, but every one matters.

If I could sit down with all of them, I know exactly what I would say:

Trust yourself exactly as God made you. Let your tics pass over you without fear or shame. Let them lead you along your own extraordinary journey. It's true what that doctor told my mother all those years ago: Tourette comes with its own beautiful flip side. It gives you gifts. Mine was soccer, goalkeeping. You have something, too.

The world will not always understand.

But your TS gives you a window into people's hearts. You know, better than anyone, that what lies on people's surface isn't the thing that's real and true about them.

Your brain is extraordinary. You are extraordinary.

Everything—I promise you, everything—is possible.

EPILOGUE

LIVERPOOL, ENGLAND
AUGUST 23, 2014

It's the start of a new season and I'm standing in the tunnel at Goodison Park ready to step on to the field.

Prayer for my kids.

Pray they'll be safe. Pray they'll know how much I love them.

The *Z-Cars* theme starts playing. It's our cue to start walking out.

Don't touch the HOME OF THE BLUES SIGN. Do touch the grass. Make a cross.

Seeing the home crowd again—all those crazies in Gladwys, all those blue scarves flying—I realize how long it feels since the last time I was here.

It's the opening home game of the 2014–2015 season. Our opponents are Arsenal, the first team I'd ever played against in the Premier League. That was 11 years ago.

I've accomplished a lot since then, but I'm hardly done. I want this team to win some silverware while I'm here, something to cement my legacy in Everton soccer history.

For the past two decades, I've crisscrossed the world again and again, going straight from the pressure-cooker of the Premier League season into equally intense tournaments for the U.S. and back again. Over the summer, I made the tough decision to take a year off from playing for the national team. I have always believed that representing my country is a gift that's not to be squandered.

But Ali and Jacob: they are gifts, too, and I've missed out on too much of their lives already.

I'm going to take care of myself. Keep working hard. Maybe, if all goes well, I'll have one more World Cup in me. Maybe there will be a chance to take the U.S. to the quarterfinals.

But I'm beginning to envision a life beyond soccer. After Brazil, I signed a contract with NBC to broadcast Premier League games on television. Next week, I'll be stepping into the broadcasting booth at Etihad Stadium to help call the Manchester City–Liverpool match.

Might I coach? It's a tantalizing possibility, especially now that soccer seems to be making great strides in the U.S. The number of MLS teams has doubled since my MetroStars days; the league has been attracting high-level players from around the world—and losing fewer of our homegrown stars to Europe. MLS games now draw an average audience of 18,000—eclipsing figures for both the NBA and the NHL.

So maybe the MLS hasn't seen the last of me.

Whatever I do, the paramount thing that will decide my future is time.

At some point, I want to wake up to an entire day—or week,

or month—during which I can be there for my kids, wholly and completely. I want to drive them to school and to soccer and basketball practice and to horseback riding lessons. I want to be that parent who's at every game, cheering from the sidelines, as my kids—and my mom—have done for me.

I'm looking forward to making dinner for Jacob and Ali and their friends, Trey's kids among them. I'll flip burgers on the backyard grill while all the kids splash in the pool and the warm Memphis sun sets through the trees.

Every so often, maybe a friend of mine will visit—Carlos or Landon or Dan or Romelu or Mulch. We'll crack open beers and talk about the good old days, distilling all those memories into a highlight reel: the glorious last-minute heroics, the clowning around in the locker room, those magnificent pileups after we'd scored. Never mind the long waits in airports, the endless bus rides, the bruised muscles and the constant fear of injury, the stomach-churning anticipation of the next day's game, the families we couldn't see for months on end. The bad memories will recede in time.

To the kids, we'll sound like old guys going on about When We Were Young. Exactly.

After all that, we'll go inside to catch a game on TV. On the way, maybe we'll stop to look at my trophies, finally out of their boxes. Then we'll sit around some more, cheering for whoever's playing. Anyone, that is, but Liverpool or Mexico.

If this is what my future holds, it will be enough.

I don't know if I'll marry again. I can't quite imagine how another person would fit into this tight-knit but unconventional extended family of ours—with the kids moving fluidly between Laura and Trey's home and my own. If I can't find the right person to embrace that life, I think I'll be fine on my own.

This future I'm envisioning isn't far away. But it's not here yet. Right now I'm still on the field; the present is still in play. I take a few steps back and forth in goal, feeling the turf beneath my cleats. I look out to the stands, then back to the center circle, where a team in bright blue and a team in red take up their positions. I see Romelu and Kevin, and I think how nice it is to have them back on *my* side again.

Behind me, in Gladwys, someone shouts, "Come on, Blue Boys!" I make the final cross over my chest.

The whistle is about to blow.

ACKNOWLEDGMENTS

Writing a book requires, by necessity, selecting just a few stories while leaving others untold. My life has been filled with remarkable people, with whom I've shared extraordinary moments. I wish I could include all in these pages. If you've been a part of my life—if you've been among those who supported me and laughed with me and rooted for me—please know that you're in my heart, even if you're not in these pages.

I am the player I am because of the teammates I've had, both past and present. To my teammates on Everton and the U.S. National Team: You are my brothers, my fellow comrades, my friends. Thank you for giving me more incredible memories than one man deserves in his lifetime. Thank you, too, to my teammates on the MetroStars, the Imperials, and to all my youth and school teams . . . right down to the North Brunswick Recreation Rangers. My experiences with all of you helped shape me.

To fans of U.S. Soccer and Everton: you are the 12th man on that field, and we'd be nothing without you. Special thanks, too, to the American Outlaws, who helped America discover the beauty and thrill of this game. I really do believe that we will win.

To the entire Everton staff: you have truly become my family. Special thanks to Sue Palmer, Bill Ellaby, Paula Smith, David Harrison, Tony Sage, Danny Donachie, Darren Griffiths, Jimmy Comer, Richie Porter, Matt Connery, Robert Elstone, and Jimmy Martin. I'll bleed blue for the rest of my life.

And most of all to Bill Kenwright: your faith in me continues to be an honor.

It's been a privilege to represent my country on the world stage. I'm grateful to U.S. Soccer for giving me the opportunity and for helping this New Jersey kid's dreams come true. I'd like to offer a special debt of gratitude to Dan Perkins, Michael Kammerman, Ivan Pierra, Dr. George Chiampas, Jon Fleischman, Jessie Bignami, Andreas Hertzog. Also, Sunil Gulati, Dan Flynn, and Don Garber, and so many others at MLS and U.S. Soccer who work every day toward taking American soccer to new heights.

To Dan Segal, the most humble, practical, hard-working guy I know. You've had my back in this book, as you have everywhere else.

To Brendan Meyer, who does a great job managing my social media accounts, and to Casey Wasserman and the rest of the crew at Wasserman Media Group who have provided helpful support throughout my career.

To Daren Flitcroft and Allison Brill, thank you for your research, feedback, and insights.

To my assistant, Amber: without your hard work and dedication, my life would descend into chaos. Thank you, sincerely, for saving me from that fate.

To Mulch: it is fair to say that this book, and indeed my whole life, would be very different—and far less—without you. You've been a coach, a mentor, and a dear friend. You are with me every time I take my place in the box. Here's to the 732.

To my many coaches: Bruce Arena, Bob Bradley, Alex Ferguson, Jürgen Klinsmann, David Moyes, Roberto Martinez, and my goalkeeping coaches, Peter Mellor, Inaki Bergara, and Chris Woods. Thank you for trusting me, and for pushing me.

This book comes from the indefatigable passion and support of my editor, David Hirshey. Thank you for your uncompromising vision, your unflagging energy, and your unyielding focus on excellence. And to Sydney Pierce: your efforts in shepherding this manuscript on its narrow timeline, with so many parties involved, have been nothing short of heroic.

To Ali Benjamin, thank you for your steadfast and tireless commitment to my cause. Our deadline was tight and my schedule was crazy, yet you captured my thoughts, ideas, and tales in a book that I am proud to share with the world.

To NBC Sports, which has given me the honor of broadcasting Premier League games, and to my commercial sponsors, past and present, who support me and also support the sport of soccer. Special mention goes to my long-standing partner, Nike, who helped make me a pro in the first place with the Project 40 program and has been with me my whole career.

To the million or so other people who helped shape my story: Chris Brienza, Rob Skead, Ross Paule, Clint Mathis, Rob Vartughian, Steve Senior, Ed Breheny, Stan Williston, James Martin, and Reverend Hooper. I'm so honored to have shared time with you. And to the admirable people I've met through the TS community: Faith and Kim Rice, Marisa Lenger, the Kowalski family, and everyone at the New Jersey Center for Tourette Syndrome and the Tourette Syndrome Association: thanks for sharing your stories and for helping change the world.

I'm endlessly grateful to my family. To my father: thank you for your love and support.

To Chris: you're the warrior, my brother.

To my grandparents—Poppa, Momma, and Nana. I love you, and I know I'll see you all again one day.

To my mom—my rock, my inspiration, my unconditional support.

To Laura. I'm so grateful to you, both for who we once were, and for who we still are today. We made two miracles. If I scoured the whole world, I could never find a better mother for Jacob and Alivia.

And, finally, to my beautiful children: my blessings, my heartbeats. Everything has been for you. Always.

ABOUT THE AUTHOR

TIM HOWARD is the goalkeeper for Everton in the English Premier League and the U.S. Men's National Team. He previously played for the MetroStars in Major League Soccer and for the storied club Manchester United. In July 2014, he broke the record for most saves (15) in a World Cup game. He also works as a soccer broadcaster on NBC's weekly coverage of the EPL.

ALI BENJAMIN is the coauthor (with Paige Rawl) of *Positive* the acclaimed memoir about teen bullying. She lives in rural Massachusetts with her husband and two children, all ardent soccer fans.